CHARMING SMALL HOTELS & RESTAURANTS

SOUTHERN FRANCE

CHARMING SMALL HOTELS & RESTAURANTS

SOUTHERN FRANCE

NEW EDITION EDITED BY

Fiona Duncan & Leonie Glass

❋
NEW TO THIS EDITION,
THE CHARMING SMALL HOTELS
TRAVEL SERVICE. SEE PAGE 7.

DUNCAN PETERSEN

HUNTER
PUBLISHING

This new, expanded and redesigned 2002 edition
conceived, designed and produced by
Duncan Petersen Publishing Ltd,
31 Ceylon Road, London W14 0PY
E-mail: dp@appleonline.net
Website: http://www.charmingsmallhotels.co.uk

3rd edition

Editorial Director Andrew Duncan
Editors Fiona Duncan and Leonie Glass
Contributing Editors Peter Henson, Jan Dodd
Production Editor Nicola Davies
Designer Don Macpherson

Sales representation and distribution in the UK and Ireland by
Portfolio Books Ltd
Unit 5, Perivale Industrial Park
Horsenden Lane South
Greenford UB6 7RL
Tel: 0208 997 9000 Fax: 0208 997 9097
E-mail sales@portfoliobooks.com

A CIP catalogue record for this book is available
from the British Library

ISBN 1 903301 20 3

Published in the USA by
Hunter Publishing Inc.,
130 Campus Drive, Edison, N.J. 08818.
Tel (732) 225 1900 Fax (732) 417 0482

For details on hundreds of other travel guides
and language courses, visit Hunter's Website at
http://www.hunterpublishing.com

ISBN 1-58843-293-9

DTP by Duncan Petersen Publishing Ltd
Printed by G. Canale & C., Italy

Contents

mendations – the stars, as it were, of our collection – BUT the short entries (four to a page) on pages 144 to 180 are equally charming and could be described as the all-important supporting cast.

When in France...

Hotel-keeping is a respected profession in France at all levels. Many small hotels are family-run and have been for generations. There are times when these establishments are very busy, when all the resources of a limited staff are being pushed to the limit and these are not times to make unnecessary demands on the management. The French enjoy and cherish their social formalities and can become very agitated if unable to conform to them.

As a basic rule, for example, it is asking for trouble to turn up at a hotel around noon, and expect instant service at reception, for this is when lunch is beginning. The French are famous for taking food seriously and eat early. If you want to have a pleasant meal, it is dangerous to leave going into the restaurant for lunch much after noon and by 1 pm you may well be turned away. Dinner can be served as early as 7 pm, particularly in country areas; hotels will expect you to be having an aperitif any time from 6 pm. Hoteliers will not be distracted from what they consider to be their crucial duty – getting meals to the table – and at these times visitors can find themselves in potentially embarrassing and even explosive situations if they present themselves at the reception desk asking unwelcome questions. This is how many misunderstandings arise. It is not that anyone wishes to be unpleasant. If faced with obstruction to what is considered to be the main business of the day, hotel owners or staff feel angry and frustrated because they cannot give their restaurant customers the service they deserve, and also because they cannot give proper service at the reception desk.

The afternoon can also be sensitive. This is when it appears that all useful people in the hotel disappear and the place seems deserted. This is not a good time to turn up and expect to be cordially received, either.

We have found on our travels that in many hotels, even those towards the coast, the social formality ethic also extends to dress. This is not an easy one, for it is really an understanding, not a written rule (except in some cases). Unless eating by the pool, guests are expected to dress correctly at meals and in the public rooms of the hotel: that is, not in swimming costumes or sunbathing attire. Towelling robes are often provided in the rooms precisely for the purpose of covering up en route for the pool. In the Vaucluse, one of our inspectors witnessed a group of scantily-clad guests fooling around on the stairs of a hotel in a listed historic building. (They were sent packing.)

Some hotels ask their guests to 'dress' for dinner; this does not mean long skirts or black ties, but is a request to wear something befitting a meal (which may be candle-lit) that has been prepared with great care by the chef and served in a manner worthy of it.

Chambres d'hôtes

Chambres d'hôtes, originally conceived in France as a way of giving town and city people a chance to stay in the country in simple, reasonably-priced accommodation, have become much more sophisticated of late. More and more professional people – of all nationalities – are choosing to open up their own houses – often beautifully decorated and furnished with treasured personal possessions, to paying guests. Staying in a *chambre d'hôte* can be a most interesting and rewarding experience, but it is not, in any way, like staying in an hotel. Guests do not have the same freedom as in an hotel or the same right to expect a certain standard of service (even though they may sometimes be paying more). Always bear in mind that you are a guest in a private house. Do not arrive without booking; telephone if you have been held up and are going to be late. In the *Charming Small Hotel Guide* series we publish a completely separate guide to French *chambres d'hôte* – see page 222 for ordering details.

Children

It is a popularly held belief that the French love their children. They do – but not always in hotels. We always ask the question 'Do you accept children?'; the answer is generally 'Of course'. But not, by any means, in every case. Many, quite understandable, reasons are given for not accepting them: our hotel is filled with treasured family furniture, fragile *objets* and porcelain; we have many regular guests who come for the peace and quiet we offer here; silence is golden; many of our guests are of a certain age; many of our guests have come to escape from their own children. Some hotels specify that they accept 'well-behaved' children. To avoid disappointment or a difficult situation, be quite sure how the hotel feels about children before booking.

Pets

We ask whether hotels accept pets and, in a country that now owns more cats and dogs even than Britain, the answer is normally in the affirmative. Often one of the most entertaining moments in the daily life of a French hotel is the after-dinner ritual of walking the dog: one's fellow guests take on a different guise when heard whistling and calling to their pets through the darkness.

But hotels have a wide variety of rules relating to pets. Some allow dogs in the restaurant, some don't. Some prefer dogs to stay in rooms for as much of the day as possible; some would rather dogs stay in rooms for as little of the day as possible and never alone, because of scratching damage to doors and furnishings. Some establishments will only take cats. In general, dogs are not allowed anywhere near swimming pools – in particular, large dogs with a liking for water.

Air conditioning

Air conditioning is by no means common in French hotels, but little by little it is being introduced. Air conditioners often make a noise and are useless if the windows are open. It is, nevertheless, a boon in very hot weather, because it helps you get a good night's sleep. It is well worth finding a hotel with air conditioning – if only for one night – when driving south in the summer months; after a long, hot, tiring day in your car and the prospect of another, the benefits of a restful night will make paying the bill considerably less painful.

Historic houses

The more faithful the renovation work, the more likely it is that some of the bedrooms may not resemble what you expect. It may sound like fun to stay in a converted abbey, but a week in a windowless monks' cell could turn out to be a little grim. Be very sure what you are getting when you book. In the busy high season, there is little chance of moving rooms after arriving.

The same principle applies to bathrooms. Although we have paid careful attention to bathrooms in our inspections, some less-than-perfect ones are bound to have slipped through our net. Bathrooms in towers, for example, may sometimes not be as quite as romantic as they sound.

Breakfast

Generally, breakfast in a French hotel will consist of coffee (or tea), a basket of bread, rolls, croissants and, perhaps, brioche, jam (often home-made) and some butter. But – and mostly you aren't told this – there are usually a number of alternatives, such as eggs (boiled, scrambled, fried), fruit and, in some places (normally with non-French owners), ham, bacon or cheese. Always ask what is available. French breakfasts are now reaching record-breaking prices – a small survey we conducted found that 16 Euros is not unusual.

How to find an entry

The guide is divided into seven geographical regions (see the maps, pages 19-31) but within that the arrangement is alphabetical, by village or town or city.

The 112 full-page entries are on pages 33-143, organized as described above – first regionally, and alphabetically within each regional section.

The shorter entries are on pages 144-180, arranged in the same way.

The restaurants are on pages 181-209, also arranged in the same way.

To find a hotel or restaurant in a particular area, look through the headings at the top of the pages until you find that area – or use the maps, pages 19-31, which show the place name and number of the page on which that hotel is described.

To locate a specific hotel in a specific place, use one of the three indexes at the back of the book. One index lists the hotels by their names; one by the name of the place in which it is located; and the third by its *département*.

How to read a full-page entry

At the top of each full-page entry is a coloured bar giving the name of the town or village where the establishment is found. Below the photograph is the name of the hotel, along with a categorization which gives some clue to its character. Then follows the address in another coloured bar. In some cases, it might be in remote countryside or in a small village or hamlet. A detailed map is always useful: we recommend the Michelin Motoring Atlas of France or the IGN (Institut Géographique National) regional tourist maps. The description follows the address.

At the foot of the description is the fact box containing information that should help you to decide if the hotel is in your price range and has the facilities you want.

Tel

Under tel we give the telephone number. In this guide, the two-digit area codes that prefix all telephone numbers in France are 04 for South-East France and 05 for South-West France. To make internal calls, dial the ten-figure number. To dial from outside the country, use the international code for France (00 33) and omit the zero of the area code.

Fax

We are able to give a fax number for the majority of our recommended hotels, but there are still a few places that – for a variety of reasons – do not have a fax machine.

E-mail and **website** addresses are listed if available. Please note that people frequently change their e-mail addresses.

Car parking

We were impressed, on our travels for this guide, with the concern shown by hoteliers for the safety of guests' cars. Since large numbers of cars were stolen or vandalized in the more popular parts of Provence and the Côte d'Azur a few years ago, many hoteliers have made secure car parks with high wire mesh fences and security gates that are closed at night – or indeed during the day – and infra-red alarm systems.

Prices

In this guide we have adopted the system of price bands, rather than giving actual prices. This is because prices are often subject to change after we go to press. The price bands refer to a standard double room (high season rates, if applicable) with breakfast for two people. They are as follows:

€	under 90 Euros
€€	90-140 Euros
€ € €	140-185 Euros
€ € € €	185-275 Euros
€ € € € €	over 275 Euros

To avoid unpleasant surprises, always check what is included in the price (for example, tax and service, breakfast and afternoon tea) when making the booking. Many hotels have special off-peak rates, and some require a minimum stay of more than one night. Half-board may also be obligatory, but this is usually only the case in country guesthouses or restaurants-with-rooms.

Credit cards

We list the following credit cards:

AE	American Express
DC	Diners Club
MC	Mastercard
V	Visa

The least often accepted credit cards – particularly in smaller establishments – are American Express and Diners Club.

Useful information
Public holidays in France

January 1st; Easter Day; Easter Monday; Labour Day, May 1st; VE Day, May 8th; Whit Monday; Bastille Day, July 14th; Assumption Day, August 15th; All Saints Day, November 1st; Remembrance Day, November 11th; Christmas Day

Information centres

All over France, there are 5,000 *Offices de Tourism* and *Syndicats d'Initiative*, which give advice on accommodation, restaurants, hotels and local transport.

Drinking and driving

It is not wise to drink and drive in France, where the limit is 0.05 per cent alcohol and random breath tests are frequent. There are stiff penalties.

Police are authorized to impose and collect on-the-spot fines from drivers who violate traffic regulations. For minor infractions, other than parking violations, a 30 per cent reduction of the amount of the fine may be granted to drivers who pay immediately or within 24 hours. If the motorist considers he is not at fault, he will be asked to pay a deposit (*amende forfaitaire*) which varies according to the offence. Police are required to issue a receipt showing the amount paid.

Speeding fines

On-the-spot fines may be imposed for exceeding the speed limit by 30 to 40 kilometres an hour. A new category of offence has been created in the penal code for drivers who 'deliberately put the lives of others in danger'. This applies when a third person has been put in direct danger of injury or death through the driver's disregard for safety precautions.

Points to remember

- In built-up areas, the *priorité à droite* still applies: you must give way to anybody coming out of a side-turning on the right. However, the *priorité* rule no longer applies at roundabouts, which means you give way to cars already on the roundabout: watch for signs and exercise great caution.
- No driving on a provisional licence.
- Seat belts must be worn by the driver and *all* the passengers.
- Children under ten may not travel in the front of the car unless sitting in a specially approved fitted seat facing backwards.
- Stop signs mean stop. Creeping slowly in first gear will not do. Come to a complete halt.
- There must be no stopping on open roads unless the car is driven off the road.
- Overtaking where there is a solid single line is heavily penalized.
- Headlight beams must be adjusted for driving on the right-hand side of the road. Yellow-tinted headlights are not compulsory for tourist vehicles.
- If a driver flashes his lights in France, he is generally indicating that he has priority and that you should give way.

Motorways

There are more than 8,000 kilometres of motorway in France, mostly toll roads (or *autoroutes à péages*). Prices per kilometre vary.

Every two kilometres there is an orange emergency telephone; parking and rest areas are every 10 or 20 kilometres. Approximately every 40 kilometres are 24-hour petrol stations, which offer a basic maintenance service. Most credit cards are accepted as payment for tolls and at service stations.

The charge for assistance on motorways is fixed by the French government. Motorists may only call the police or the official breakdown service operating in that area, and cannot request help from their own assistance company, if they break down on a motorway. The same applies on the Paris *périphérique*.

Speed limits

Unless otherwise posted and on dry roads:

- 130 km/h on toll motorways.
- 110 km/h on dual carriageways and non-toll motorways.
- 90 km/h on other roads.

- 50 km/h in towns. The limit begins at the red-bordered roadside sign giving the name of the town and ends where you see a diagonal bar through the place name sign.

On wet roads:

- 110 km/h on toll motorways.
- 100 km/h on dual carriageways and non-toll motorways.
- 80 km/h on other roads.
- There is a new speed limit of 50 km/h on motorways in foggy conditions, when visibility is less than 50 metres.

Hotel bookings

When booking you will be asked for a deposit (*arrhes*) equal to 25 per cent of the bill. If you cancel you lose your deposit. If the owner or hotelier cancels, he must pay you double the amount of deposit paid. If you are asked for payment on account (*acompte*), you are more firmly committed: if you cancel you are liable for payment for the whole stay. Make sure these conditions are absolutely clear before making your booking.

To avoid disappointment, the traveller is advised to book in advance. The most satisfactory way is to do this by fax. Bear in mind that the French often put the month first when writing dates, as in 6.14.02 (June 14th, 2002).

Your booked room will normally be kept for you until 6 pm, so it is sensible to telephone ahead if you are likely to arrive at the hotel much after that time.

Payment and credit cards

Most major credit cards are accepted in shops, hotels, restaurants, petrol stations and hypermarkets. The most widely accepted are Mastercard and Visa. When paying by credit card, check the amount which appears on the receipt.

Recently French cards have started to carry personal information, designed to reduce the risk of fraud, in a chip rather than on a magnetic band. If your card is queried because this information can't be read, have your bank's or credit card company's telephone number ready so that you and your card can be verified.

Remember that cards can be used to withdraw cash from machines all over France – of course they need to bear the appropriate symbol.

Service and tips

Service is included in restaurant bills, but you may also wish to leave a tip as a mark of appreciation. It is usual to give porters, doormen, theatre and cinema usherettes, guides, taxi drivers and hairdressers a tip of about 2 Euros.

French holiday dates

The French continue to prefer to take their holidays in July and August and take to the roads in their hundreds of thousands, if not millions, at certain times over the summer. If possible, try to avoid travelling on 1st July, the weekends of 14th July, 31st July, 1st August, and the weekend of the 15th August. These are known as 'black' weekends.

With thanks to the French Tourist Office.

Bon voyage.

MENU DECODER

A selection of the words and phrases that visitors find hardest to understand on French menus:

Abats	offal
Aiglefin, aigrefin, eglefin	haddock
Aiguille	needlefish, garfish
Ail	garlic
Airelles	cranberries, whortleberries, bilberries
Allache	large sardine
Alsacienne, à la	with choucroute, ham and frankfurter sausages
Ananas	pineapple
Andouillettes	small chitterling sausages, usually served hot with mustard
Ange de mer, angelot	angel fish, resembling skate
Anguille	freshwater eel
Arachide	peanut
Araignée de mer	spider crab
Arapède	limpet
Arlésienne à l'	fish or meat with tomatoes, onions and olives
Armoricaine à l'	fish or lobster with brandy, white wine, herbs, tomatoes and onions
Baie de ronce	blackberry
Bar, badèche, cernier, bézuque, loup de me	sea bass
Barbadine	passion fruit
Barbue	brill
Baudroie	monkfish
Bécasse, bécasseau	woodcock
Bécassine	snipe
Beignets	fritters
Belon	breton oyster
Bergère, à la	chicken or meat with ham, mushrooms, onions and potatoes
Betterave	beetroot
Bifteck	steak
Blanchaille	whitebait
Bonite	bonito fish, resembling tuna
Bordelaise, à la	in red wine sauce with shallots, tarragon and bone marrow
Boudin noir	black pudding
Bouillabaisse	mediterranean fish stew
Boulangère, à la	oven baked, with potatoes
Boule de neige	sponge or ice-cream covered with whipped cream
Bourgeoise, à la	braised meat or chicken with bacon, carrots and onions
Bourride	white fish stew
Brandade de morue	dried salt cod mousse
Bretonne, à la	in onion sauce with haricot beans
Bretonneau	turbot
Brochet	pike
Brochet de mer	barracuda
Broufado	beef stew with vinegar, capers and anchovies
Cabillaud	cod
Caille, cailleteau	quail
Camarguaise, à la	with tomatoes, garlic, herbs, orange peel olives and wine or brandy
Canard, caneton, canardeau	duck
	cranberry

MENU DECODER

Canneberge	sardine
Cardeau, celan	plaice
Carrelet	pork, mutton or lamb, cooked with
Cassoulet	haricot beans, bacon and sausage
Cèpe	wild boletus mushroom
Cervelas	smoked pork sausage with garlic
Cervelle	brain
Chasseur	with wine, mushrooms and shallots
Chèvre	goat
Chevreuil	venison
Chicon	chicory
Chou-navet	swede
Ciboule	spring onion
Citrouille	pumpkin
Civet	thick meat stew, thickened with blood
Clafoutis	baked cherry batter pudding
Colimaçon	snail
Colin	hake
Coquillages	shellfish
Coquille Saint-Jacques	scallops
Cornichon	gherkin
Cotriade	fish stew with onions, potatoes and cream
Couissinet	cranberry
Crécy, à la	soup with carrots
Crème Anglaise	egg custard
Crépinette	small flat sausage, encased in caul
Crevette	shrimp, prawn
Croque Monsieur	toasted ham and cheese sandwich
Crudités	raw vegetables
Cuisseau	leg of veal
Cuisses de grenouille	frogs' legs
Darne	thick fish steak
Daube	braised meat in red wine, herbs, carrots and onions
Daurade, dorade	sea bream
Dieppoise, à la	fish, often sole with shellfish, in white wine sauce
Dinde	turkey
Ecrevisse	crayfish
Encornet	squid
Espadon	swordfish
Esprot	sprat
Esquinade	spider crab
Estouffade	pot-roasted met
Exocet (poisson volant	flying fish
Faisan, faisandeau	pheasant
Faséole	kidney beans
Faux-filet	sirloin steak
Fermiére, à la	meat or chicken braised with vegetables
Flétan	halibut
Galantine	loaf-shaped chopped meat, fish or vegetables set in natural jelly
Galette	breton buckwheat pancake
Garbure	soup with root vegetables and bacon
Gibier	game
Gigot	leg of lamb
Grecque, à la	mushrooms, aubergines and other vegetables poached in oil and herbs

MENU DECODER

Grenade	pomegranate
Groseille	redcurrant
Hareng	herring
Homard	lobster
Huître	oyster
Ile flottante	soft meringue on egg custard sauce
Italienne, à la	with pasta, tomato and mushrooms
Langue	tongue
Lièvre	hare
Lotte de mer, baudroie	monkfish
Lyonnaise, à la	with onions
Maquereau	mackerel
Marcassin	young wild boar
Merlan	whiting
Merluche	hake
Mode, à la	marinated meat braised in wine with bacon, calf's foot and vegetables
Mouclade	mussel stew
Mûre	mulberry
Myrtille	bilberry
Navet	turnip
Normande, à la	with apples, cream, cider or calvados
Palombe	woodpigeon
Palourde	clam or cockle
Pamplemousse	grapefruit
Panais	parsnip
Perdreau	partridge
Persil	parsley
Pintade	guinea fowl
Pipérade	scrambled egg with red peppers, onions and tomatoes
Plie	plaice
Pochade	freshwater fish stew with carrots
Poireau	leek
Pot-au-feu	boiled beef with turnips, leeks, carrots and
Potiron	pumpkin
Poulpe	octopus
Pouvron	sweet pepper
Praire	clam
Prune	plum
Pruneau	prune
Quenelle	poached, chopped fish or white meat, like dumplings
Raie	ray, skate
Ramereau, ramier	woodpigeon
Rave	turnip
Reine, à la	with chicken
Rillettes	shredded, potted meat
Ris	lamb or veal sweetbreads
Rognon	kidney
Rosbif	cold, rare beef
Rouget	red mullet
Salmis	game casserole
Sanglier	wild boar
Soupe au pistou	vegetable soup with basil paste
Tarte Tatin	upside down apple pie
Thon	tuna
Truffado	potatoes with garlic, bacon and chesse
Veau	veal
Vigneron, à la	in wine sauce, with grapes

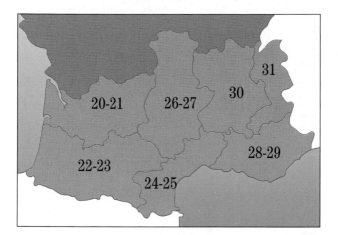

Key to the maps of hotel and restaurant locations and visitor information

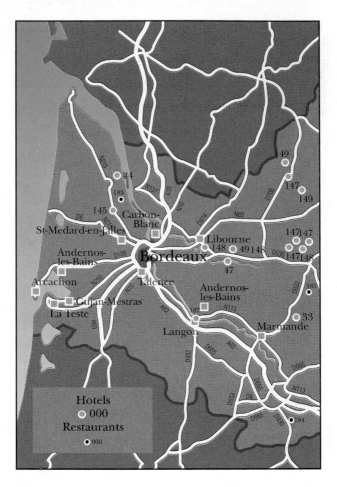

Bordeaux is perhaps one of the best-known parts of France because of the wines that take their name from the villages and chatêaux of the famous vinyards. For many travellers it is also the gateway to the green, fertile hinterland generally known as the Dordogne, with pretty pastoral landscapes that seem to have changed little in hundreds of years.

Many of our most charming small hotels are on the winding rivers of the Dordogne and the Lot. With abundant truffles and *foie gras*, the region is a paradise for gourmets.

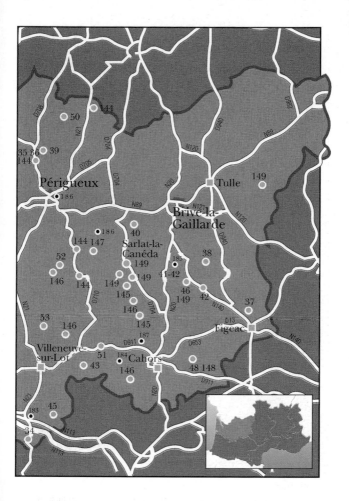

50 144
35 36 39
144
Périgueux
186
186 40
144 147 Sarlat-la-
52 Canéda
146 144 149
149
145
146
53 145
146 187
Villeneuve- 184 Cahors
sur-Lot 51 146
43
45
183
34

Tulle 149
Brive-la-
Gaillarde
38
185
41-42
46 42 37
149
Figeac
48 148

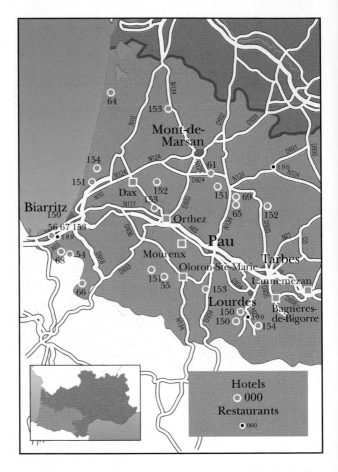

With Atlantic beaches, the strange, immense expanses of the Landes, the Basque country, the Pyrenees and the Spanish border, and fine examples of midieval towns, villages and fortified *bastides*, this is a region rich in diversity, tradition and history. You can also eat memorably – the area is renowned throughout France for its gastronomy and is fiercely proud of its reputation.

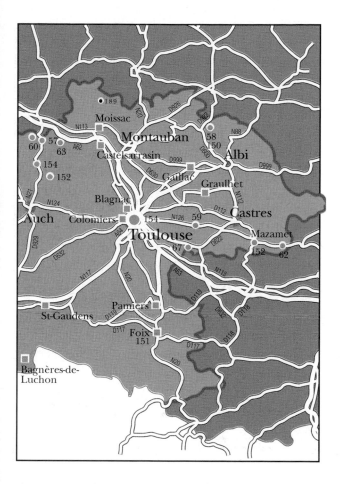

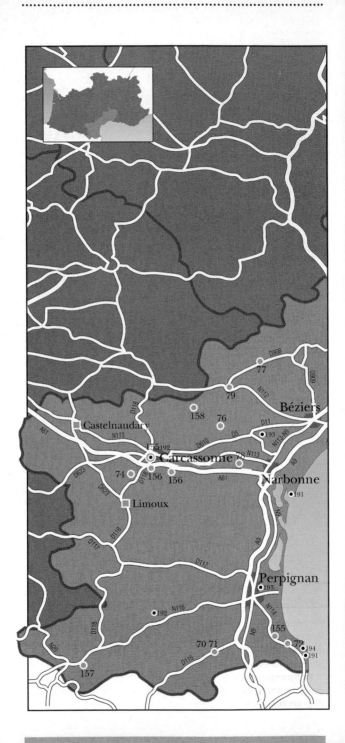

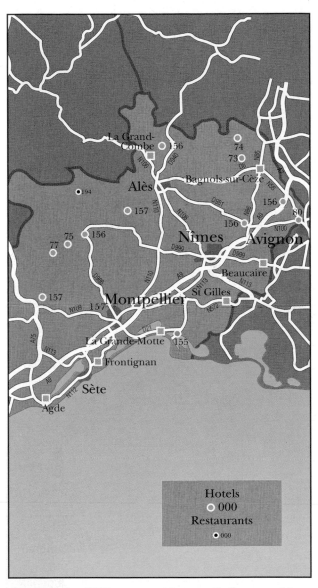

La Grand-Combe
156
74
73
Bagnols-sur-Cèze
194
Alès
157
156
156
156
80
75
Nîmes
77
156
Avignon
Beaucaire
157
157
Montpellier
St Gilles
La Grande-Motte
155
Frontignan
Sète
Agde

Hotels
○ 000
Restaurants
● 000

Set between the wild Cévennes mountain ranges, the Pyrenees and the Mediterranean, the region bears many similarities to Provence _ on the other side of the Rhône – being a sun-baked land of vineyards, olive groves and dry, scrubby *garrigue*.

Romanesque buildings, Roman remains and palaces of popes and cardinals are among its architectural treasures, and rugby pitches and bull-rings are emlems of local passions.

The Auvergne is at the very heart of France, in the rugged, high Massif Central, with its impressive scenery of mountain ranges, volcanic formations, larva rock, lakes and valleys. Heavily depopulated in the past – many of Paris's bars and cafés are run by *auvergnat* families – the region has been opened up to tourism by modern communications, and ski resorts attract visitors from all over Europe. The area is also well known for cheeses, such as Saint-Nectaire and Auvergne blue.

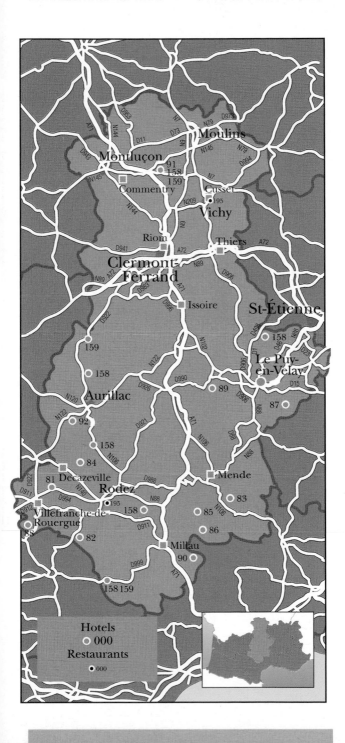

Moulins

Montluçon

Commentry

Cusset

Vichy

Riom

Thiers

Clermont-Ferrand

Issoire

St-Étienne

Le Puy-en-Velay

Aurillac

Mende

Decazeville

Rodez

Villefranche-de-Rouergue

Millau

Hotels
○ 000
Restaurants
● 000

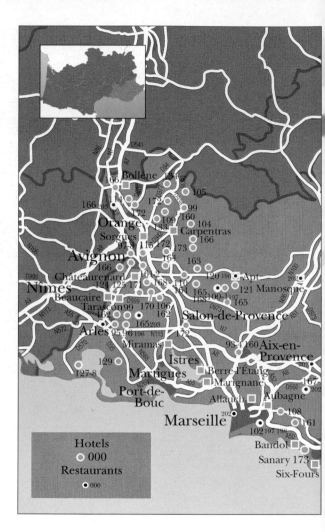

The allure of Provence – sun, sparkling sea, blue skies, wine, the easy Mediterranean way of life, and a light that has inspired painters through the centuries – continues to work its magic. Not surprisingly, our largest concentration of recommendations is here. Provence is prettiest in spring, when the flowers are at at their best, apart from the fields of lavender, which should be seen in midsummer.

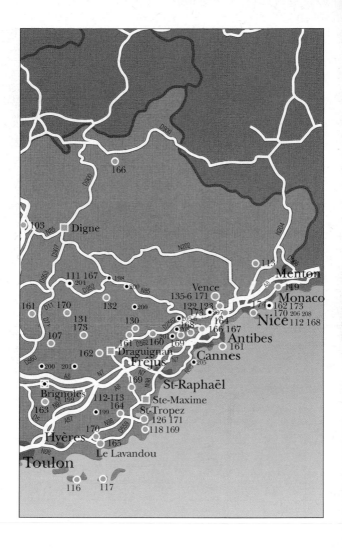

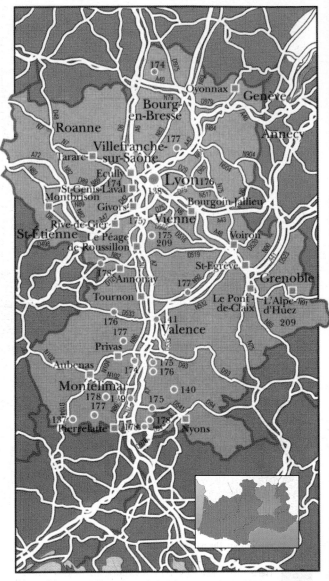

Many visitors see this region only briefly – through the window of a car or a coach – and therefore miss much. Lyon is the gastronomic centre of France, with chefs able to draw on local fish, game, vegetables and fruit, and the wines of the Beaujolais vineyards and the Côtes-du-Rhône villages. The enterprising traveller will want to find time to stop on the route south, to sit under the trees or on a terrace and watch one of the great rivers of Europe go by.

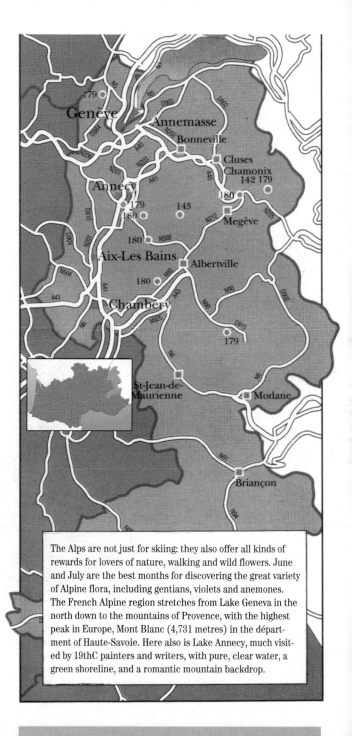

The Alps are not just for skiing: they also offer all kinds of rewards for lovers of nature, walking and wild flowers. June and July are the best months for discovering the great variety of Alpine flora, including gentians, violets and anemones. The French Alpine region stretches from Lake Geneva in the north down to the mountains of Provence, with the highest peak in Europe, Mont Blanc (4,731 metres) in the départment of Haute-Savoie. Here also is Lake Annecy, much visited by 19thC painters and writers, with pure, clear water, a green shoreline, and a romantic mountain backdrop.

REPORTING TO THE GUIDE

Please write and tell us about your experiences of small hotels, guesthouses and inns, whether good or bad, whether listed in this edition or not. As well as hotels in France, we are interested in hotels in Italy, Spain, Austria, Germany, Switzerland, Greece and the U.S.A. We assume that reporters have no objections to our publishing their views unpaid.

Readers whose reports prove particularly helpful may be invited to join our Travellers' Panel. Members give us notice of their own travel plans; we suggest hotels that they might inspect, and help with the cost of accommodation.

The address to write to us is:

Editor, *Charming Small Hotel Guides*,
Duncan Petersen Publishing Limited,
31 Ceylon Road,
London W14 0PY.

Checklist
Please use a separate sheet of paper for each report; include your name, address and telephone number on each report.

Your reports will be received with particular pleasure if they are typed, and if they are organized under the following headings:

Name of establishment
Town or village it is in, or nearest
Full address, including postcode
Telephone number
Time and duration of visit
The building and setting
The public rooms
The bedrooms and bathrooms
Physical comfort (chairs, beds, heat, light, hot water)
Standards of maintenance and housekeeping
Atmosphere, welcome and service
Food
Value for money

We assume that in writing you have no objections to your views being published unpaid, either verbatim or in an edited version. Names of major outside contributors are acknowledged, at the editor's discretion, in the guide.

BORDEAUX AND THE DORDOGNE

AGNAC

CHATEAU DE PECHALBET

~ COUNTRY HOUSE HOTEL ~

47800 Agnac (Lot-et-Garonne)
TEL/FAX 05 53 83 04 70
E-MAIL pechalbet@caramail.com **WEBSITE** www.eymet-en-perigord.com

WHEN HENRI PEYRE AND HIS WIFE, Françoise, fled from the crowded shores of the Riviera in 1995 in search of somewhere quiet in the country, their initial idea was to provide *chambres d'hôte* with breakfast only. But they found that guests were most reluctant to tear themselves away from the huge rooms and peace of this beautiful 17thC château to go out to eat in restaurants at the end of the day and last year Mme Peyre gave in to pressure and now cooks dinner. "It's very pleasant," says her husband. "We all gather on the terrace to watch the sunsets, then eat by candlelight and talk and talk. It's sometimes very difficult to get our guests to bed." Prices are kept deliberately low to encourage people to come for several days, or even weeks, at a time. There is a huge amount of space – rooms, furnished with charming antiques, are enormous and all open on to the terrace – and the house has an intriguing history. Sheep graze in the park, when autumn comes around logs crackle in the massive stone fireplace and there is mushrooming in the woods. For guests M. Peyre has his own list of what he claims are entirely secret places that he has discovered himself to be visited nearby, and he and his wife offer the warmest of welcomes. Reports please.

~

NEARBY Eymet (4 km); Bergerac (25 km).
LOCATION on 40-hectare country estate; signposted S of Eymet on D933 to Miramont; ample car and garage parking
FOOD breakfast, dinner
PRICE ⓔ
ROOMS 5 double and twin, all with bath or shower
FACILITIES 2 sitting rooms, billiard room, bar, dining room, terrace, gardens, swimming pool
CREDIT CARDS not accepted **CHILDREN** welcome
DISABLED no special facilities **PETS** accepted **CLOSED** Dec to Apr
PROPRIETOR Henri Peyre

BORDEAUX AND THE DORDOGNE

ASTAFFORT

LE SQUARE
~ VILLAGE HOTEL ~

5/7 place de la Craste, 47220 Astaffort (Lot-et-Garonne)
TEL 05 53 47 20 40 **FAX** 05 53 47 10 38 **E-MAIL** Latrille.Michel@wanadoo.fr
WEBSITE www.latrille.com

WARM OCHRE AND SIENNA-WASHED EXTERIORS, blue shutters and striped awnings on a little *place* filled with roses and pergolas really make you feel you are heading south. There have been recent improvements at this charming little hotel since Agen chef Michel Latrille and his wife, Sylvie, took over. Now there is a satisfying combination: M. Latrille's excellent traditional local cuisine and stylish, comfortable, spacious bedrooms with shining bathrooms, all set off by Mme Latrille's vivacity. No expense has been spared on the high quality renovation of two adjoining houses and the smart Kenzo fabrics, painted furniture, modern uplighting and glistening tiled bathrooms are pleasingly fresh and uplifting. This little hotel is just the right size and the Latrilles have created an easy informality, while assuring that there are no slips in their standards. Nooks and crannies of the hotel are filled with interesting detail; a small Moorish-style patio with olive tree helps to give the impression you are not far away from the road to Spain and there's a large, leafy outside terrace on the first floor for eating on summer evenings. Outside, dogs bark, old men play *boules* and children scamper in the square.

NEARBY Agen (18 km); *bastides*; Garonne river.
LOCATION in village centre; garage and street parking
FOOD breakfast, lunch, dinner
PRICE €€€
ROOMS 14; 12 double and twin, 2 suites, 11 with bath, 3 with shower; all rooms have phone, TV, air conditioning, minibar, safe, hairdrier
FACILITIES sitting room, dining room, lift, terrace
CREDIT CARDS AE, DC, MC, V
CHILDREN accepted
DISABLED 1 specially adapted room
PETS accepted
CLOSED 15 days in Jan; 1 week in Nov
PROPRIETORS Michel and Sylvie Latrille

BORDEAUX AND THE DORDOGNE

BRANTOME

✳ DOMAINE DE LA ROSERAIE ✳

∽ COUNTRY HOTEL ∽

route d'Angoulême, 24310 Brantôme (Dordogne)
TEL 05 53 05 84 74 **FAX** 05 53 05 77 94 **E-MAIL** domaine.la.roseraie@wanadoo.fr
WEBSITE www.domaine-la-roseraie.com

IT IS SOME TIME SINCE THE DOMAINE DE LA ROSERAIE looked like a 17thC monastery and the courtyard surrounded by restored one-storey buildings is now almost swamped by flowers and plants. There are roses in abundance, as the name implies, and everywhere you look there are little troughs and pots full of blooms, which give the air a heavy scent. Evelyne Roux is fastidious about her *domaine*, constantly doing her rounds to check that all is in place and there is nothing that guests might find less than perfect. All her rooms face south, have old family furniture, spotless bathrooms and independent entrances. The most popular, Bagatelle, is turned out in yellow *toile de Jouy* – and is charming. In one room Mme Roux painted the *trompe l'oeil* herself and when she made a mistaken blob on another wall artfully turned that into a butterfly. Her taste will suit those who appreciate high, comfortable beds, immaculate bathrooms, prettiness and peace and quiet. The swimming pool is discreetly hidden behind greenery and breakfast can be taken outside at little tables. M. Roux's local cooking is served in the evenings in the beamed dining room with stone fireplace and picture windows or among the roses on the terrace. For nature lovers.

∽

NEARBY Brantôme (1 km); Bourdeilles; Richemont; Puyguilhem.
LOCATION in countryside on 4 hectares of gardens and grounds; ample car parking
FOOD breakfast, dinner **PRICE** €€ **ROOMS** 9 double and twin, all with bath and shower; all rooms have phone, TV, hairdrier; 2 have air conditioning **FACILITIES** sitting room, dining room, bar, terrace, garden, swimming pool **CREDIT CARDS** AE, MC, V **CHILDREN** welcome

DISABLED 1 specially adapted room
PETS not accepted
CLOSED mid-Nov to mid-Mar
PROPRIETORS Evelyne and Denis Roux

BORDEAUX AND THE DORDOGNE

BRANTOME

✳ MOULIN DE L'ABBAYE ✳
∼ CONVERTED MILL ∼

1 route de Bourdeilles, 24310 Brantôme (Dordogne)
TEL 05 53 05 80 22 **FAX** 05 53 05 75 27 **E-MAIL** moulin@relaischateaux.com
WEBSITE www. relaischateaux.com

'ALTHOUGH WE ARRIVED RATHER LATE (8.30 pm), without a booking and clad in leather, we were welcomed with open arms. We stayed in one of their buildings across the river, and were upgraded to a junior suite (without us asking) on the top floor which had a fabulous view to the Moulin. There was a huge bathroom with a circular marble bathtub. The room was tastefully decorated in colonial style. We would love to have stayed there longer and felt it was worth the money.' So write a very satisfied pair of motorcyclists about this exquisite little mill.

The setting is the thing. The shady riverside terrace, illuminated in the evening, is an idyllic place for a drink or a meal while admiring Brantôme's unusual angled bridge, the tower of the abbey or the swans gliding by. Wonderful views over the river and the old houses of one of the prettiest villages in France are also to be had from many of the bedrooms – all comfortably furnished, some with four-poster beds and antiques, others in more modern style.

Traditional Périgord dishes with a creative touch earn the restaurant 16/20 from GaultMillau and a star from Michelin. The dining room makes a pleasant setting for this excellent cuisine in cooler weather, although we can raise no enthusiasm for the 'Monet-style' colour scheme.

NEARBY Antonne-et-Trigonant (3 km); Bourdeilles (10 km).
LOCATION on edge of town, 20 km N of Périgueux; garage parking across road
FOOD breakfast, lunch, dinner; room service **PRICE** €€€€-€€€€€
ROOMS 17 double and twin, 3 apartments, all with bath, all rooms have phone, TV, air conditioning, minibar, hairdrier **FACILITIES** sitting room, restaurant, terrace

CREDIT CARDS AE, DC, MC, V
CHILDREN welcome
DISABLED no special facilities
PETS accepted
CLOSED Nov to May
MANAGER Bernard Dessum

BORDEAUX AND THE DORDOGNE

CARDAILLAC

CHEZ MARCEL
~ VILLAGE INN ~

rue du 11 Mai 1944, 46100 Cardaillac (Lot)
TEL 05 65 40 11 16 **FAX** 05 65 40 49 08

BUILT AS AN *auberge* and stables in the mid-19th century and now the local bar-restaurant of a small village north of Figéac, this has been run for the past three years by Bernard Marcel, who took it over on the death of his father, André. Time has barely touched it and from the minute you find yourself among the red-and-white gingham tablecloths and lace curtains of the handsome ground-floor rooms you are enveloped by the authentic rustic charm of days long gone by. The barely believable prices and unspoiled simplicity of the place have proved a winner for the Marcel family, but some very small changes are planned, though nothing that could be described as radical. Mme Marcel, Gisèle, who speaks English, is slowly adding to the delightful collection of country antiques in the bedrooms and her husband is contemplating the possibility of replacing the plastic curtain in the shower with a glass door, but he's not in any hurry. Nothing to frighten the horses, so Chez Marcel fans, of which there are many, will not get any unwelcome shocks when they return. The chef, Jacky Fabre, has been there for 22 years and bread comes in fresh from the baker just up the road. There's plenty of life in the bar in the evenings and a pretty little village to visit.

~

NEARBY Figéac (9 km); Cahors (60 km); valley of the Lot.
LOCATION in country village; car parking in large public car park and street
FOOD breakfast, lunch, dinner
PRICE €
ROOMS 5; 4 double and 1 triple; all rooms have washbasins and share shower and WC on landing
FACILITIES restaurant, bar, terrace
CREDIT CARDS MC, V **CHILDREN** accepted
DISABLED no special facilities **PETS** accepted
CLOSED 15 days in Feb
PROPRIETOR Bernard Marcel

BORDEAUX AND THE DORDOGNE

CARENNAC

HOSTELLERIE FENELON
~ VILLAGE INN ~

46110 Carennac (Lot)
TEL 05 65 10 96 46 **FAX** 05 65 10 94 86

MME RAYNAL WAS, with her characteristic attention to detail, busy gardening and planting out geraniums in the plentiful window boxes on this jolly-looking, family-run, colourful *logis*, with red roof and red-and-white striped awnings, when we called. She likes the place to be a riot of flowers and her warm welcome and the friendly and unobtrusive service of her staff have won her many admirers among our readers. Traditionalists will be happy to know that son, Philippe, is now in the kitchen and continues his father's highly commended and generous *cuisine du terroir*. In the middle of the Haut-Quercy, Carennac is a delightful, riverside medieval village, full of charm, and quite a few of Mme Raynal's neat, clean bedrooms – conventionally decorated with reproduction furniture and flowery prints – look over the pointed Perigordan roof of a little gingerbread house on the banks of the Dordogne river. The beamed restaurant, too, overlooks the river, though meals are served, as well, on the paved terrace at the front of the hotel, which is shielded from the quiet road by a tall hedge. Use of the swimming pool is reserved for guests. Excellent value for money and a homely ambience make this a perfect staging post for touring the area.

~

NEARBY Carennac priory; Rocamadour (30 km); Gouffre de Padirac (10 km).
LOCATION in village centre; ample car parking
FOOD breakfast, lunch, dinner
PRICE €
ROOMS 15 double and twin, all with bath or shower; all rooms have phone, TV
FACILITIES sitting room; dining room, bar, terrace, garden, swimming pool
CREDIT CARDS DC, MC, V **CHILDREN** accepted
DISABLED access difficult **PETS** accepted
CLOSED mid-Jan to mid-Mar
PROPRIETORS M. and Mme Raynal and sons

BORDEAUX AND THE DORDOGNE

CHAMPAGNAC-DE-BÉLAIR

MOULIN DU ROC
~ CONVERTED MILL ~

24530 Champagnac-de-Bélair (Dordogne)
TEL 05 53 02 86 00 **FAX** 05 53 54 21 31 **E-MAIL** moulinroc@aol.com
WEBSITE www.moulin-du-roc.com

THIS DELECTABLE OLD WALNUT-OIL MILL with its Michelin-starred restaurant belongs to that rare breed of hotels that gives you the sense of being pampered without costing a fortune. The setting on the banks of the Dronne is truly romantic: the gardens are lush, secluded, shady and bursting with colour. A Japanese-style bridge crosses the river to a grassy area with scattered seating and discreetly positioned swimming pool and tennis court. Inside the rough-stone 17thC building, oak beams, stone fireplaces, mill machinery, rich fabrics and a wealth of antiques – oil paintings, silverware and solid Périgord dressers – combine with abundant flower arrangements to create an intimate yet highly individual style. Some may find it slightly heavy. The same cannot be said of the food: in the land of *foie gras*, Alain Gardillou manages to build on culinary traditions to produce remarkably light and inventive dishes. Herbs and vegetables come from the hotel gardens, and there's a dazzling choice of wines. Breakfasts, too, are a treat, with home-baked rolls, fresh fruit, eggs and yoghurt, beautifully served. Bedrooms vary in size, but do not disappoint. Many are pretty, cosy and filled with their share of antiques; several have four-posters. Others have recently been redesigned to create fewer, more spacious rooms, including large and immaculate bathrooms.

~

NEARBY Brantôme (6 km); Bourdeilles (15 km).
LOCATION in village, on D82 and D83, 6 km NE of Brantôme; car parking
FOOD breakfast, lunch, dinner
PRICE €€€-€€€€
ROOMS 13; 8 double and twin, 4 junior suites, 1 suite, all with bath or Jacuzzi bath; all rooms have phone, TV, minibar, hairdrier, 8 rooms have air conditioning
FACILITIES sitting room, dining room, terrace, garden, covered swimming pool, tennis **CREDIT CARDS** AE, DC, MC, V **CHILDREN** welcome
DISABLED 2 rooms on ground floor **PETS** accepted **CLOSED** Jan to Mar
PROPRIETORS M. and Mme Gardillou

BORDEAUX AND THE DORDOGNE

COLY

MANOIR D'HAUTEGENTE

~ MANOR HOUSE HOTEL ~

Coly, 24120 Terrasson (Dordogne)
TEL 05 53 51 68 03 **FAX** 05 53 50 38 52
E-MAIL hotel@manoir-hautegente.com **WEBSITE** www.manoir-hautegente.com

A READER ONCE DESCRIBED this creeper-clad manor house as 'so good that I wouldn't tell you about it if it were not already in the guide'. The house, set in beautiful wooded grounds in the heart of the Périgord Noir, has been in the Hamelin family for about 300 years, and is now run by Edith Hamelin and her son, Patrick. It was built as a forge in th 13th century, later became a mill (using the stream that runs beside it), was then embellished and turned into a family residence and was finally converted into a hotel – but with the feeling of a private house skilfully retained. Public rooms and the spacious, comfortable bedrooms are imaginatively decorated with family antiques and paintings.

Dinner in the pretty vaulted dining room is a five-course affair – 'first-class cuisine' which inevitably includes home-produced *foie gras*, another of the Hamelins' commercial successes. The present chef, Bernard Villain, is a particular find. Wines are reasonably priced.

In the pleasant grassy grounds there is a smart pool that gets plenty of sun. There is also a pond, and fishing is available on the local river. The Hamelins are natural hosts and a warm welcome awaits guests to their family home.

~

NEARBY châteaux; Lascaux (15 km); Sarlat (25 km).
LOCATION in countryside, 6 km SE of Le Lardin on D62, in own grounds; ample car parking
FOOD breakfast, dinner
PRICE €€€
ROOMS 15 double and twin, all with bath; all rooms have phone, TV, hairdrier
FACILITIES sitting room, dining room, terrace, garden, swimming pool
CREDIT CARDS MC, V **CHILDREN** welcome
DISABLED 1 ground-floor room **PETS** accepted **CLOSED** Nov to Easter
PROPRIETORS Edith Hamelin and Patrick Hamelin

BORDEAUX AND THE DORDOGNE

LACAVE

CHATEAU DE LA TREYNE

~ CHATEAU HOTEL ~

Lacave, 46200 Souillac (Lot)
TEL 05 65 27 60 60 **FAX** 05 65 27 60 70
E-MAIL treyne@relaischateaux.com **WEBSITE** www.relaischateaux.com/treyne

WE'VE HAD OUR EYE on this little château beside the Dordogne since an inspector came back a few years ago with a report littered with emphatically underscored adjectives – 'gorgeous... impeccable... exceptionally comfortable'. Of course, it is not cheap; perhaps we should be grateful that elevation to Relais & Châteaux status has not pushed prices up further.

Michèle Gombert-Deval's house has made a splendid small hotel. It starts with the advantage of a beautiful position, in woods on a low cliff cut by the meandering river Dordogne. But the compelling attraction of the château is the near-ideal balance struck between the impressiveness of a fortified manor house and the intimacy of a genuine home. The building dates from the early 14th century, but was substantially rebuilt in the 1600s; it is now tastefully equipped with a happy mix of furnishings – comfy sofas in front of an open fire, as well as grand antiques.

There are long walks to enjoy in the grounds, and a very beautiful formal garden before which you can take breakfast. Excellent regional food is served – on the delightful terrace perched above the river in good weather.

~

NEARBY Souillac (6 km); Rocamadour; Sarlat.
LOCATION 3 km W of village on D43, 6 km SE of Souillac, in large grounds beside river; ample car parking
FOOD breakfast, lunch, dinner; room service
PRICE €€€€
ROOMS 16; 14 double and twin, 2 suites, all with bath; all rooms have phone, TV, air conditioning, hairdrier
FACILITIES 3 sitting rooms, dining room, bar, billiard room, lift, terrace, garden, swimming pool, tennis **CREDIT CARDS** AE, DC, MC, V **CHILDREN** welcome
DISABLED access difficult **PETS** accepted
CLOSED mid-Nov to Easter
MANAGER Philippe Bappel

BORDEAUX AND THE DORDOGNE

LACAVE

PONT DE L'OUYSSE
~ RIVERSIDE HOTEL ~

46200 Lacave (Lot)
TEL 05 65 37 87 04 **FAX** 05 65 32 77 41
E-MAIL Pont.Ouysse@wanadoo.fr

THE *RAISON D'ETRE* of this peaceful, small *auberge* is its magnificent dining terrace overlooking the river, shaded by horse chestnut and lime trees. The approach, via a long, private drive, gives a first impression of total seclusion. (This privacy is especially valued by guests; our inspector spotted a celebrated French news anchorman on one visit.) There's a riverside walk with benches and a new pool discreetly tucked away from the main bustle of the hotel. There is not a sound here of traffic, only birdsong and the murmuring of the river.

The large house has been in Mme Chambon's family for generations and still feels in many ways like a private home. Rooms are decorated with pretty English wallpapers and matching fabrics; some have angled ceilings and authentic beams. It is always a good sign when the restaurant draws local as well as hotel guests and Daniel Chambon's cooking packs the dining room with people from as far away as Sarlat. His creative talents are complemented by his liberal use of fresh local produce (which includes eel from the Ouysse). Our reporter was enchanted: 'Beautiful setting, great food and charming hosts.'

~

NEARBY Souillac (8 km); Sarlat (35 km); Rocamadour (30 km).
LOCATION in 5-hectare grounds on the river Ouysse; car parking
FOOD breakfast, lunch, dinner
PRICE €€
ROOMS 12 double and twin, 2 suites, all with bath; all rooms have phone, TV, minibar, safe, hairdrier
FACILITIES sitting room, dining room, terrace, garden, swimming pool
CREDIT CARDS AE, DC, MC, V **CHILDREN** accepted
DISABLED no special facilities **PETS** accepted
CLOSED mid-Nov to Mar
PROPRIETORS M. and Mme Chambon

BORDEAUX AND THE DORDOGNE

HOSTELLERIE LE VERT
~ FARMHOUSE HOTEL ~

Mauroux, 46700 Puy L'Evêque (Lot)
TEL 05 65 36 51 36 **FAX** 05 65 36 56 84

L E VERT GOES FROM STRENGTH TO STRENGTH. The attractions of this secluded
17thC farmhouse have been greatly increased by the construction of a
swimming pool. Whatever the changes, however, it will doubtless remain
the kind of hotel you look forward to returning to at the end of the day; it
also looks set to become the kind you're disinclined to leave at all.

There is just a small side door to lead you inside. Within, all is original
stone walls and beams ('just about perfect', comments a reader). The dining room opens out on to a terrace with wide views; through an arch at one
end is a small sitting room – ideal for an aperitif. The bedrooms are all
comfortably and tastefully modernized, and have lovely views. The largest
are quite grand and furnished with antiques. But the most attractive are in
the little annexe a couple of yards from the entrance – the lower one
stone-vaulted, the upper one beamed, with a marble floor. The garden has
chairs and tables, and is improving in colour despite dry summers. The
owners are a friendly and hard-working couple – M. Philippe cooks (inter-
estingly and competently), Mme Philippe serves (and also speaks excellent English).

~

NEARBY Bonaguil (15 km); Biron (35 km); Monpazier (50 km).
LOCATION in countryside, off D5, 10 km SW of Puy-L'Evêque, 10 km SE of Fumel;
ample car parking
FOOD breakfast, lunch, dinner
PRICE €
ROOMS 7 double and twin, all with bath or shower; all rooms have phone, TV
FACILITIES sitting room, dining room, terrace, garden, swimming pool
CREDIT CARDS AE, MC, V **CHILDREN** welcome
DISABLED no special facilities **PETS** accepted
CLOSED mid-Nov to mid-Feb
PROPRIETORS Eva and Bernard Philippe

BORDEAUX AND THE DORDOGNE

PAUILLAC

✳ CHATEAU CORDEILLAN-BAGES ✳

～ CHATEAU HOTEL ～

route des Châteaux, 33250 Pauillac (Gironde)
TEL 05 56 59 24 24 **FAX** 05 56 59 01 89 **E-MAIL** cordeillan@relaischateaux.com
WEBSITE www.relaischateaux.com/cordeillan

THE RESTAURANT AND TERRACE at Cordeillan-Bages look directly out on to rows of vines – neighbours are Latour, Lafite, Mouton-Rothschild and many other distinguished names in the history of wine. Built in the purest 17thC style, the château is in the heart of the Médoc. (There's a small boutique selling good vintages.) The lovely, pale-stone, well-proportioned single-storey house was completely restored in 1989 and the decoration is stylish and restful. There is something of the feel of an English country house about the intimate sitting rooms and elegant dining room. The bedrooms are very comfortable, with the sure hand of the interior designer given full rein. In the kitchen, chef Thierry Marx uses his skills to create new dishes based on seasonal produce, as well as traditional regional food. The wine list is encyclopaedic. The château is home to the Ecole de Bordeaux, which offers a wide choice of courses for both professional and amateur wine lovers and organizes visits to other vineyards in the area. The hotel slightly lacks the character it might have in private hands, but it is a charming house and the high standard of service lives up to its four star expectations.

～

NEARBY Château Mouton-Rothschild (5 km); Bordeaux (40 km).
LOCATION in own vineyards, in wine village on D2, 40 km N of Bordeaux; ample car parking **FOOD** breakfast, lunch, dinner; room service
PRICE €€€-€€€€
ROOMS 25; 24 double and twin, 1 suite, all with bath; all rooms have phone, TV, minibar, safe, hairdrier **FACILITIES** sitting rooms, dining room, boutique, lift, terrace, garden **CREDIT CARDS** AE, DC, MC, V **CHILDREN** accepted

DISABLED access possible
PETS accepted
CLOSED mid-Dec to Feb; restaurant closed Mon, Sat dinner
MANAGER Thierry Marx

BORDEAUX AND THE DORDOGNE

PUYMIROL

LES LOGES DE L'AUBERGADE
~ VILLAGE HOTEL ~

52 rue Royale, Puymirol (Lot-et-Garonne)
TEL 05 53 95 31 46 **FAX** 05 53 95 33 80
E-MAIL trama@aubergade.com **WEBSITE** www.aubergade.com

'**E**XCELLENCE PAR EXCELLENCE' enthused a visitor to this handsome former residence of the Counts of Toulouse, dating from the 13th century and in a little fortified village. The lodestones to Puymirol are chef Michel Trama (two Michelin stars) for his superb food, wine and cigars, and his wife Maryse, with whom he has created this international-class hotel-restaurant. The building has stone walls, high ceilings, beams, a 17thC oak staircase and is decorated with impeccable style. The extensive kitchens are impressive and full of activity with M. Trama very much in personal charge. A special feature is a large smoking room with a glass-fronted, fully humidified cabinet containing a collection of the very best Cuban cigars – not for show but for smoking.

A terrace garden, leading off the dining room, has attractive canvas umbrella sunshades and is discreetly illuminated through trees and bushes after dark. Bedrooms, in contemporary style, are large and elegant and bathrooms have whirlpool baths. The overall feeling inside is one of light and airiness, predominantly white (much original stone), with white furniture offset with green and the colours of the abundant floral decorations.

NEARBY Agen (17 km); Moissac (32 km); Villeneuve-sur-Lot (31 km).
LOCATION in middle of small fortified village, 20 km E of Agen; car parking and garage
FOOD breakfast, lunch, dinner; room service
PRICE €€€€-€€€€€
ROOMS 10 double and twin, all with whirlpool bath or massage shower; all rooms have phone, TV, video, air conditioning, minibar, hairdrier
FACILITIES sitting room, dining room, terrace
CREDIT CARDS AE, DC, MC, V **CHILDREN** accepted
DISABLED 2 rooms on ground floor **PETS** accepted
CLOSED 5 weeks Feb-Mar
PROPRIETORS Michel and Maryse Trama

BORDEAUX AND THE DORDOGNE

ROCAMADOUR

DOMAINE DE LA RHUE
~ CONVERTED STABLES ~

46500 Rocamadour (Lot)
TEL 05 65 33 71 50 **FAX** 05 65 33 72 48 **E-MAIL** domainedelarhue@rocamadour.com
WEBSITE www.rocamadour.com/us/hotels/LaRhue/index.htm

O N OUR MOST RECENT VISIT we came away more enthusiastic than ever about this truly charming place. A former stable block next to the handsome, family-owned château, it's set in peacefully rolling countryside, down a long drive, where you're assured complete silence. Above all, the Jooris's are exceptional hosts: they have time for everyone, even when demands press in. Helpful and good humoured, they never intrude: the atmosphere is always good.

Their formula is simple: they serve no meals other than breakfast and light lunches (on request) by the pool, but guests are welcome to make themselves at home and spend the day relaxing by the pool if they feel like it. There's a proper reception area and large sitting areas for guests' use. Rooms are comfortable and pretty; several are ideal for families, some with kitchenettes and their own garden entrances.

Eric Jooris is a hot-air balloon pilot and will take guests for flights, weather permitting. With Gallic nonchalance, he calmly pushes away branches as the basket brushes against them on the way up out of Rocamadour's deep gorge. But he's very safe. If you like that sort of thing, don't miss a flight. In short, a brilliant place.

~

NEARBY Rocamadour (7 km); Padirac (15 km); Carennac (20 km).
LOCATION in countryside, on N140, 7 km N of Rocamadour; car parking
FOOD breakfast, light lunch
PRICE €€
ROOMS 14; 12 double and twin, 2 family, 12 with bath, 2 with shower; all rooms have phone, fan; some rooms have minibar, kitchenette, hairdrier
FACILITIES sitting room, terrace, swimming pool
CREDIT CARDS MC, V **CHILDREN** accepted
DISABLED no special facilities **PETS** accepted
CLOSED mid-Oct to Easter
PROPRIETORS M. and Mme Jooris

BORDEAUX AND THE DORDOGNE

RUCH

CHATEAU LARDIER
~ COUNTRY HOUSE HOTEL ~

route de Sauveterre, Ruch, 33350 Castillon-la-Bataille (Gironde)
TEL 05 57 40 54 11 **FAX** 05 57 40 72 35
E-MAIL chateau.lardier@free.fr **WEBSITE** www.chateau.lardier.free.fr

THE PAGES PRODUCE their own AOC Bordeaux Rouge and Rosé (bottles attractively displayed everywhere and available to accompany your own supper cooked on the barbecue by the pool) from the vineyards that surround this elegant 17th/18thC house, with its rows of white shutters and long ivy-clad stone façade. Relaxed and informal, it is the kind of place that is immediately welcoming, with spacious, airy ground-floor rooms, bedrooms with views over neat rows of vines and a pleasant garden area at the rear next to the pool. If you don't want to go out in the evenings to eat locally, there's a communal barbecue under the chestnut tree and swings for children. Rooms, reached up a wide, stone staircase, are simple and basic, but antique beds have pretty cotton covers and tables have marble tops. There's a good choice of sleeping arrangements, with extra beds available, and it is hard to beat for value, given the swimming pool and the other amenities. Peace, quiet and birdsong are in abundance. A set of large sitting and games rooms is set aside on the ground floor for guests. There are plenty of country lanes to explore and walks through the vineyard at the end of a long, hot day by the pool.

~

NEARBY Castillon-la-Bataille (10 km); Dordogne river; St-Emilion (20 km).
LOCATION among vineyards; ample car parking
FOOD breakfast
PRICE €
ROOMS 7; 5 double and twin, 2 triple, 3 with bath, 4 with shower; all rooms have phone, TV
FACILITIES 2 sitting rooms, billiard room, terrace, garden, swimming pool
CREDIT CARDS MC, V **CHILDREN** welcome
DISABLED no special facilities **PETS** accpeted
CLOSED Nov to Mar
PROPRIETORS Jean-Noël and Evelyne Pagès

BORDEAUX AND THE DORDOGNE

ST-CIRQ-LAPOPIE

LA PELISSARIA
~ VILLAGE INN ~

St-Cirq-Lapopie, 46330 Cabrerets (Lot)
TEL 05 65 31 25 14 **FAX** 05 65 30 25 52
E-MAIL lapelissariahotel@minitel.net **WEBSITE** www.quercy.net

RECENT REPORTS LEAVE US IN NO DOUBT that the Matuchets' distinctive little
hotel is as compelling as ever. The 13thC house clings to the steep hillside on the edge of the lovely medieval hilltop village of St-Cirq-Lapopie. It
was lovingly restored by the Matuchets themselves, and its quirky character is such that you descend the stairs to the bedrooms which look out on
to the tiny garden and enjoy stunning views over the Lot valley. The bedrooms – two of them detached from the house, down the garden – are
light, airy and comfortable, with close attention to detail in the furnishings. Three large bedrooms, with two double beds in each, are located in
an old house next door to the main one. The place is simply and artistically decorated, its thick stone walls painted white, with old wooden beams
and tiled floors.

Although Mme Matuchet no longer cooks dinner, there are plenty of
good restaurants in St-Cirq-Lapopie to which the couple will direct you.
Breakfast is served *alfresco* or in your room if you prefer.

M. Matuchet, who is a musician, provides a pleasant musical background with tapes of his own music. The *salon* is graced by a piano and
various stringed instruments.

~

NEARBY Pêche-Merle caves and museum; Cahors (35 km).
LOCATION in village, 30 km E of Cahors; car parking difficult
FOOD breakfast
PRICE €€€
ROOMS 10; 8 double and twin, 6 with bath, 2 with shower, 2 suites with bath; all
rooms have phone, TV
FACILITIES sitting room, dining room, terrace, garden, small swimming pool
CREDIT CARDS MC, V **CHILDREN** welcome
DISABLED 1 suitable bedroom **PETS** accepted
CLOSED mid-Nov to Apr
PROPRIETORS Marie-Françoise and François Matuchet

BORDEAUX AND THE DORDOGNE

ST MICHEL-DE-MONTAIGNE

LE JARDIN D'EYQUEM
~ CASTLE HOTEL ~

24230 St Michel-de-Montaigne (Dordogne)
TEL 05 53 24 89 59 **FAX** 05 53 61 14 40 **E-MAIL** jardin-eyquem@wanadoo.fr
WEBSITE www.perso.wanadoo.fr/jardin-eyquem

AN UNUSUAL RECOMMENDATION for us, but this is such a well thought-out idea that we felt we should not leave it out. The Le Morvans – he was a pilot, she a teacher – moved here from Paris 10 years ago to provide for others what they always hoped to find for themselves on their travels – somewhere pretty, small, calm and somewhere with a small kitchen, so that if you wanted to stay in all day you could. Both passionate about Montaigne, they have converted a farmhouse in the village where the great philosopher was born and named it after his family; in winter you can see through the trees the château of Montaigne's brother. A delightful, thoughtful air prevails. The house faces south and the swimming pool among the vines is in full sun all day. The largest apartment is the old beamed hayloft, but all are spacious with the kitchen section hidden behind cotton curtains made by Danièle, tables, chairs and even egg cups for meals, and painted furniture. When we visited, any fabrics in what could be considered dull colours were being thrown out and replaced by yellow, "for the gaiety of life" said Madame. Breakfast is served in a large ground-floor room with handsome stone fireplace.

House rule: The pool must always be a quiet, peaceful place.

NEARBY Montaigne's Tower (short walk); St Emilion (18 km); *bastides* of Ste-Foy and Libourne.
LOCATION among vineyards on edge of village; ample car parking
FOOD breakfast
PRICE ©©©
ROOMS 5 apartments, double or twin, 3 with bath, 2 with shower; all rooms have phone, TV, kitchenette
FACILITIES sitting room, library, breakfast room, terrace, garden, swimming pool
CREDIT CARDS MC, V **CHILDREN** welcome
DISABLED 1 suitable apartment
PETS not accepted **CLOSED** Nov to Apr
PROPRIETORS Danièle and Christian Le Morvan

BORDEAUX AND THE DORDOGNE

St-Saud-Lacoussiere

HOSTELLERIE ST-JACQUES

~ VILLAGE INN ~

24470 St-Saud-Lacoussière (Dordogne)
Tel. 05 53 56 97 21 **Fax** 05 53 56 91 33

THE MORE WE LEARN about the Babayous' enterprise, the more thoroughly impressed we are by their sure understanding of holidaymakers' needs and priorities.

The front of the creeper-clad 18thC building gives little clue to what lies within – or, more to the point, what lies behind: the Babayous' 'summer sitting room', which consists of lovely sloping gardens, with masses of colourful flowers, a fair-sized pool, tennis court and plenty of shade and space for children. Inside there is an unusually large dining room/bar decorated in bright blue and yellow, with big windows which open on to the terrace above the garden. All the bedrooms are comfortable, spacious and attractively decorated; several can accommodate families.

The food is rich and varied; even the basic menu is probably enough to satisfy most appetites. A buffet breakfast/brunch is served in the garden or by the pool. Occasionally there are lively evenings with dancing and games, or communal dinners devoted to exploration of regional cuisine. Not your cup of tea? Just give it a try: you might be surprised.

~

Nearby Château de Richemont; Montbrun (15 km); Brantôme (30 km); Rochechouart (45 km).
Location in quiet village, 30 km N of Brantôme; car parking
Food breakfast, lunch, dinner
Price €
Rooms 22 double and twin, 2 suites, all with bath or shower; all rooms have phone, some have TV, minibar
Facilities 2 dining rooms, bar, TV room, terrace, garden, swimming pool, tennis
Credit cards AE, MC, V **Children** welcome
Disabled no special facilities **Pets** accepted
Closed Nov to Mar and Sun dinner, Mon
Proprietor Jean-Pierre Babayou

BORDEAUX AND THE DORDOGNE

TOUZAC

HOSTELLERIE DE LA SOURCE BLEUE
∽ RIVERSIDE HOTEL ∽

Moulin de Leygues, 46700 Touzac (Lot)
TEL 05 65 36 52 01 **FAX** 05 65 24 65 69
E-MAIL sourcebleue@wanadoo.fr **WEBSITE** www.hotelsourcebleue.free.fr

SET PEACEFULLY beside the Lot in a grove of weeping willows, this hotel is an oasis of verdant tranquillity in a quiet corner of Quercy. The property has been in the family of M. Bouyou for more than 600 years and consists of three mills built in the 11th, 13th and 17th centuries. The trio of large rooms under the eaves in the main 700-year-old paper mill have been renovated with particular sensitivity and taste, and even the lowest-priced rooms are reasonably spacious and endowed with charm. A smaller mill is used for art exhibitions. The hotel's rustic dining room and pool are added attractions. A terrace overlooks a cobalt-coloured pool – 'the blue spring' – bubbling from an underground spring rich in magnesium.

Guests have the freedom of a large park; there are long walks along paths following the river and through a plantation of giant bamboo and a birch forest. Smaller guests will enjoy the children's garden and the hotel has a leisure centre, a library, a room for tea, and a boat. There is also a kitchen garden, and home-grown cherries, apricots, hazelnuts and raspberries feature at mealtimes. Salmon and *rôti de lotte* in a fresh tomato sauce are specialities of the house.

∽

NEARBY Puy L'Evêque (20 km); Cahors (48 km).
LOCATION in 3-hectare grounds on the banks of the Lot; car parking
FOOD breakfast, lunch, dinner
PRICE €€€
ROOMS 17 double and twin, 16 with bath, 1 with shower; all rooms have phone, TV
FACILITIES sitting rooms, dining room, terrace, fitness centre, sauna, boat, Japanese garden
CREDIT CARDS AE, DC, MC, V **CHILDREN** accepted
DISABLED 1 suitable room **PETS** accepted
CLOSED Jan to Apr
PROPRIETORS Siân and Jean-Pierre Bouyou

BORDEAUX AND THE DORDOGNE

TREMOLAT

✳ LE VIEUX LOGIS ✳
~ VILLAGE HOTEL ~

24510 Trémolat (Dordogne)
TEL 05 53 22 80 06 **FAX** 05 53 22 84 89 **E-MAIL** vieuxlogis@relaischateaux.com
WEBSITE www.relaischateaux.com/vieuxlogis

WE CONTINUE TO LIST this glorious old hotel, one of the most civilized in a region with many attractive hotels, despite a recent postbag of readers' letters, which, though broadly complimentary, had some niggles too. On the complimentary side, all our correspondents marked out for special praise the 'happy and smiling, well-trained staff' and the warm atmosphere they engendered. The food, too, was praised, including the 'spectacular' buffet breakast. Irritations included problems with hot water on a couple of occasions, tired decoration in the bedroom and bathroooom, and an exorbitant charge for a single brandy. All our correspondents, however, said they would return.

Owners the Giraudel-Destords have lived in this complex of farm and village houses for nearly 400 years. The part which is now the dining room once held pigs and wine barrels. Now all has been designer-decorated to produce comfort of a high degree. Bedrooms, some with four-posters, are done in a cosy sophisticated-rustic style; public rooms (some little used) are elegant and comfortable, with plenty of quiet nooks. The open fire in the small *salon* is much appreciated by guests. The galleried dining room looks out on to the green and flowery garden where you can breakfast.

NEARBY Les Eyzies-de-Tayac (25 km); Monpazier (30 km); Beynac (30 km).
LOCATION in village, 15 km SW of Le Bugue; car and garage parking
FOOD breakfast, lunch, dinner; room service
PRICE €€€€ **ROOMS** 24; 18 double and twin, 6 suites, all with bath; all rooms have phone, TV, minibar, hairdrier
FACILITIES 3 sitting rooms, 2 dining rooms, bar, terrace, garden, swimming pool
CREDIT CARDS AE, DC, MC, V
CHILDREN welcome
DISABLED 1 specially adapted room **PETS** accepted
CLOSED never
MANAGER Didier Bru

✳ **BOOK THIS HOTEL**
✳ **BOOK FERRY/EUROTUNNEL**
✳ **SAVE MONEY**
TEL: (UK) 01892 55 98 66
e-mail: enquiries@chs-travelservice.com

BORDEAUX AND THE DORDOGNE

VILLERÉAL

CHATEAU DE RICARD
~ COUNTRY HOUSE ~

route de Beaumont, 47210 Villeréal (Lot-et-Garonne)
TEL 05 53 36 61 02 **FAX** 05 53 36 61 65

EVERYTHING IS IMMACULATE about this renovated *castella de petit seigneur*, built in H-form with four pigeonnier-style turrets in 1830 (it opened to guests in mid-1995) and elegantly set in spacious grounds. The garden has manicured lawns, abundant floral display under mature trees, weeping willows reflected in lakes and even a swamp cypress.

In the main house, there is a fine *salon*, library, billiard room (French), dining room and laundry facilities – all for use by guests as in their own home. Upstairs are three magnificent bedrooms – with excellent bathrooms. The stable block has been cleverly adapted for a charming breakfast room overlooking one of the lakes, a dining room and two suites. The owners are connoisseurs of fabrics, wall coverings and tiles and their taste and expertise embellish all the rooms down to the last detail. Bed linen is changed daily; books are everywhere and for use. Breakfast is sumptuous, whether taken inside or on the large terrace by the pool. Evening meals are by arrangement for the very reasonable, inclusive price of 25 Euros for good regional food and wine. Some may find it a bit too tidy.

~

NEARBY Bastide de Villeréal (1 km); Bergerac (30 km).
LOCATION in countryside on D676 N of Villeréal; car parking
FOOD breakfast; dinner 4 nights a week
PRICE €€
ROOMS 5; 3 double and twin, 2 suites, all with bath; suites with terrace
FACILITIES sitting room, library, billiard room, dining room, laundry room, terrace, garden, swimming pool, tennis, fishing
CREDIT CARDS not accepted **CHILDREN** accepted
DISABLED access difficult **PETS** not accepted
CLOSED Nov to Easter
PROPRIETORS M. and Mme Deguilhem

THE SOUTH-WEST

AINHOA

OHANTZEA
~ VILLAGE HOTEL ~

64250 Ainhoa, (Pyrénées-Atlantiques)
TEL 05 59 29 90 50 **FAX** 05 59 29 89 70

A WARM WELCOME AWAITS in this unpretentious, seriously Basque hotel dating back to the 17th century and in the same family for the past three centuries. The timbered and shuttered building in the centre of a picturesque village is typical of the region. Inside, you step back in time, with bare, worn wooden flooring, beamed ceilings, old pictures, shelves of antique kitchen utensils, copper kettles, pewter jugs – and no concession to modern materials or ornament. French windows look out to the garden from the spacious dining room. Bedrooms are large and convey the same mood of established solidarity and family farmhouse comfort. Mme Ithurria modestly explains that "this is not a modern house and we have no formula, except to provide the atmosphere of a family home and fair prices". It is not surprising that it is much patronized by our readers. The food, too, caters to old-fashioned tastes with large helpings of succulent baby lamb and other local products. Great value for money.

The area is renowned for its mild climate; Edmond Rostand, author of *Cyrano de Bergerac*, came here to take the spa waters and liked it so much that he built a house nearby, Villa Arnaga (open to visitors on the D932).

~

NEARBY Spanish border (2 km); Villa Arnaga; St-Pée-sur-Nivelle (10 km); Sare (10 km).
LOCATION in middle of village, 10 km SW of Cambo-les-Bains; car parking
FOOD breakfast, lunch, dinner
PRICE €
ROOMS 10; 8 double and twin, 2 family, all with bath; all rooms have phone
FACILITIES sitting room, dining room, garden **CREDIT CARDS** AE, DC, MC, V
CHILDREN welcome
DISABLED no special facilities **PETS** accepted
CLOSED mid-Nov to mid-Feb
PROPRIETOR Marcel Ithurria

THE SOUTH-WEST

BARCUS

CHEZ CHILO
~ VILLAGE HOTEL ~

64130 Barcus (Pyrénées-Atlantiques)
TEL 05 59 28 90 79 **FAX** 05 59 28 93 10
E-MAIL martine.chilo@wanadoo.fr

IT IS WELL WORTH making a detour to enjoy the delights of this small hotel on the borders of the verdant Basque and Béarn country. The expertise of three generations has created a place of welcome, comfort and wonderful food. The attractive building harmonizes with the surrounding village, with a delightful garden and children's play area, and a discreetly located swimming pool with mountain views. The rooms have all been recently refurbished, and are bright and friendly without extravagance. Downstairs is an L-shaped dining room with open fireplace, a large sitting room with a bar, reminiscent of an English country inn, and a main dining room with picture windows on to the garden. This is the setting for a memorable meal. Early each morning the freshest and best of local produce is delivered straight from the market, ready to be transformed by Pierre Chilo into dishes of exceptional refinement and quality. This is a refreshing, reasonably-priced, efficient and very enjoyable stopping-place for the traveller and Martine and Pierre Chilo specialize in a warm Basque welcome. Note that they have recently acquired another hotel, the Bidegain, with period Basque interior, in nearby Mauléon (tel 05 59 28 16 05).

~

NEARBY Pau (50 km); the Spanish border.
LOCATION in village, on D24 between Oloron Ste-Marie and Mauléon; ample car parking
FOOD breakfast, lunch, dinner
PRICE (€)
ROOMS 10; 7 double and twin, 3 family, 6 with bath (3 Jacuzzi), 4 with shower
FACILITIES sitting room/TV room, bar, restaurant, terrace, garden, swimming pool
CREDIT CARDS AE, DC, MC, V **CHILDREN** welcome
DISABLED 1 specially adapted room **PETS** accepted
CLOSED Jan
PROPRIETORS Pierre and Martine Chilo

THE SOUTH-WEST

LEHEN TOKIA
~ SEASIDE GUESTHOUSE ~

chemin Achotarreta, 64500 Ciboure (Pyrénées-Atlantiques)
TEL 05 59 47 18 16 **FAX** 05 59 47 38 04
E-MAIL info@lehen-tokia.com **WEBSITE** www.lehen-tokia.com

THE UNUSUAL NAME means 'first house' in the strange language of the
Basques, whose origins still baffle the experts. A splendid example of
neo-Basque architecture, it was built in 1925 by the architect Hiriart who
is credited with coining the expression 'Art Deco'. The house embodies
many features in this style, notably stained glass windows by Jacques
Grüber, and is a *Monument Historique*. It is certainly special.

On a recent visit we found that the new proprietor, Yan Personnaz, has
done much to make the house lighter, fresher and more welcoming and
comfortable without sacrificing any of its spirit or charm. It still feels like
a home, an atmosphere enriched by its display of personal belongings,
books and paintings. All the rooms have been refurbished, and each one is
different (see the hotel's excellent website). Only breakfast is served, but
other meals can be delivered by a local caterer. The rose garden and pretty
summer house and terrace look out to the ocean while retaining an intimate seclusion. Ideal for golfing enthusiasts: there are seven courses within a radius of 15 kilometres, and golfing trips can be organized.

~

NEARBY St-Jean-de-Luz; Spanish border; Biarritz (16 km).
LOCATION in Ciboure, across river Nivelle from St-Jean-de-Luz, well-signposted in
residential street within walking distance of beach and town centre; street car
parking
FOOD breakfast
PRICE €€
ROOMS 7; 6 double and twin, 1 suite, 5 with bath, 2 with shower; all rooms have
phone, TV, minibar
FACILITIES sitting rooms, terrace, garden, swimming pool
CREDIT CARDS AE, DC, MC, V **CHILDREN** accepted
DISABLED access difficult **PETS** not accepted
CLOSED mid-Nov to mid-Dec
PROPRIETOR Yan Personnaz

THE SOUTH-WEST

TROIS LYS
~ TOWN HOTEL ~

38 rue Gambetta, 32100 Condom (Gers)
TEL 05 62 28 33 33 **FAX** 05 62 28 41 85
E-MAIL hoteltroislys@minitel.net **WEBSITE** www.gascogne.fr/htroislys

THIS BEAUTIFULLY RESTORED 18thC town house is an old favourite of ours for its restrained elegance both externally and within. It is a real oasis of calm and quiet despite its location in the centre of a busy market town. Its new owner, Pascal Miguet, is as dedicated as his predecessor and draws on long experience working in international hotels. A charming new dining room gives a feeling of space and at the same time initimacy, as does the friendly new bar. The hotel is now air-conditioned throughout. In summer the entrance courtyard which leads off the pedestrian precinct is decorated with shrubs and flowers and set with chairs and tables. You can eat here when the weather permits. The kitchen specializes in fresh local produce cooked with care and expertise, but without pretension.

Despite another new feature, a fully equipped meeting room, the Trois Lys continues to feel more like a home than a hotel. All is light and restful, with Versailles parquet floors, original moulded wood panelling – and a perfect wide stone staircase with wrought-iron balustrade. The bedrooms are in keeping, each with a different colour scheme, with antique or reproduction furniture. Outside there is a large swimming pool and terrace, discreetly hidden behind a wall, and shaded.

~

NEARBY Cathédrale St-Pierre; Musée d'Armagnac.
LOCATION in town centre; car parking
FOOD breakfast, lunch, dinner
PRICE €€
ROOMS 10; 9 double and twin, 1 single, 8 with bath, 2 with shower; all rooms have phone, TV, air conditioning, hairdrier
FACILITIES dining room, terrace, swimming pool
CREDIT CARDS V **CHILDREN** welcome
DISABLED access difficult **PETS** accepted
CLOSED never
PROPRIETOR Pascal Miguet

THE SOUTH-WEST

CORDES-SUR-CIEL

LE GRAND ECUYER
∽ MEDIEVAL INN ∽

Grande-Rue Raimond VII, 81170 Cordes-sur-Ciel (Tarn)
TEL 05 63 56 01 03 **FAX** 05 63 56 18 83

AT THE INSTIGATION OF the novelist Prosper Mérimée, this former hunting lodge of the Counts of Toulouse was classified as a historic monument in the 19th century. It has been transformed into a comfortable and dependable hotel, with stone walls, beamed ceilings and paved floors. It is furnished with heavy oak antiques and tapestry-upholstered furniture, oil paintings, suits of armour, paved floors, rich damask and velvet wall coverings, blackamoor lampholders and four-poster beds. Parts of it are rather gloomy, though the bedrooms are quiet and inviting (if you like monumental stone fireplaces), with modern bathrooms.

Cordes-sur-Ciel – a remarkably preserved 13thC fortified hilltop village, with little cobbled streets and a busy tourist attraction – is the gastronomic domain of pastry chef Yves Thuriès, who has a Michelin star and is something of a celebrity. Le Grand Ecuyer is his base, though recent visitors feel he might be doing less in the kitchen now than in the past. The service is excellent and the chandeliered, plum-coloured dining room has been conceived as a prestigious setting for his cuisine. Our reporter dined well, and was struck by the helpfulness and knowledge of the wine waiter.

NEARBY Fôret Grésigne; Albi (27 km); Villefranche-de-Rouergue (47 km).
LOCATION in middle of village; car parking nearby
FOOD breakfast, lunch, dinner
PRICE €€€
ROOMS 13; 10 double, 2 triple, 1 suite, all with bath; all rooms have phone, TV; some rooms have air conditioning
FACILITIES sitting room, restaurant, breakfast room, bar **CREDIT CARDS** MC, V
CHILDREN accepted
DISABLED no special facilities **PETS** accepted
CLOSED mid-Oct to Apr; restaurant lunch Mon to Fri
PROPRIETOR Yves Thuriès

THE SOUTH-WEST

CUQ-TOULZA

CUQ-EN-TERRASSES

~ COUNTRY HOTEL ~

Cuq Le Château, 81470 Cuq-Toulza (Tarn)
TEL 05 63 82 54 00 **FAX** 05 63 82 54 11
E-MAIL Cuq-en-Terrasses@wanadoo.fr **WEBSITE** www.cuqenterrasses.com

IN 1990 TWO LONDON DESIGNERS, Tim and Zara Whitmore, bought a semi-abandoned old presbytery and spent the next few years hard at work on the conversion which produced this successful hotel. The house, in a hilltop village square, is on a series of south-facing levels – from the street downwards – with more terraces of garden tumbling down the hillside below. Although Tim and Zara sold up in 2000, the new owners continue to run the hotel in much the same way, confirmed by a spate of complimentary readers' letters. Our latest reads: 'We were captivated by this charming location and hotel. We had a wonderful dinner and were extremely comfortable there.'

The entrance hall leads to the upstairs rooms via a balustraded staircase and a superb beamed ceiling, uncovered during the building work. Kitchen, dining room and beautiful outside terrace (with barbecue) for summer meals are two floors down. The swimming pool is on another terrace. All quite stunning. The decoration and furnishing are original without eccentricity – clean, fresh and colourful.

The view, particularly from the terraces, is breathtaking. It's not hard to see why the local name for this small pocket of fertile country is Le Pays de Cocagne (the land of plenty). An ideal place in which to relax and enjoy the peace.

~

NEARBY Castres (35 km); Toulouse (37 km).
LOCATION in a hilltop hamlet by the church, 3 km from Cuq-Toulza; car parking
FOOD breakfast, lunch, dinner (by reservation)
PRICE €€
ROOMS 8; 7 double, 1 family, 6 with bath, 2 with shower; all rooms have phone, TV
FACILITIES dining room, terraces, garden, swimming pool, badminton
CREDIT CARDS AE, DC, MC, V **CHILDREN** accepted
DISABLED no special facilities **PETS** accepted **CLOSED** early Jan to early Apr
PROPRIETORS Philippe Gallice and Andonis Vassalos

THE SOUTH-WEST

✳ CHATEAU DE FOURCES ✳
～ CHATEAU HOTEL ～

32250 Fourcès (Gers)
TEL 05 62 29 49 53 **FAX** 05 62 29 50 59
E-MAIL chatogers@aol.com **WEBSITE** www.chateau_fources.com

T HE ORIGINS OF THIS FORTIFIED CASTLE are traced back to the 12th century. It stands guarding the entrance to a circular *bastide* (very popular with tourists in summer) with typical half-timbered houses and covered arcades near the river Azoue. Thanks to the energy, dedication and flair of its present owner, Patrizia Barsan, it has been meticulously restored and transformed into a delightful hotel which successfully blends the requirements of modern man into an ancient setting. The massive stone masonry of the high walls and turret – in excellent condition – dominate, but they are softened by Renaissance mullion windows which allow in plenty of light. The central square spiral staircase was one of the first to be built in France. By some miracle an efficient lift has been installed, and leads to charmingly arranged bedrooms. A sitting room opening on to a terrace has vestiges of an old wine press. Stairs lead down to a spacious dining room where a good choice of menus is on offer. Breakfast can be served in your room if you wish. The château is surrounded by a park bordering the river which is fringed by magnificent stands of weeping willow. The swimming pool sits beside a covered terrace. Mme Barsan is a memorable hostess. Reports please.

～

NEARBY Condom (13 km); *bastides*.
LOCATION 5.5 km NE of Montréal via RD29; car parking
FOOD breakfast, lunch, dinner **PRICE** €€-€€€€ **ROOMS** 17; 12 double and twin, 5 suites, all with bath; all rooms have phone, TV, minibar, safe
FACILITIES sitting room, bar, dining room, billiard room, lift, terrace, swimming pool, fishing

CREDIT CARDS AE, DC, MC, V
CHILDREN accepted
DISABLED no special facilities
PETS accepted
CLOSED Oct to Dec
PROPRIETOR Mme Barsan

THE SOUTH-WEST

GRENADE-SUR-L'ADOUR

PAIN ADOUR ET FANTAISIE
~ RIVERSIDE HOTEL ~

14-16 place des Tilleuls, 40270 Grenade sur l'Adour (Landes)
TEL 05 58 45 18 80 **FAX** 05 58 45 16 57
E-MAIL pain.adour.fantaisie@wanadoo.fr

WHEN DIDIER OUDILL left for the Café de Paris, Biarritz, he was succeeded as chef/*patron* of this distinguished hotel/restaurant by Philippe Garret, who has worked here since its creation. Both served under Michel Guérard at Eugénie-les-Bains and this tutelage is evident as much in the taste and quality in the design and furnishings of the rooms as in the refinement and authority of the cuisine and service. One half of the building was an 18thC *maison de maître* and boasts a superb stone staircase and fine oak panelling and carved fireplace in part of the dining room. The other half is 17th century, with original arcading on to the market square and half-timbered walls. Much care has gone into selecting appropriate antique furniture and the atmosphere is enhanced with original paintings and fine mirrors. On the south side is a handsome wide terrace overhanging the river: a very romantic setting for a summer's evening, with elegantly-laid tables and green-and-white parasols. Bedrooms are spacious; the best are furnished in a modern style and have views over the river and whirlpool baths. They have fanciful names, such as Clair de Lune. The food is much vaunted – M. Garret has a Michelin star.

~

NEARBY Pau (60 km); Mont-de-Marsan (14 km); Biarritz.
LOCATION 15 km SE of Mont-de-Marsan on river Adour; car parking and garage
FOOD breakfast, lunch, dinner
PRICE €€€-€€€€
ROOMS 11 double, all with bath; all rooms have phone, TV, hairdrier; 8 have air conditioning, minibar, safe, whirlpool bath
FACILITIES sitting room, restaurant, terrace **CREDIT CARDS** AE, DC, MC, V
CHILDREN accepted
DISABLED 1 ground-floor room **PETS** accepted
CLOSED 2 weeks Feb, Sun eve, Mon in winter
PROPRIETOR Philippe Garret

THE SOUTH-WEST

DEMEURE DE FLORE

~ COUNTRY HOTEL ~

106 Route Nationale, 81240 Lacabarède (Tarn)
TEL 05 63 98 32 32 **FAX** 05 63 98 47 56
E-MAIL demeure.de.flore@hotelrama.com **WEBSITE** www.hotelrama.com/flore

THIS HOTEL IN THE FOOTHILLS of the Haut-Languedoc was opened in 1992 by Monike and Jean-Marie Tronc to realize their dream of creating a perfect hotel. Having done that, in 1999 they decided to sell to a sophisticated Italian, Francesco Di Bari, who has spent almost a million francs on redecoration, creating a new restaurant, and landscaping the garden.

The 19thC *maison de maître* may be an undistinguished building, but it sits prettily in a mature, wooded *jardin anglais*, far enough from the passing RN112 to feel secluded. And within, there is a delightful ambience, mercifully unchanged since M. Di Bari took over. Stylish floral prints are set against warm, plain backgrounds. The house is full of floor-to-ceiling windows, and the general impression is light and fresh. Carefully chosen antiques and ornaments give the feel of a lived-in but cared-for family home. The eleven bedrooms are individually furnished in the same careful way, with knick-knacks and fresh flowers. You could easily be staying with friends.

Perhaps not surprisingly the cooking combines Provençal and Italian styles, and the menu changes every day depending on what's in season. In summer, 'a bite of lunch' can be had by the smart little pool or on the terrace overlooking the garden. More reports please.

NEARBY Castres (35 km); Albi (60 km); Toulouse (100 km).
LOCATION opposite service station on outskirts of village on RN112 between St-Pons and Mazamet; car parking
FOOD breakfast, lunch, dinner
PRICE ⓔⓔ
ROOMS 11; 10 double, 1 suite, all with bath; all rooms have phone, TV, hairdrier
FACILITIES sitting room, dining room, meeting room, garden, swimming pool
CREDIT CARDS MC, V **CHILDREN** accepted
DISABLED 1 specially adapted room **PETS** accepted **CLOSED** 3 weeks Jan
PROPRIETOR Francesco Di Bari

THE SOUTH-WEST

LECTOURE

HOTEL DE BASTARD
∼ COUNTRY TOWN MANSION ∼

rue Lagrange, 32700 Lectoure (Gers)
TEL 05 62 68 82 44 **FAX** 05 62 68 76 81
E-MAIL hoteldebastard@wanadoo.fr **WEBSITE** www.hotel-de-bastard.com

LECTOURE RISES ON A HILL overlooking the beautiful valley of the Gers. It is a town of rich archaeological finds and fine architecture. So it is fitting that its best hotel stands proudly displaying all its 18thC elegance as a former private mansion. A paved upper terrace is a lovely setting for summer meals. Protected by a semi-circle of warm stone buildings, it has views over the unspoiled countryside. A lower level includes a swimming pool, and plenty of room to relax around it, with a new *salon*/bar in a separate building. Judiciously placed trees, shrubs and flowers add to the picture.

Gascony has a well-deserved reputation for its local produce – *foie gras*, duck and goose in all its forms, vegetables, fruit (including superb melons and prunes) – but rarely are they presented with such imagination and variety as here. "The best place to eat for miles around", says one knowledgeable local resident. The dining room is made up of three *salons*, each opening into the other and full of light.

Inside the hotel is decorated in sympathy with its 18thC character, with polished wood floors and pretty antique furniture. Bedrooms are mostly small; ask for one on the first floor (*premier étage*), rather than on the second, with its mansard roof. They are, however, along with the food, very good value for money.

∼

NEARBY Musée Lapidaire; tannery; *bastides*; Auch (35 km).
LOCATION in town, 35 km N of Auch; car parking and garage
FOOD breakfast, lunch, dinner
PRICE €
ROOMS 29; 24 double and twin, 3 triple, 2 suites, all with bath or shower; all rooms have phone, TV, hairdrier
FACILITIES sitting room, bar, restaurant, terrace, swimming pool
CREDIT CARDS AE, DC, MC, V **CHILDREN** welcome
DISABLED no special facilities **PETS** accepted **CLOSED** mid-Dec to Feb
PROPRIETOR Jean-Luc Arnaud

THE SOUTH-WEST

MIMIZAN

AU BON COIN DU LAC

~ LAKESIDE HOTEL ~

29 avenue du Lac, 40400 Mimizan (Landes)
TEL 05 58 09 01 55 **FAX** 05 58 09 40 84

WE ARE HAPPY TO REPORT that we continue to see no sign of slippage in the high standards of Jean-Pierre Caule, the third generation of his family to run Au Bon Coin, or, indeed, the exacting standards of Mme Caule, who oversees things front of house. There is no pretence here – everything is genuine and it starts with the smile with which Madame greets you on arrival – it clearly comes from within.

Beside a large freshwater lake away from the noise and bustle of the seaside town, the hotel is a refuge of calm and repose, yet less than a kilometre from the sandy dunes and beaches for which this region is known. It is the gastronomic Mecca for this part of the Landes and amply justifies its reputation. Our inspector's dinner was 'a delight of refined dishes of an individuality not without surprises'. M. Caule, who has a Michelin star, buys his own fish in nearby Arcachon. The dining room is light and welcoming, with a terrace outside shaded by trees and awning, all looking over a smooth green lawn to the water, rowing boats and ducks. Bedrooms are unobtrusively furnished, cosy and restful. Ideal for those who want solicitous treatment, a relaxed atmosphere and excellent food.

NEARBY Bordeaux (98 km); Arcachon (65 km); Dax (70 km).
LOCATION on edge of lake, 2 km N of Mimizan; car parking
FOOD breakfast, lunch, dinner
PRICE €-€€€
ROOMS 8; 4 double and twin, 4 suites, all with bath; all rooms have phone, TV, fridge, hairdrier
FACILITIES sitting room, restaurant, terrace, garden
CREDIT CARDS AE, MC, V
CHILDREN accepted
DISABLED rooms on ground floor **PETS** not accepted
CLOSED never
PROPRIETORS Jean-Pierre and Jacqueline Caule

THE SOUTH-WEST

CHATEAU DE PROJAN
~ CHATEAU GUESTHOUSE ~

32400 Projan (Gers)
TEL 05 62 09 46 21 **FAX** 05 62 09 44 08 **E-MAIL** chateaudeprojan@libertysurf.fr

WHEN GLOBETROTTING art lover Bernard Vichet acquired this historic château he had a dream of creating something which would bring a breath of life into hotel-keeping. His key words are 'welcome, art and conviviality'. An entry in the guest book reads 'from the moment we entered I knew I was in a very special home – the cultural quality was so exciting for me', indicating how he has succeeded. The setting is magnificent, with panoramas of timeless natural beauty, the château sedate and sure in its classic grace. Inside all is light and airy, and harmoniously juxtaposes the old with the new. One enters a hall to be faced by a superb antique wooden staircase hung with highly colourful modern paintings and a floor featuring bright comtemporary mosaic in marble and granite of symbolic geese taking flight. For conviviality there is a grand piano, a lovely terrace and belvedere for dancing, and a library of art books open to all. The bedrooms each display original paintings by different modern artists. The château is run with expertise by Christine Poullain. In autumn, her husband Richard runs weekend courses on how to buy and prepare fattened ducks for the table – appropriate for the home of *foie gras*.

~

NEARBY Aire sur l'Adour (15 km); Eugénie-les-Bains; Pyrenees.
LOCATION in own grounds, on rocky spur overlooking the two Lees valleys, 15 km S of Aire sur l'Adour, signposted off D134 to Sarron; car parking
FOOD breakfast; dinner on request
PRICE €-€€€
ROOMS 9 double and twin, 4 with bath or shower, 5 sharing shower room
FACILITIES sitting room, dining room, library, terrace, garden
CREDIT CARDS MC, V **CHILDREN** accepted
DISABLED no special facilities **PETS** accepted **CLOSED** Fri Jan to May
MANAGER Christine Poullain

THE SOUTH-WEST

ST-ETIENNE-DE-BAIGORRY

✷ ARCE ✷
~ RIVERSIDE HOTEL ~

64430 St-Etienne-de-Baigorry (Pyrénées-Atlantiques)
TEL 05 59 37 40 14 FAX 05 59 37 40 27
E-MAIL hotel-arce@wanadoo.fr WEBSITE www.hotel-arce.com

A FAVOURITE OF OUR INSPECTORS AND OUR READERS, recently redecorated and refurbished to maintain its impeccable standards. The setting – by a river in a typical Basque village – is a magical one, best appreciated from the dining terrace, which juts out over the water and is sheltered by a canopy of chestnut trees. Nestled there, one feels both intimate and secluded and nothing could be more pleasant than a relaxed breakfast by the water's edge. Inside, the public rooms are spacious: a smart dining room with picture windows, and a beamed library with books in a variety of languages. The green, white and red colours of the Basque flag predominate. Some of the bedrooms are impressively large, with apartment-sized sitting areas; others open on to small terraces with mountain views. A sizeable blue-tiled swimming pool is hidden in a green enclosure on the far side of a wooden bridge across the river.

Management of the hotel is now in the capable hands of the fifth generation of the family Arcé. The much-appreciated cooking emphasizes fresh local ingredients, with an interesting wine list at reasonable prices. There is plenty to do in the area – walking, fishing, cycling, riding, canoeing – and the Atlantic coast is only half an hour away.

~

NEARBY Pyrenees; Spanish border; Atlantic coast.
LOCATION in village, 10 km W of St-Jean Pied-de-Port; car parking
FOOD breakfast, lunch, dinner **PRICE** €€ **ROOMS** 23; 22 double and twin, 20 with bath, 2 with shower, 1 single with shower; all rooms have phone, TV, hairdrier
FACILITIES sitting rooms, dining room, library, games room, terrace, garden, swimming pool, tennis

CREDIT CARDS DC, MC, V
CHILDREN welcome
DISABLED 1 ground-floor room
PETS accepted **CLOSED** mid-Nov to mid-Mar
PROPRIETORS Arcé family

THE SOUTH-WEST

LA DEVINIERE
~ SEASIDE GUESTHOUSE ~

5 rue Loquin, 64500 St-Jean-de-Luz (Pyrénées-Atlantiques)
TEL 05 59 26 05 51 **FAX** 05 59 51 26 38

L A DEVINIERE is discreetly tucked away in a pedestrian precinct with
nothing more than a modest signboard artistically spelling out the
name in Basque green. Other than that, there is little to betray that this
house is in fact a hotel. Its owners describe it as a 'charming old English
hotel', and that's how it feels, an elegant and traditional privately owned
town house in the centre of this historic and picturesque resort. The spell
is cast as soon as you enter the beautifully furnished reception area with
shelves of leather-bound books and a view through to a sitting room with
comfortable chairs and a grand piano. It is the creation of former lawyer
Bernard Carrère and his wife, an expert in antiques.

Although there is no restaurant, a fairly new addition is that of a
delightful tea room in complete harmony with the rest of the house and
the concept of a hotel as a private home, surrounded by personal things. It
may be for the discriminating, but nevertheless it has an air of freshness
and warm welcome. A small garden lies behind the house. There is parking
close by but final access is by foot – well worth the small effort.

~

NEARBY Spanish border; Biarritz (15 km).
LOCATION in pedestrian precinct in town centre; car parking nearby
FOOD breakfast
PRICE €€
ROOMS 8 double and twin, all with bath; all rooms have phone
FACILITIES sitting room, library, tea room, garden
CREDIT CARDS AE, DC, MC, V **CHILDREN** welcome
DISABLED not suitable **PETS** accepted
CLOSED mid-Nov to Dec
PROPRIETORS M. and Mme Carrère

THE SOUTH-WEST

ARRAYA
~ RIVERSIDE HOTEL ~

64310 Sare (Pyrénées-Atlantiques)
TEL 05 59 54 20 46 **FAX** 05 59 37 40 27
E-MAIL hotel@arraya.com **WEBSITE** www.arraya.com

WITH ITS TIMBERED, white-painted houses adorned with red or green shutters, Sare can claim to be the prettiest of all the extremely pretty Basque villages. In the heart of the village, this 17thC house was once an overnight resting place for pilgrims on their way across the Pyrenees to Santiago de Compostela. Behind the slightly severe frontage on the main road lies a country-style hotel of great character, now run by the third generation of the charming Fagoaga family. Inside all is spick and span and immaculately cared for – clean, airy and light, with much old, dark, burnished wood. The beamed sitting room and dining room – and every nook and cranny on stairways and landings – are filled with glorious old Basque furniture; sofas and chairs are comfortable and inviting and flowers are everywhere.

A handsome curved wooden staircase leads to bedrooms of different sizes (some border on the small), all expertly decorated using colourful fabrics and bedspreads made by a member of the family. Some look out over the verdant garden, others have a view of the village square. The restaurant is excellent, with a well-chosen wine list; in summer meals are taken on the terrace. A new boutique on the ground floor sells local products, including delicious *gâteau basque*.

~

NEARBY Aïnhoa (10 km); St-Jean-de-Luz (14 km); Biarritz (29 km).
LOCATION in middle of village, 14 km SE of St-Jean-de-Luz; car parking
FOOD breakfast, lunch, dinner
PRICE €-€€
ROOMS 22; 20 double and twin, 2 single, 19 with bath, 3 with shower; all rooms have phone, TV, safe, hairdrier
FACILITIES sitting room, dining room, boutique, terrace, garden
CREDIT CARDS AE, DC, MC, V **CHILDREN** welcome
DISABLED ground-floor rooms **PETS** not accepted
CLOSED mid-Nov to Apr; restaurant closed Sun dinner, Mon lunch
PROPRIETORS Fagoaga family

THE SOUTH-WEST

DOMAINE DE BASSIBE
~ COUNTRY HOTEL ~

32400 Ségos (Gers)
E-MAIL bassibe@relaischateaux.com
WEBSITE www.relaischateaux.com/bassibe

'S O MANY RELAIS & CHATEAUX HOTELS can't resist exuding a superior air,' comments our first inspector to this new entry, ' but here one feels very much wrapped up and safe'.

One simply has to admire the flair and taste of Sylvie and Olivier Lacroix, and their success in providing their guests with all the comforts of a first-class hotel in the ambience of a private and very friendly country house. Set in a park and garden running riot with cascades of flowers, the main house is an 18thC *maison de maître* with a long two-storeyed wing which was originally stabling but is now fitted out with delightful suites. Alongside stands the former *chai* – another lovely stone building – once a centre of activity in this huge agricultural *domaine* and now housing the kitchens, restaurant and wine stock. In the garden a newer construction in white and blue, La Maison des Champs, contains more rooms and suites, each decorated in different colours, all bright and light. Close by a stand of impressive centenarian oaks (the oldest more than 300 years old) is a large open-air pool with terrace and enclosed fitness area. The food is exceptional as is the carefully selected wine list. In short – a place where the best is offered with simplicity and warmth. No wonder the extravagant wistaria flowers no less than three times a year.

~

NEARBY Aire-sur-l'Adour (8 km); Pau (30 km).
LOCATION on large farming estate, signposted from Ségos; car parking
FOOD breakfast, lunch, dinner; room service
PRICE €€€
ROOMS 18; 11 double and twin, 7 suites, all with bath; all rooms have phone, TV
FACILITIES sitting room, dining room, fitness centre, terraces, garden, swimming pool **CREDIT CARDS** AE, DC, MC, V **CHILDREN** welcome
DISABLED no special facilities **PETS** accepted
CLOSED Jan to Apr
PROPRIETORS Sylvie and Olivier Lacroix

LANGUEDOC-ROUSSILLON

CERET

LE MAS TRILLES

~ COUNTRY HOTEL ~

Le Pont de Reynes, 66400 Céret (Pyrénées-Orientales)
TEL 04 68 87 38 37 **FAX** 04 68 87 42 62

L ASZLO BUKK IS A Lithuanian-born, Swiss-trained hotelier, whose experience includes spells working in Canada and Australia. He and his Breton wife, who has carried her artistic and design talents into the world of refined cuisine, make an accomplished team. In a labour of love, they transformed this 17thC *mas* into a delightful, welcoming hotel – blending past and present and endowing it with their own very personal aura. The massive warm stone structure overlooks the fast-flowing River Tech – a tiny path brings you down to a stretch between two bends where the clear water looks almost still – an unspoiled natural sanctuary. A terrace beside the house leads down to a delightfully uncomplicated garden with lawn and swimming pool, mature trees and flowering shrubs.

Bedrooms are practical, immaculately kept and all have either a terrace or a small private garden. The atmosphere in the public rooms is informal and relaxed, so guests feel very much at home in them.

The menu for dinner is chalked up on a board but Mme Bukk is always willing to provide alternative dishes for those with special requirements. She is justifiably proud of her kitchen.

~

NEARBY Perpignan (26 km); Castelnou (30 km); beaches.
LOCATION in countryside on the D115, 2 km from Céret; car parking
FOOD breakfast, dinner
PRICE €€
ROOMS 10 double with bath; all rooms have phone, TV
FACILITIES sitting room, dining room, garden, swimming pool, table tennis
CREDIT CARDS MC, V
CHILDREN accepted
DISABLED 1 specially adapted room
PETS accepted
CLOSED mid-Oct to Easter
PROPRIETORS M. and Mme Bukk

LANGUEDOC-ROUSSILLON

CÉRET

LA TERRASSE AU SOLEIL

~ COUNTRY HOTEL ~

route de Fontfrède, 66400 Céret (Pyrénées-Orientales)
TEL 04 68 87 01 94 **FAX** 04 68 87 39 24
E-MAIL terrasse-au-soleil.hotel@wanadoo.fr   **WEBSITE** www.la.terrasse-au-soleil.com

THE ORIGINAL PART OF THE HOTEL was an 18thC *mas* but already a hotel when the present owners acquired it in 1980. Since then two annexes have been added for extra bedrooms and suites. The setting is lovely, higher up the mountains than nearby Céret, with splendid views over unspoiled hills.

Bedrooms vary in size, but the biggest are very spacious and all are tastefully furnished and decorated (some have their own private verandas). There is plenty of individuality in the interior design – much of it the legacy of Charles Trenet (the house at one time belonged to his agent and was a haunt of show-business personalities): unusual terracotta and ceramic tiling and imported African wood carvings, as in the huge bar. Colour and warmth in abundance introduce intimacy and cosiness not normally found in four-star hotels. Picasso is said to have sat on the terrace to enjoy the views of Mont Canigou.

The restaurant, La Cerisaie, has an enviable reputation and a young chef from Paris. At lunchtime, there is a tempting *carte brasserie* as a lighter alternative to the more serious food served at dinner.

~

NEARBY Perpignan (26 km); Castelnou (30 km); beaches.
LOCATION in Pyrenean foothills above the town, SW of Perpignan; car parking
FOOD breakfast, brunch, dinner; room service
PRICE €€€€
ROOMS 21; 14 double, 7 suites, all with bath; all rooms have phone, TV, air conditioning, minibar, hairdrier
FACILITIES sitting room, dining room, bar, garden, swimming pool, tennis, table tennis, helipad, pétanque, golf practice area
CREDIT CARDS AE, DC, MC, V **CHILDREN** accepted
DISABLED some specially adapted rooms
PETS accepted
CLOSED never
PROPRIETOR M. Leveille-Nizerolle

LANGUEDOC-ROUSSILLON

COLLIOURE

HOTEL CASA PAIRAL

~ SEASIDE TOWN HOTEL ~

impasse des Palmiers, 66190 Collioure (Pyrénées-Orientales)
TEL 04 68 82 05 81 **FAX** 04 68 82 52 10
E-MAIL hotelsmascasa@wanadoo.fr **WEBSITE** www.roussillhotel.com

TUCKED AWAY IN A SMALL *impasse,* this quiet, elegant hotel has a magical situation just 150 metres from the busiest part of Collioure, close to the harbour and main beach with their many seaside cafés, restaurants, and narrow packed streets winding up the hill. A period-piece Catalan-style house built in the mid-19th century, it has a lush, picturesque interior garden with 100-year-old palm trees and pines shading a courtyard with tables and chairs and (somewhat apart) a swimming pool. The attractive ground-floor *salon* has a tiled floor and looks out to the courtyard and a fountain backed by oleanders and a huge magnolia. There is also a larger 1930s-style *salon* with a television and card table. The breakfast room (down a stone staircase) is captivating – and surprising; in one corner is the trunk of a vast oak tree which grows out through the roof, while opposite, large windows frame beautiful views of the garden.

Bedrooms in the main house combine old-world charm in the sleeping area with modern bathroom facilities. Our inspector was overcome by nostalgia: 'It reminded me of how good hotels used to be, but with all the up-to-date comforts. A place full of charm.'

~

NEARBY Port-Vendres (4 km); Argelès-sur-Mer (6.5 km); Perpignan (27 km).
LOCATION in the centre of town 150 m from the port and beach; car parking
FOOD breakfast
PRICE €
ROOMS 28 double and twin, 23 with bath, 5 with shower; all rooms have phone, TV, air conditioning, minibar
FACILITIES 2 sitting rooms, breakfast room, garden, swimming pool
CREDIT CARDS AE, DC, MC, V
CHILDREN accepted
DISABLED some ground-floor rooms **PETS** accepted
CLOSED Nov to Apr
PROPRIETOR Mme de Bon

LANGUEDOC-ROUSSILLON

CORNILLON

LA VIEILLE FONTAINE
~ HILLTOP VILLAGE HOTEL ~

30630 Cornillon (Gard)
TEL 04 66 82 20 56 **FAX** 04 66 82 33 64
E-MAIL vieillefontaine@libertysurf.fr

BUILT WITHIN THE WALLS of the ruined château of a medieval fortified village, with cobbled streets and ivy-clad ramparts, this little hotel is full of charm. *Patron* and chef, M. Audibert, is a Marseillais; his *gratinée de langoustines* and *chou farci à la provençale*, accompanied by the local Tavel *rosé*, have long been the restaurant's attractions. The hotel is the creation of Mme Audibert, a native of this once semi-abandoned village. Inspired by the Louvre pyramid, she has, with great flair, clad the exterior circular staircase to the bedrooms with an elegant glass structure, at which one can gaze in wonder over breakfast in the courtyard.

Her decorating style is simple and pretty: tiled bathrooms, Provençal fabrics, furniture from local *antiquaires*. One room contains a great chunk of the old château wall. Most have terraces; Nos 7 and 8 have views way over the top of the castle wall to the south. A steep flight of stone steps through terraced gardens leads to the pool: water gushes down from the hillside, and it is like bathing in a mountain stream.

The welcome is spontaneous and warm, and dinner on the terrace looking over the hills and vineyards of the Gard is a delight.

~

NEARBY Orange (44 km); Avignon (45 km); Gorges de l'Ardèche.
LOCATION in the heart of the village, with limited access by car; car parking outside village
FOOD breakfast, lunch, dinner
PRICE €€€
ROOMS 8 double with bath; all rooms have TV, phone
FACILITIES sitting room, dining room, terrace, garden, swimming pool
CREDIT CARDS AE, DC, MC, V **CHILDREN** welcome
DISABLED not suitable
PETS accepted
CLOSED mid-Dec to mid-Mar
PROPRIETORS M. and Mme Audibert

LANGUEDOC-ROUSSILLON

GINCLA

HOSTELLERIE DU GRAND DUC

~ VILLAGE HOTEL ~

2 route de Boucheville, 11140 Gincla (Aude)
TEL 04 68 20 55 02 **FAX** 04 68 20 61 22
E-MAIL host-du-grand-duc@ataraxie.fr

THE GRAND DUC IS THE EAGLE OWL, presiding (stuffed) over the fireplace in the beamed dining room of this delightful, modest little *logis*. A refurbished *maison de maître* (the *maître* made his living from the surrounding forests), it was opened more than a decade ago as a restaurant by the son of the Bruchet family, a chef, whose father is a wine inspector from Burgundy. The wide central hallway has original stone walls and the fine old staircase has terracotta tiles with oak nosings and wrought-iron balustrade. There's a large dining room and a superb modern kitchen with the latest German electronic oven, where they make their own bread.

The bedrooms are large, but somewhat disappointing with fussy wallpaper, which comes as an aesthetic let-down after the fine, clean lines and whitewashed walls of the dining room.

Admirers return year after year to write flattering remarks in the visitors' book: 'Gets better all the time – everything, reception, service, food and comfort is excellent.' Our inspector – wallpaper excepted – found it charming. There's a pleasant terrace, looking on to a fountain and old lime trees; in summer, you dine outside by candlelight.

~

NEARBY Perpignan (63 km); Quillan (23 km); Forêt de Fanges.
LOCATION in the village NW of Perpignan; car parking
FOOD breakfast, lunch, dinner
PRICE ⓔ
ROOMS 12 double, twin and family, all with bath or shower; all rooms have phone, TV, hairdrier, safe
FACILITIES sitting room, bar, restaurant, terrace
CREDIT CARDS MC, V
CHILDREN accepted
DISABLED no special facilities
PETS accepted
CLOSED mid-Nov to mid-Mar
PROPRIETORS M. and Mme Bruchet

LANGUEDOC-ROUSSILLON

MADIERES

CHATEAU DE MADIERES

~ CHATEAU HOTEL ~

Madières, 34190 Ganges (Hérault)
TEL 04 67 73 84 03 FAX 04 67 73 55 71
E-MAIL madieres@wanadoo.fr WEBSITE www.hotelvision.com/madieres-chateau

'Exceptional,' enthused our inspector, after visiting this 14thC fortress, perched above the Vis river gorge and rescued from decay in the mid-1980s by the previous owner, Mme Brucy. After a career in fashion design in Paris, she transferred her artistic talent and expertise to more durable materials and, with her husband, created a remarkably successful and exciting blend of ancient and modern beauty. Since her death last year, the hotel has been taken over by M. Guyrat, and we would welcome new reports.

Comfortable rooms have been made within the existing framework of medieval walls and arches, with no loss to the historic feel of the place. No two bedrooms are alike; there's luxury and light and colour in abundance. All have modern bathrooms. The best are spacious and delightfully furnished, with bold colourful fabrics against white walls and oriental rugs on tiled floors. The public rooms are superb. The galleried sitting room has a vast Renaissance fireplace. The vaulted dining room, jutting out of the main building and with a terrace above, has spectacular views across the gorge through arched windows. A courtyard leads to a swimming pool with fitness room, and terraces go down to the river below. The food is excellent and the welcome, warm. An ideal place to relax both mind and body.

~

NEARBY Cirque de Navacalles; Grottes des Demoiselles; Ganges.
LOCATION on hillside overlooking village, on crossroads of D48 and D25; car parking
MEALS breakfast, lunch, dinner
PRICE €€€€
ROOMS 12; 8 double, 4 apartments, all with bath or shower; all rooms have TV, phone, minibar, hairdrier
FACILITIES 3 sitting rooms, restaurant, 3 terraces, garden, swimming pool, fitness room, table tennis CREDIT CARDS AE, DC, MC, V CHILDREN accepted
DISABLED no special facilities PETS accepted CLOSED Nov to late Mar
PROPRIETOR M. Guyrat

LANGUEDOC-ROUSSILLON

MINERVE

RELAIS CHANTOVENT

~ VILLAGE HOTEL ~

MINERVE, AN OLD CATHAR REFUGE, is that rare thing – a 14thC fortified hilltop town unspoiled, as yet, by the tourist business. Tourists there are, but the industry has not yet taken over and the small town continues to have an ongoing organic life which is very appealing. With only two narrow streets up and down, cars have to be left below. It is no effort (except for the handicapped) and well worth the inconvenience.

The hotel is really in three parts, each equally attractive. There is a restaurant and stunning terrace looking across a deep gorge to a layered limestone cliff populated by birds and with vineyards on the top level. Then there's a separate building with bedrooms and, around the corner in the next street, an old village house, restored with care and charm, with sitting room and fireplace, furnished in period harmony.

All the decoration is done with attention to detail, but no fuss – light walls, uncluttered, attractive etchings and paintings. The Evenous – he is a Breton and an expert in preparing abundant local produce for the table – are a totally dedicated couple, with taste and finesse and a real love for their home.

~

NEARBY Carcassonne (45 km); Narbonne (32 km); St-Pons (29 km).
LOCATION in small historic town NW of Carcassonne with no access by car; car parking outside town
FOOD breakfast, lunch, dinner
PRICE €
ROOMS 10 double, 1 with bath, 9 with shower
FACILITIES sitting room, dining room, terrace
CREDIT CARDS MC, V
CHILDREN accepted
DISABLED not suitable
PETS accepted
CLOSED mid-Dec to mid-Jan
PROPRIETORS M. and Mme Evenou

LANGUEDOC-ROUSSILLON

OLARGUES

DOMAINE DE RIEUMEGE
~ COUNTRY HOTEL ~

17 Grande Rue, 34210 Minerve (Hérault)
TEL 04 68 91 14 18 **FAX** 04 68 91 81 99

IN A LOVELY, NATURAL SETTING of hills, rock, water, trees, shrubs and soft green grass, this sensitively restored 17thC stone house is in the middle of the Haut Languedoc national park and close to Olargues, one of the villages classed as the most beautiful in France. It is a perfect place for a stroll after dinner or before breakfast. There are few hotels in this area and, although there is a road nearby, little traffic noise filters through. Deep, restful calm prevails. The attractive high-ceilinged beamed restaurant retains, even after restoration, its country barn origins. (The food our inspector had was excellent; the 'pleasant, not-too-professional service' was also much appreciated).

Bedrooms are simply furnished with respectable antique pieces – and comfortable. The beamed sitting room, with open fire in cooler weather and oil lamps, is cosy, with some handsome antique furniture. A smaller separate building has been adapted to provide a luxury room and suite, complete with its own garden and private swimming pool. There is a wide range of accommodation here; three categories offer 'comfort', 'superior' and 'prestige', so there is something for all pockets. M. Henrotte took over from the Sylvas two years ago. Reports please.

~

NEARBY St-Pons (17 km); Castres (70 km); Béziers (50 km).
LOCATION in countryside 3 km outside Olargues; car parking
FOOD breakfast, lunch, dinner
PRICE €€
ROOMS 14; 10 double, 3 family, 1 suite, all with bath or shower; all rooms have phone; TV on request
FACILITIES sitting room, dining room, garden, swimming pool, tennis
CREDIT CARDS AE, MC, V **CHILDREN** accepted
DISABLED no special facilities
PETS accepted
CLOSED Jan to Mar
PROPRIETOR M. Henrotte

LANGUEDOC-ROUSSILLON

ORNAISONS

LE RELAIS DU VAL D'ORBIEU

~ CONVERTED MILL ~

11200 Ornaisons (Aude)
TEL 04 68 27 10 27 FAX 04 68 27 52 44 E-MAIL Relais.Du.Val.Dorbieu@wanadoo.fr
WEBSITE www.perso.wanadoo.fr/relais.du.val.dorbieu/

THIS HOTEL HAS BEEN cleverly designed to provide everything which the overnight traveller or long-stay holidaymaker could wish for – made to measure. Extensions with red-tiled roofs have been added to the original old mill to form an integrated complex of rooms and suites, four sides of which enclose a lush, secluded cloister. Rooms are bright, modern and newly decorated – 15 have their own terrace. The choice of accommodation is particularly flexible for families with children. Although parts of the hotel are old, there's no feeling of a museum but rather a highly efficient and comfortable hostelry. There is ample room for everyone in the spacious grounds. The swimming pool is equally serious and professional and is flanked by impressive stands of oleander. The excellent cooking – fish dishes are recommended – and wine cellar reflect the personal passion of the owner, M. Gonzalvez, the son of a vigneron. Quite a number of English wine merchants make this hotel their base to sample the wines of the Corbières. Another regular booking is by American cyclists who tour the region on two wheels. There's a full-time gardener and home-grown vegetables and herbs feature prominently on the menus.

~

NEARBY Narbonne (14 km); Carcassonne (44 km).
LOCATION in countryside outside Ornaisons; car parking
FOOD breakfast, lunch, dinner
PRICE €€€-€€€€
ROOMS 20; 14 double, 6 family suites, all with bath; all rooms have phone, TV, minibar, hairdrier
FACILITIES sitting room, dining room, meeting room, garden, swimming pool, tennis, practice golf, table tennis CREDIT CARDS AE, DC, MC, V
CHILDREN accepted
DISABLED 1 specially adapted room
PETS accepted
CLOSED Dec; restaurant lunch Nov to Feb
PROPRIETORS M. and Mme Gonzalvez

LANGUEDOC-ROUSSILLON

ST-PONS-DE-THOMIERES

LES BERGERIES DE PONDERACH

~ COUNTRY HOTEL ~

route de Narbonne, 34220 St-Pons-de-Thomières (Hérault)
TEL 04 67 97 02 57 **FAX** 04 67 97 29 75

ST-PONS-DE-THOMIERES is a pleasant little town in the Parc Régional de Haut Languedoc, in these parts an area of gentle wooded hills. This restaurant-hotel, just under a kilometre outside the town, with large grounds, a charming courtyard, and peaceful rural surroundings, has been fashioned out of an 18thC farmhouse, retaining all its character and adding many comforts. Bedrooms are smart and bright, with exposed beams. Each has its own terrace and views over the orchard and river.

M. Lentin, the proprietor, used to own an art gallery, and paintings are a major feature of the attractive drawing room and dining room. Food, however, is probably the high point: there are four menus from which to choose, the cheapest offering value for money. Fresh local produce, especially pork, takes precedence, and the wine list has an interesting selection of country wines. A recent English visitor went for one night but stayed for three – for the 'marvellous food and wonderful warm hospitality'. (M. Lentin is an Anglophile who once nearly married an English girl.) We hope your reports will confirm our view that this place offers charm and delicious food at notably fair prices.

~

NEARBY Castres (52 km); Béziers (51 km).
LOCATION 0.8 km outside town; car parking
FOOD breakfast, lunch, dinner
PRICE €€
ROOMS 7 double with bath
FACILITIES sitting room, restaurant, terraces, garden
CREDIT CARDS DC, MC, V
CHILDREN accepted
DISABLED no special facilities
PETS accepted
CLOSED early Nov to Mar
PROPRIETOR M. Lentin

LANGUEDOC-ROUSSILLON

VILLENEUVE-LEZ-AVIGNON

HOTEL DE L'ATELIER

~ TOWN HOTEL ~

5 rue de la Foire, 30400 Villeneuve-lez-Avignon (Gard)
TEL 04 90 25 01 84 **FAX** 04 90 25 80 06
E-MAIL hotel-latelier@libertysurf.fr

THIS BED-AND-BREAKFAST in a 16thC cardinal's house has long been a stalwart of our Southern France guide, but we'd heard it had become a little *fatigué*, which was indeed how Agnès Berméjo and Gui Lainé, the charming new owners, found it when they took over in August 2000. Coming from the worlds of cinema and advertising, Agnès and Gui used their ingenuity and skill, with the help of their friend Dominique, to create a hotel of great character and style without spending a fortune. They were lucky to inherit so many splendid features: the stone staircase, huge battered wooden doors, beamed ceilings and ancient fireplace, to which they have added fresh decoration and fabrics, pretty lamps and wall-lights, a mixture of wooden and painted furniture, sisal flooring and paintings and objects. Some of the latter will be part of the temporary art exhibitions that Agnès likes to host here. Bedrooms are all different, simple yet elegant. The four newest weren't even finished when we visited.

At the back of the house is a lovely courtyard, where you can eat breakfast under the shade of fig trees and a vine, and through a stone gateway beyond is a gloriously overgrown 'secret garden', a riot of oleander, geraniums and climbing roses in early summer. It's hard to believe that Avignon is only a 10-minute bus-ride across the Rhône.

~

NEARBY Avignon; Fort St-André; Chartreuse du Val de Bénédiction.
LOCATION in the town centre; car parking
MEALS breakfast
PRICE €
ROOMS 23 double and twin, all with bath or shower; all rooms have phone, TV, hairdrier
FACILITIES sitting room, breakfast room, garden **CREDIT CARDS** AE, DC, MC, V
CHILDREN accepted
DISABLED not suitable **PETS** accepted
CLOSED Nov to mid-Dec
PROPRIETORS Agnès Berméjo and Gui Lainé

AUVERGNE & MASSIF CENTRAL

BELCASTEL

HOTEL RESTAURANT DU VIEUX PONT

~ RESTAURANT-WITH-ROOMS ~

12390 Belcastel (Aveyron)
TEL 05 65 64 52 29 **FAX** 05 65 64 44 32
E-MAIL hotel-du-vieux-pont@wanadoo.fr

THE NAME REFERS TO A medieval cobbled bridge linking the two compo-
nents of this much-lauded restaurant-with-rooms. On one side of the
river stands a solid rough-stone house, the Fagegaltier sisters' childhood
home, now the restaurant; on the other side, the sisters have rescued a
tumbledown building next to the church to create seven comfortable, stylish bedrooms. Above, Belcastel's picture-postcard houses cling to a cliff
with a castle crowning its summit.

Michèle Fagegaltier is the manager, while her sister Nicole and Nicole's
husband Bruno Rouquier are responsible for the cooking. Their imaginative versions of local dishes, such as *boeuf de l'Aubrac à la réduction de
banyuls*, served with *un concassé de pommes de terre à la ventrèche et
au roquefort*, have won them much praise, including a Michelin star and a
Gault Millau heart and 16 points. Through picture windows, diners can
spot trout rising if the Aveyron isn't flowing too fast.

The sisters have imparted some of their own elegance to both restaurant and hotel, and nowhere is this more evident than in the bedrooms.
They are just the kind we like; simply decorated, some with cream walls,
bedspreads and curtains and French windows on to the small garden; all
furnished with hand-picked antiques.

~

NEARBY Rodez (23 km); Sauveterre-de-Rouergue (26 km).
LOCATION in the village beside the river, 8 km SE of Rignac; car parking
FOOD breakfast, lunch, dinner
PRICE €
ROOMS 7 double and twin with bath or shower; all rooms have phone, TV, air
conditioning, minibar, hairdrier
FACILITIES restaurant, garden, fishing **CREDIT CARDS** MC, V
CHILDREN accepted
DISABLED 1 specially adapted room **PETS** accepted
CLOSED Jan to mid-Feb; restaurant Mon, Sep to Jun Sun dinner
PROPRIETORS Michèle and Nicole Fagegaltier

AUVERGNE & MASSIF CENTRAL

CHATEAU DE CASTELPERS
~ MANOR HOUSE HOTEL ~

Castelpers, 12170 Léderques (Aveyron)
TEL 05 65 69 22 61 **FAX** 05 65 69 25 31

YOLANDE TAPIÉ DE CELEYRON, of the old and distinguished family that owns this beautiful house, handed over the reins to her daughter, Mme de Saint-Palais, after 30 years. Our inspector found it a 'real delight' to share their home full of memories and objects of continuous history. On the stairs is a portrait of Mme Tapié's great-grandfather, an *'intendant militaire'* of Napoleon. Her grandfather (an engineer who pioneered the building of dams to harness water power and whose car licence plate was 9) restored and built on to the remains of a 17thC mill at the end of the 19th century. The result is not a grandiose château but something more like an unspoiled country house, kept as it has matured and been lived in. Its rooms are full of fine old furniture and pictures. Many of the beds are four-posters.

The taste here is timeless; the charm effortless. The park is enchanting – tall trees shading a long stretch of lawn running between a river and a stream. There are swings for children. It is a 'peaceful, timeless place, happy to be just itself', in the words of our inspector. His dinner and choice of wine were excellent. The inexpensive prices, especially for week-end breaks, are an added appeal.

~

NEARBY Château du Bosc; Sauveterre-de-Rouergue (20 km).
LOCATION in countryside 9 km SE of RN88, 10 km S of Naucelle; car parking
FOOD breakfast, lunch, dinner (residents only)
PRICE €-€€
ROOMS 8; 2 double, 4 twin, 2 family, 3 with bath, 5 with shower; all rooms have phone; some have TV
FACILITIES sitting room, 2 dining rooms, garden, fishing
CREDIT CARDS AE, DC, MC, V **CHILDREN** welcome if well behaved
DISABLED 1 ground-floor room
PETS accepted
CLOSED mid-Oct to mid-Apr; restaurant occasional eve or days
PROPRIETOR Mme de Saint Palais

AUVERGNE & MASSIF CENTRAL

COCURES

✳ LA LOZERETTE ✳
~ VILLAGE INN ~

48400 Cocurès (Lozère)
TEL 04 66 45 06 04 **FAX** 04 66 45 12 93
E-MAIL lalozerette@wanadoo.fr

THE DRIVING FORCE behind this village inn is the charming Pierrette Agulhon, the third generation of her family to own and run it. Her grandmother opened the house as an *auberge*, and clearly passed her hotel-keeping skills on to her granddaughter, who manages La Lozerette with calm efficiency, helped by an able, friendly staff. Although it's on a fairly busy road (by day) on the historic route taken by Robert Louis Stevenson and his donkey Modestine, the wild mountainous landscape of the Cévennes National Park surrounds it, with signs of cultivation – vineyards and orchards – dotted here and there. The best of the views are from the large, wood-floored bedrooms. Painted in spring colours, with co-ordinating floral, checked or striped fabric, they are never fussy, but clean-cut and fresh-looking.

Several downstairs rooms have been knocked together to make the large dining room, the heart of the hotel, which, with its wood-panelled ceiling, cane chairs and cheerful yellow curtains, is cosy despite its size. The menu is regional – you might find *foie gras de canard, chataignes, charcuterie de pays*, river trout or *ceps* on the menu – and so highly regarded that it keeps the restaurant almost permanently full. Leave your choice of wines to Pierrette, who – in addition to her other talents – is a qualified *sommelier*.

~

NEARBY corniche des Cévennes; gorges du Tarn; Mende (42 km). **LOCATION** in village, 6 km NE of Florac; car parking **FOOD** breakfast, lunch, dinner **PRICE** € **ROOMS** 21; 20 double and twin, 1 single, all with bath or shower; all rooms have phone, TV **FACILITIES** 2 sitting rooms, restaurant, bar, garden **CREDIT CARDS** AE, DC, MC, V **CHILDREN** accepted **DISABLED** 1 specially adapted room **PETS** accepted **CLOSED** early Nov to Easter **PROPRIETOR** Pierrette Agulhon

AUVERGNE & MASSIF CENTRAL

GRAND-HOTEL STE-FOY

~ VILLAGE HOTEL ~

Conques, 12320 St-Cyprien-sur-Dourdou (Aveyron)
TEL 05 65 69 84 03 **FAX** 05 65 72 81 04
E-MAIL hotelsaintefoy@hotelsaintefoy.fr **WEBSITE** www.hotelsaintefoy.fr

H OTEL STE-FOY is a lovingly restored, partly timbered 17thC inn which takes its name from the great abbey church directly opposite (with a remarkable tympanum and treasury). It is in the lovely, old village of Conques, and for centuries it has been one of the main stopping places for pilgrims on the route to Santiago.

Marie-France and Alain Garcenot have been the proprietors since they took over from an aunt in 1987. In 1993 it was promoted to four stars. Today they are justifiably proud of their achievement, but the facilities that allow its four-star rating are not the sole basis of the hotel's appeal.

The house has been beautifully furnished with close attention to detail and to preserving the character of the building. Glowing wood is everywhere. The large two-part sitting room is particularly well furnished with antiques. Bedrooms are highly individual, tasteful and large, with views either over the church or the flowery courtyard garden.

You can dine here or in the intimate but pleasantly spacious rooms inside. The increasingly inventive cooking (daily changing menus) gets impressive reviews.

~

NEARBY Rodez (36 km); Figéac (44 km).
LOCATION in the heart of the village; car parking
FOOD breakfast, lunch, dinner; room service
PRICE €€€-€€€€
ROOMS 17; 15 double, 2 suites, all with bath; all rooms have phone, hairdrier; suites have air conditioning; TV on request
FACILITIES sitting room, 3 dining rooms, bar, conference room, interior patio, 2 terraces
CREDIT CARDS AE, DC, MC, V **CHILDREN** accepted
DISABLED 1 specially adapted room
PETS accepted
CLOSED mid-Oct to Easter
PROPRIETORS Marie-France and Alain Garcenot

AUVERGNE & MASSIF CENTRAL

LA MALÈNE

MANOIR DE MONTESQUIOU
∼ MANOR HOUSE HOTEL ∼

48210 La Malène (Lozère)
TEL 04 66 48 51 12 **FAX** 04 66 48 50 47
E-MAIL montesquiou@de-lozere.com **WEBSITE** www.manoir-montesquiou.com

SET DRAMATICALLY between two sheer rock faces in the Gorges du Tarn, this attractive family-run castle-like 15thC manor house offers historical interest as well as excellent value for money. When Louis XIII ordered all rebel fortresses to be razed, the noble Montesquiou family saved their home by carrying out 'special favours' for the king, but worse misfortunes were to follow. A later fire destroyed part of the house and, during the Revolution, Gabriel de Montesquiou was imprisoned and his terrified wife hid herself in a cave; when she re-emerged she was blind.

Today, the house is having happier times. Heavily creepered, it has an inner courtyard and bedrooms in the turret, with stunning views. Larger ones have four-poster canopied beds and rich velvet upholsteries. There's much highly-polished dark furniture, which suits the surroundings, but it is an unassuming, comfortable hotel and guests are well looked after, with good humour and consideration, by owners M. and Mme Guillenet, who have been running the place and providing tasty regional fare for more than 30 years. 'Good-sized rooms, good food, very good views', reports a contented reader.

∼

NEARBY river trips; fishing; bathing; Ste-Enimie (15 km).
LOCATION small village in the Gorges of the Tarn; car parking
FOOD breakfast, lunch, dinner **PRICE** €€
ROOMS 12; 10 double and twin, 2 suites, 7 with bath, 5 with shower; all rooms have phone, TV; hairdrier on request
FACILITIES sitting room, 2 dining rooms, bar, garden, 2 terraces
CREDIT CARDS DC, MC, V
CHILDREN accepted
DISABLED access difficult
PETS accepted
CLOSED Nov to early Apr
PROPRIETORS M. and Mme Guillenet

AUVERGNE & MASSIF CENTRAL

MEYRUEIS

CHATEAU D'AYRES

~ COUNTRY HOTEL ~

48150 Meyrueis (Lozère)
Tel 04 66 45 60 10 **Fax** 04 66 45 62 26
E-MAIL Alliette@wanadoo.fr **WEBSITE** www.chateau-d-ayres.com

THE LOVELY, STONE, mainly 18thC, white-shuttered château stands on the site of a 12thC Benedictine monastery, now in the heart of the Cévennes National Park and in its own beautiful wooded grounds, with mature sequoias and oaks. Inside it is handsome, with walnut and chestnut panelling in some rooms, vaulted ceilings and a profusion of good antiques and pictures. Bedrooms are well appointed, with elegant, traditional furniture and carved mouldings. Some of the larger rooms have interesting bathrooms – extended into round towers or elevated on a mezzanine. Staff are friendly and helpful. The food is excellent. The chef, Jacqui Joubin, specializes in Languedoc cuisine using plenty of local produce. M. de Montjou is a knowledgeable *sommelier*.

The house has a relaxed, convivial atmosphere and is extremely quiet. The garden is superb, with a lake, tennis court, swimming pool made out of local stone, a small whirlpool bath, and five horses, kept specially for guests to ride. There are plenty of alluring, shady places to which you can retreat with a chair and a book on long, hot afternoons – at 750 metres, the air is fresh and pure.

~

NEARBY Meyrueis (1 km); Gorges du Tarn; Mont Aigoual (1,387 m).
LOCATION 1 km SE of Meyrueis; car parking
FOOD breakfast, lunch, dinner
PRICE €€
ROOMS 27; 21 double and twin, 6 suites, 24 with bath, 3 with shower; all rooms have phone, TV, hairdrier
FACILITIES sitting room, library, 3 dining rooms, garden, terrace, swimming pool, tennis, riding
CREDIT CARDS AE, DC, MC, V **CHILDREN** accepted
DISABLED no special facilities
PETS accepted
CLOSED mid-Nov to late Mar
PROPRIETOR M. de Montjou

AUVERGNE & MASSIF CENTRAL

MOUDEYRES

LE PRE BOSSU
~ FARMHOUSE HOTEL ~

43150 Moudeyres (Haute-Loire)
TEL 04 71 05 10 70 **FAX** 04 71 05 10 21

MOUDEYRES IS A REMOTE village of thatched stone cottages and farm buildings, high (1,200 m) in the volcanic Mézenc massif, surrounded by fields of wild flowers in the spring and mushrooms in the autumn. It is a long way off the beaten track, but our inspector found it well worth the journey: 'Rarely have I seen a more beautiful location.' It is very rugged and difficult to get to.

The conscientious Flemish owners, the Grootaerts, have worked extremely hard to create an attractive and comfortable house. To original beams, wooden floors and old-fashioned, open fireplaces, they've added antique dressers, lace curtains, wild flowers when they are available – dried flowers when they are not – and books. Pots of home-made jam and artisan products are (subtly) for sale.

Some of our reports suggest that the hospitality may occasionally lack warmth, while others enthuse over the comfort and high standard of the food. By Easter 2002, M. Grootaert should have completed his project to knock together some of the ten original bedrooms to create five splendid large double rooms and one family room. Picnic baskets are provided for lunching out. Smoking is not allowed in the dining room.

NEARBY Le Puy-en-Velay (25 km); Yssingeaux (35 km).
LOCATION on the edge of the village, SE of Le Puy, beyond Laussonne; car parking
FOOD breakfast, lunch (Sun only), dinner
PRICE €
ROOMS 6; 5 double and twin, 1 family, all with bath or shower; all rooms have phone
FACILITIES bar, TV room, dining room, garden
CREDIT CARDS AE, MC, V
CHILDREN accepted
DISABLED no special facilities **PETS** accepted
CLOSED Nov to Easter; restaurant lunch Mon-Sat
PROPRIETOR Carlos Grootaert

AUVERGNE & MASSIF CENTRAL

NAJAC

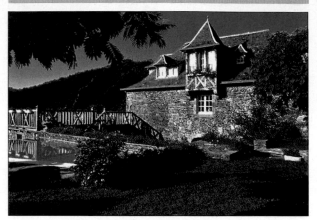

LONGCOL

~ COUNTRY HOTEL ~

La Fouillade, 12270 Najac (Aveyron)
TEL 05 65 29 63 36 **FAX** 05 65 29 64 28
E-MAIL longcol@relaischateaux.fr **WEBSITE** www.relaischateaux.fr/longcol

THIS SPLENDID, TURRETED, restored medieval farmhouse – with added buildings in the same bell-shaped slate-roofed style – is set in isolated grandeur in a forested valley of the Gorges de l'Aveyron.

Solid and dignified, the overall effect is delightful. Much skill and taste has gone into the architecture, fittings and furnishings and there are antiques in every room. Quite a few of the pieces are European, but mostly they are from Asia: huge carved and studded Indian doors, exotic wood carvings and bronzes from India, Burma and Thailand, Indian miniature paintings on silk and ivory, all cleverly lit and displayed. One could be in a luxury hotel in India. The original Belgian owner, Fabienne Luyckx, began work on the site in 1982 with her mother (who died before completion), and although she is no longer in charge, it was her passion for Asian art and antiques that dictated the hotel's style.

Added to all this is a sense of great comfort and professionalism. Seafood and regional dishes are served in a light and airy dining room or on the little walled terrace in summer – or by the angular swimming pool, which has views of woods. Food is taken seriously and there is an excellent wine list.

~

NEARBY Najac (5 km); Villefranche-de-Rouergue (20 km).
LOCATION between Monteils and La Fouillade on D638, NE of Najac; car parking
FOOD breakfast, lunch, dinner
PRICE €€€
ROOMS 19 double, 17 with bath, 2 with shower; all rooms have phone, TV, minibar
FACILITIES sitting room, restaurant, billiard room, garden, terrace, swimming pool, tennis court
CREDIT CARDS DC, MC, V
CHILDREN welcome
DISABLED no special facilities **PETS** welcome
CLOSED Nov to Easter; restaurant Mon, Tue and lunch Wed
PROPRIETORS Luyckx family

AUVERGNE & MASSIF CENTRAL

ST-ARCONS-D'ALLIER

LES DEUX ABBESSES

~ VILLAGE HOTEL ~

Le Château, 43300 St-Arcons-d'Allier (Haute-Loire)
TEL 04 71 74 03 08 **FAX** 04 71 74 05 30
E-MAIL direction@les-deux-abbesses.fr **WEBSITE** www.les-deux-abbesses.fr

ONCE YOU ARRIVE in St-Arcons-d'Allier, a picturesque medieval village perched above the river which gives it the second half of its name, there's no point in asking where the hotel is because you are already standing in the middle of it. Laurence Perceval and Bernard Massas have breathed new life into a well-nigh abandoned village by converting six of the houses into 10 bedrooms for their hotel centred on the château whose origins stretch back more than a thousand years. The streets are cobbled with stones taken from the river bed, and as visitors' cars are excluded to preserve the peace and undeniable charm of the village, you and your luggage will be taken to your lodging by Mini Moke.

The restoration has been done sensitively, and creature comforts have been installed without marring the pleasing simplicity of the buildings. The traditional plantings in the gardens, warm stonework and glimpses of the countryside beyond the village all contribute to the atmosphere of rustic peace. Breakfast and dinner are civilized meals, eaten in the château; the latter by candlelight in the baronial dining room. Dishes at dinner are prepared using fresh local produce, flavoured with herbs from the hotel's own garden. An elegant but comfortable *salon* offers a place to linger after dinner before you walk home.

~

NEARBY Le Puy-en-Velay (47 km); St-Flour (57 km); riding; golf.
LOCATION 6 km SE of Langeac, left off the D585 to Saugues; car parking
FOOD breakfast, dinner (by reservation only)
PRICE €€-€€€€; 2-night minimum stay Fri to Sun
ROOMS 10; 5 double, 1 twin, 3 triple, 1 family, 9 with bath, 1 with shower
FACILITIES sitting room, dining room, terraces, garden, swimming pool
CREDIT CARDS AE, MC, V **CHILDREN** accepted over 10
DISABLED not suitable
PETS accepted
CLOSED never
PROPRIETORS Laurence Perceval and Bernard Massas

AUVERGNE & MASSIF CENTRAL

ST-JEAN-DU-BRUEL

HOTEL DU MIDI-PAPILLON

~ RIVERSIDE HOTEL ~

12230 St-Jean-du-Bruel (Aveyron)
TEL 05 65 62 26 04 **FAX** 05 65 62 12 97

EVERY YEAR WE RECEIVE a long handwritten bulletin from Jean-Michel Papillon, the fourth generation of Papillons to run this old coaching inn, reporting on the latest developments. Readers share our enthusiasm for the place, telling us that nothing changes, the food remains 'wonderful', the welcome 'faultless', the value 'outstanding'. Our inspector, to his pleasure, finds everything just right: 'The Papillons go on doing what they have been doing for the last 150 years – providing a lively welcome, lodging and food to grateful travellers.' The hotel still bears features of its past and is the sort of traditional unpretentious *auberge* that is getting harder and harder to find; this one stands out for the quality of its food and the warmth of the welcome. There is an excellent dining room – the domain of Mme Papillon – and a view from most tables of the river and a little medieval stone humpbacked bridge. There is also a terrace (though sometimes one may not always be able to sit where one wishes). Jean-Michel Papillon cooks with vegetables from the garden and home-raised poultry, and makes his own jam, croissants, and *charcuterie*. This is the rural, family-run inn at its best.

~

NEARBY Gorges de la Dourbie (10 km); Montpellier-le-Vieux.
LOCATION by river, in village on D991, 40 km SE of Millau; car parking
FOOD breakfast, lunch, dinner
PRICE €
ROOMS 19; 8 double, 5 twin, 1 suite, 1 single, 4 family, all with bath or shower; all rooms have phone
FACILITIES sitting room, TV room, 3 dining rooms, bar, terrace, garden, swimming pool, Jacuzzi
CREDIT CARDS MC, V **CHILDREN** welcome
DISABLED access difficult
PETS accepted
CLOSED mid-Nov to Easter
PROPRIETORS Papillon family

AUVERGNE & MASSIF CENTRAL

TARGET

CHATEAU DE BOUSSAC

~ CHATEAU HOTEL ~

Target, 03140 Chantelle (Allier)
TEL 04 70 40 63 20 **FAX** 04 70 40 60 03
E-MAIL longueil@club-internet.fr **WEBSITE** www.chateau-de-boussac.com

INCREASED PUBLIC EXPOSURE – now in other British hotel guides as well as this one – has not affected the delicate balancing act conducted by the Marquis and Marquise de Longueil, who continue to welcome guests into their home with captivating charm.

The Château de Boussac lies between Vichy and Moulin, tucked away in the Bourbonnais – quite difficult to find. Solid, turreted and moated, the château could be a tourist sight in its own right; it is built around a court-yard, and the main reception rooms, furnished with Louis XV antiques and chandeliers, open on to a vast terrace with an ornamental lake and formal gardens. But the château is very much lived-in. By day the Marquis dons his overalls and works on the estate, but comes in to cook at least one course of the evening meal and chat to his guests. His wife looks after the rooms with care – there are fresh flowers everywhere, and the antiques are highly polished. Dinner *en famille* can be a rather formal affair, but the food is hard to fault and the Marquis, who speaks English, will make you feel at home. One reader was enchanted, and proclaimed it 'one of the highlights of our two-week trip'.

~

NEARBY Chantelle (12 km); Souvigny (35 km); Vichy (50 km).
LOCATION in countryside, off D42, NW of Chantelle; car parking
FOOD breakfast, dinner
PRICE €€€
ROOMS 5; 1 double, 3 twin, 1 suite, all with bath
FACILITIES sitting room, dining room, terrace, garden
CREDIT CARDS AE, MC, V
CHILDREN accepted if well behaved
DISABLED no special facilities
PETS accepted
CLOSED Nov to Feb (except by reservation in advance)
PROPRIETORS Marquis and Marquise de Longueil

AUVERGNE & MASSIF CENTRAL

VITRAC

AUBERGE DE LA TOMETTE

~ VILLAGE INN ~

15220 Vitrac (Cantal)
TEL 04 71 64 70 94 **FAX** 04 71 64 77 11
E-MAIL latomette@wanadoo.fr **WEBSITE** www.auberge-la-tomette.com

'THIS HOTEL HAS ALL THE QUALITIES of peace, welcome, attractive setting and very good food that characterize your selections,' a reader said of La Tomette – a jolly whitewashed and shuttered inn, much expanded and improved over the past 18 years, without the loss of its essential appeal. In an exceptionally pretty village in the middle of the chestnut groves of the southern Cantal, it makes a perfect base for a family holiday, with its large garden, where trees and parasols provide plenty of shade, lawns for running around and covered and heated swimming pool. There's also a health centre with Jacuzzi, sauna and steam room.

Wood-panelling gives a rustic feel to the cosy dining room, where every day a vase of freshly picked garden flowers is placed on each of the pink-covered tables. In summer, meals are served on a lovely terrace, part of which is covered for those who prefer to eat in total shade. In a separate building, the bedrooms are modern and clean but otherwise unexceptional. There is one duplex with a convenient lay-out for families.

~

NEARBY Maurs (21 km); Aurillac (22 km); Figéac (43 km).
LOCATION in village, 5 km S of St-Mamet-la-Salvetat; car parking
FOOD breakfast, lunch, dinner
PRICE €
ROOMS 15; 14 double and twin, 1 family, all with bath or shower; all rooms have phone, TV
FACILITIES sitting room, restaurant, sauna, terrace, garden, health centre, swimming pool
CREDIT CARDS AE, MC, V
CHILDREN accepted
DISABLED no special facilities
PETS accepted
CLOSED Jan to Apr
PROPRIETORS Odette and Daniel Chausi

PROVENCE-COTE D'AZUR

AIX-EN-PROVENCE

MAS D'ENTREMONT
~ FARMHOUSE HOTEL ~

Montée d'Avignon, 13090 Aix-en-Provence (Bouches-du-Rhône)
TEL 04 42 17 42 42 **FAX** 04 42 21 15 83
E-MAIL entremont@wanadoo.fr **WEBSITE** francemarket.com/mas_dentremont

THIS IS ONE OF OUR FAVOURITE HOTELS and a visit not long ago confirms our earlier impressions. The hosts here are the charming M. Marignane and his family – his brother owns the Relais de la Magdeleine at Gémenos, about which we are equally enthusiastic (see page 108). Low, red-roofed buildings are clustered around a courtyard – modern constructions, but using old materials. Within are wooden beams and pillars, rustic furniture, tiled floors and open fireplaces. Bedrooms are also rustic in style and comfortable. Many of the rooms are spread around the grounds in bungalows.

The setting is peaceful and the gardens a delight – with a big swimming pool shielded by cypresses, plenty of secluded corners, and a pond with a fountain, lilies and a number of lazy carp. Overlooking this is a beautiful summer dining room, with windows that slide away, effectively creating a roofed terrace – to which underfloor heating has now been added, allowing you to eat out even on a chilly day.

The food is excellent, with the emphasis on fish, fresh vegetables and a strong Provençal influence (although the chef is from Strasbourg).

~

NEARBY Aix-en-Provence; Abbaye de Silvacane (25 km).
LOCATION just off the RN7, 2 km from the centre of Aix, in large garden and grounds; parking
FOOD breakfast, lunch, dinner
PRICE €€€
ROOMS 17; 15 double and twin, 2 family, all with bath; all rooms have phone, TV, air conditioning, minibar, hairdrier, safe
FACILITIES dining room, gym, lift, terrace, garden, swimming pool, tennis
CREDIT CARDS MC, V **CHILDREN** welcome
DISABLED ground-floor rooms available
PETS accepted
CLOSED Nov to mid-Mar; restaurant Sun dinner
PROPRIETORS Marignane family

PROVENCE-COTE D'AZUR

AIX-EN-PROVENCE

✳ VILLA GALLICI ✳

~ TOWN VILLA ~

avenue de la Violette, 13100 Aix-en-Provence (Bouches-du-Rhône)
TEL 04 42 23 29 23 **FAX** 04 42 96 30 45
E-MAIL villagallici@wanadoo.fr **WEBSITE** www.villagallici.com

MANY PEOPLE CONSIDER the four-star Relais & Châteaux Villa Gallici to be the best hotel in Aix; a recent inspection confirms its place at the top. It is certainly beautiful, and interior-designed down to the last curtain hook. Everything, inside and out, is perfect – gardens, terraces, pool, enormous terracotta pots overflowing with flowers, white umbrellas and plenty of wrought iron. A terrace, adjoining the villa, shaded by plane trees has been converted to an outside sitting room with deep-cushioned sofas and chairs. Bedrooms are sumptuous, with marvellous French wallpapers and fabrics and elegant 18thC furniture. Most of the bathrooms are classic, and pristine white. Downstairs, a series of small, welcoming, intimate sitting rooms are filled with colour and light, prints, paintings, coffee-table books and pieces of porcelain.

Our reporter noted that the guests were as beautiful as the hotel; this is not a place for the much-loved old grey T-shirt. Perhaps there is something just a little intimidating about the grand style of the Villa Gallici for it to be entirely relaxing, but that, as always, is a matter of taste.

NEARBY Avignon (82 km); Marseille (31 km).
LOCATION in a quiet suburb, 500 m from cathedral; car parking
FOOD breakfast, lunch, dinner
PRICE €€€€€
ROOMS 22; 18 double and twin, 4 suites, all with bath; all rooms have phone, TV, video, air conditioning, minibar, hairdrier, safe
FACILITIES sitting rooms, dining room, terrace, garden, swimming pool
CREDIT CARDS AE, DC, MC, V **CHILDREN** welcome
DISABLED 1 specially adapted room
PETS welcome
CLOSED never
PROPRIETORS M. Jouve, M. Dez and M. Montemarco

PROVENCE-COTE D'AZUR

CALENDAL
~ TOWN HOTEL ~

5 rue Porte de Laure, 13200 Arles (Bouches-du-Rhône)
TEL 04 90 96 11 89 **FAX** 04 90 96 05 84
E-MAIL contact@lecalendal.com **WEBSITE** www.lecalendal.com

THIS BUSY, FRIENDLY HOTEL offers the best of both worlds: a location right next door to the great Roman arena – our inspector's room had a little balcony looking on to it – and a surprisingly large courtyard garden, a shady haven of trees (including a 400-year-old nettle tree), where on a hot day you can retreat from the dusty city. The building is 18th century, which shows through as features of the decoration, for example the rough stone walls and exposed beams downstairs. Here all the rooms have been knocked through to make one huge open-plan space, supported by pillars, with arches and steps marking the divisions between sitting and eating areas. The cosy sitting area, centred on the fireplace, is a perfect place for waiting, with armchairs and foreign-language newspapers on rods brasserie-style. You help yourself to the buffet breakfast and light lunch, which is still on offer at 5 pm.

One can't imagine being glum for long in this hotel. The colourful decoration would lift the blackest of moods. The bedrooms are different variations on a theme, mixing blues and yellows, yellows and reds or reds and greens, with pretty co-ordinating Provençal fabrics. Though small, they are well designed, with TVs on high brackets or shelves and cleverly added bathrooms, full of the fluffiest, brightest yellow towels.

~

NEARBY arena; St-Trophîme; place du Forum.
LOCATION opposite Roman arena; car parking (reserve in advance)
FOOD breakfast, light lunch, tea
PRICE €
ROOMS 38 double, twin, triple and family, all with bath; all rooms have phone, TV, air conditioning, hairdrier
FACILITIES sitting area, dining areas, garden
CREDIT CARDS AE, DC, MC, V **CHILDREN** accepted
DISABLED 3 specially adapted rooms **PETS** welcome
CLOSED 3 weeks Jan
MANAGER Mme Jacquemin

PROVENCE-COTE D'AZUR

ARLES

✳ GRAND HOTEL NORD-PINUS ✳

～ TOWN HOTEL ～

place du Forum, 13200 Arles (Bouches-du-Rhône)
TEL 04 90 93 44 44 **FAX** 04 90 93 34 00
E-MAIL info@nord-pinus.com **WEBSITE** www.nord-pinus.com

A STUNNING EXAMPLE of how a former cult hotel can, in the right hands, live again with its spirit intact but its amenities altered to suit the modern age. Anne Igou's imaginative and extravagant renovation (now 10 years old) has given back the Nord-Pinus its Bohemian past, recalling the post-war days when artists such as Picasso and Cocteau as well as bull-fighters were entertained by its charismatic owners, a cabaret dancer and her husband, a famous tightrope-walking clown. The famous yellow bar, in particular, remains a homage to those times. There are other mementoes, too, including a cabinet of souvenirs, huge posters advertising bullfights around the fine stairwell, as well as chandeliers, gilded mirrors and all the original wrought-iron beds. The lobby has a dramatic, slightly Moorish feel; the restaurant, a traditional brasserie, leads off it, although it is not currently owned by Anne Igou.

Bedrooms come in three sizes: the smallest are compact but charming, with Provençal fabrics and antique wardrobes; larger ones are very spacious; and the six suites are enormous, worth splashing out on, especially No. 10, the 'bullfighters' suite', from the window of which legendary matador Domingúin would greet the crowds below. The hotel is run in a laid-back but professional way.

～

NEARBY Arena, Théatre Antique; St-Trophîme; Les Alyscampes.
LOCATION in town centre (follow hotel signs); garage parking
FOOD breakfast **PRICE** €€€ **ROOMS** 25; 19 double and twin, 6 suites, all with bath; all rooms have phone, TV, air conditioning, minibar, hairdrier
FACILITIES sitting room, bar, adjoining restaurant, breakfast room, lift, terrace

CREDIT CARDS AE, DC, MC, V
CHILDREN accepted
DISABLED access possible
PETS accepted
CLOSED never
PROPRIETOR Anne Igou

PROVENCE-COTE D'AZUR

AVIGNON

LA MIRANDE
~ TOWN HOTEL ~

4 place de Mirande, 84000 Avignon (Vaucluse)
TEL 04 90 85 93 93 **FAX** 04 90 86 26 85
E-MAIL mirande@la-mirande.fr **WEBSITE** www.la-mirande.fr

A CLASSIC HONEY-COLOURED late 17thC façade by Pierre Mignard transformed La Mirande, which was built on the 14thC foundations of a cardinal's palace, into a *hotel particulier*. Right opposite the Palais des Papes, in a quiet cobbled square, it was seized on by the Stein family and, since 1990, has been a sumptuous hotel that looks and feels as if it had been lived in for generations by a single family endowed with money and good taste. Tiled and parquet floors, smart Provençal fabrics and chintzes, wall coverings, paint, panelling, pictures, mirrors, and furniture all come together in serene period harmony. The good news doesn't stop there: the staff are kind and courteous as well.

The central courtyard, dotted with plants and sculptures, has been covered over with a glass roof, and is surrounded by a series of public rooms any one of which you'd like to wrap up and take home with you. The bedrooms vary in size (those on the first floor being the largest) but not in their uniformly high quality. From the second-floor balconies you are treated to rooftop views across the city. Last but not least are the treats in store in the dining room: Daniel Hébet draws eager gourmets from far and wide. And, yes, there is a garage for your car.

~

NEARBY Petit-Palais; Notre-Dame-des-Doms; Calvet museum.
LOCATION opposite the Palais des Papes; car parking
FOOD breakfast, lunch, dinner
PRICE €€€€€
ROOMS 20; 19 double and twin, 1 suite, all with bath; all rooms have phone, TV, air conditioning, hairdrier
FACILITIES sitting rooms, bar, dining room, lift, terrace, garden
CREDIT CARDS AE, DC, MC, V **CHILDREN** accepted
DISABLED 1 specially adapted room
PETS accepted **CLOSED** never; restaurant Jan
PROPRIETOR M. Achim Stein

PROVENCE-COTE D'AZUR

BARTHELASSE (ILE DE LA)

L'ANASTASY
~ COUNTRY HOUSE ~

chemin des Poiriers, Ile de la Barthelasse, 84000 Avignon (Vaucluse)
TEL 04 90 85 55 94 **FAX** 04 90 82 59 40 **E-MAIL** HYPERLINK mailto:anastasy@avignon-et-provence.com **WEBSITE** www.avignon-et-provence.com/bb/anastasy

STAYING WITH THE MANGUINS on this green island just over the river from Avignon is as good as having friends with a house in Provence. Olga Manguin is a great character, a published writer who cooks like a dream in the kitchen of L'Anastasy, her old farmhouse surrounded by orchards. The house has been restored with artistic style, and if the simple bedrooms and bathrooms are showing signs of wear and tear, we think it only adds to the charm. In the sitting room there are long white curtains and plenty of comfortable sofas. On the walls are pictures by the grandfather – a French fauvist painter – of Mme Manguin's husband Henri. Guests sit together in the evenings – either at a big marble table in one of the two kitchens or out on the covered terrace – to eat whatever Mme Manguin has found in the market that day. Specialities of the house are home-made pasta and traditional dishes of Southern France, Italy and the Mediterranean, with olive oil, thyme, saffron and garlic. Fellow guests are an eclectic mix, often interesting, such as our companion on a recent visit, a singer who was staying for several weeks while starring at Avignon's opera house. Bedrooms are basic; two are downstairs. They are spare rooms in a private house and do not pretend to be otherwise. The house has a welcoming, convivial air. All the attractions and bustle of Avignon are across the river; La Barthelasse, by contrast, is an island of tranquillity (the house is hard to find; ask for directions). Prices are a bargain.

~

NEARBY Avignon (7 km); Arles (43 km); Aix-en-Provence (90 km).
LOCATION on Ile de la Barthelasse among fields and orchards; car parking
FOOD breakfast, dinner on request
PRICE €
ROOMS 4 double, 1 with bath, 3 with shower; 2 bathrooms are not en suite
FACILITIES sitting room, dining room, conservatory breakfast room, terrace, garden, swimming pool **CREDIT CARDS** not accepted **CHILDREN** accepted
DISABLED no special facilities **PETS** accepted **CLOSED** never
PROPRIETORS Olga and Henri Manguin

PROVENCE-COTE D'AZUR

LA MAISON
~ VILLAGE RESTAURANT-WITH-ROOMS ~

84340 Beaumont-du-Ventoux (Vaucluse)
TEL 04 90 65 15 50 **FAX** 04 90 65 23 29

FROM THE OUTSIDE, La Maison looks like dozens of other pretty Provençal houses – creeper-covered stone walls, blue window-shutters and doors, white wrought-iron tables and chairs, parasols and plants in terracotta pots on a shady front terrace – but a surprise lies in store. The restaurant, opened by Michèle Laurelut in June 1993, four years before she started letting rooms, is as chic as the owner herself with the kind of sophistication that you would hardly expect to find on the edge of a sleepy rural village like Beaumont-du-Ventoux. The decoration is stylishly simple: ochre-washed plaster walls, terracotta-tiled floor and heavy cream curtains at the windows. It is furnished like a private house, with massive table lamps, cushions to sit on, well-spaced tables, and artfully arranged pictures and ornaments. The focal point is an immense stone fireplace, where a fire burns on chilly autumn nights, to be replaced by a bank of hydrangeas when the weather improves.

Michèle offers a short seasonal menu, which we considered good value at around 25 Euros, and you can keep your bill down if you stick to the excellent local wine. To save driving home after dinner, you could stay in one of the large, modest bedrooms (two connect), which are immaculately kept but lack the dining room's panache.

~

NEARBY Vaison-la-Romaine (12 km); Avignon (47 km).
LOCATION in village, turn left at sign just before Mairie; car parking
FOOD breakfast, lunch, dinner
PRICE €
ROOMS 4; 2 double, 2 twin, 3 with shower
FACILITIES dining room, terrace, garden
CREDIT CARDS MC, V **CHILDREN** accepted
DISABLED not suitable **PETS** accepted
CLOSED Nov to Apr; restaurant Mon and Tue Apr to Jun, Sep and Oct; lunch Mon to Sat Jul and Aug
PROPRIETOR Michèle Laurelut

PROVENCE-COTE D'AZUR

BONNIEUX

AUBERGE DE L'AIGUEBRUN
~ COUNTRY HOTEL ~

Domaine de la Tour, RD 943, 84480 Bonnieux (Vaucluse)
TEL 04 90 04 47 00 **FAX** 04 90 04 47 01

SYLVIE BUZIER IS WARM, pretty and talented (she can paint as well as cook and decorate). Her staff are equally charming, easy-going and unobtrusively hip (her co-chef is friendly Francis Motta). They are a happy, well-knit team, and, along with the hotel's setting, they engender a rare sense of peace and well-being in their beautiful house.

The hotel lies on its own in a green oasis at the end of a steep track by a waterfall in the river Aigebrun, the only natural water in this barren region. 'When Sylvie (who previously owned a much loved restaurant near Avignon) bought it, she transformed the interior, which is now a delightful, personalized version of current Provençal decoration. Rooms are full of light: the white and cream dining room with its fresh green leaf curtains is surrounded by windows overlooking the river; the sitting room is a lovely yellow, with a well-stocked drinks tray, comfy sofas and a minah bird in an antique cage; the bedrooms are similarly full of light and colour (the family suite is excellent, with two bedrooms, one perfect for children).

The food is a highlight: a simple, delicious set menu with one or two choices using organic meat and vegetables and wild fish. Herbs and salads come from the *potager*. There is a lovely pool.

~

NEARBY Bonnieux (6 km); Lourmarin (10 km); Aix-en-Provence (45 km).
LOCATION in valley, 6 km E of Bonnieux, down a steep rutted track signposted off Bonnieux to Boux road; car parking
FOOD breakfast, lunch, dinner
PRICE €€€
ROOMS 8; 4 double and twin, 1 single, 3 suites, all with bath; all rooms have phone, TV, hairdrier
FACILITIES sitting room, dining room, terrace, garden, *potager*, swimming pool, bar
CREDIT CARDS MC, V **CHILDREN** accepted
DISABLED not suitable **PETS** not accepted **CLOSED** mid-Nov to mid-Mar; restaurant Tue, Wed lunch
PROPRIETOR Sylvia Buzier

PROVENCE-COTE D'AZUR

L'HOSTELLERIE DU PRIEURE

~ VILLAGE HOTEL ~

84480 Bonnieux (Vaucluse)
TEL 04 90 75 80 78 **FAX** 04 90 75 96 00
E-MAIL hotelprieure@hotmail.com

THIS ATTRACTIVE HOTEL at the foot of the ramparts of one of the showpiece Luberon villages has been in our Southern France guide for many years and, after our latest inspector gave a favourable report, we decided to include it in this guide too. The Prieuré's new manager, Michèle Cadillon is down-to-earth and kindly, fostering the warm, relaxed ambience for guests that her predecessor, Caroline Coutaz, made her trademark.

What is so refreshing about this former hospital – an 18thC *hôtel-Dieu* – is that it has escaped the vogue for prettification, and remains little changed since our first visit. Through massive oak doors, a splendid wide, red-tiled staircase leads up to the balustraded landing. (The former chapel is now used for storage.) What were once rooms for the patients are light with beams, antique furniture and endearingly old-fashioned wallpaper and curtains. Some overlook the pretty walled garden at the rear, where apricot and plum trees give shade from the heat, and are quieter than those at the front, which face the road going up into the village. Food is served on the covered terrace or in the dining room where the original hearth takes up an entire wall. In the spacious bar there is a wonderful antique glass case with replicas of Paris theatres in miniature, designed so that theatre-goers could choose their seats.

~

NEARBY Avignon (51 km); Aix (40 km); the villages of the Luberon.
LOCATION on a lower road of the village; car parking
FOOD breakfast, lunch, dinner
PRICE €€€
ROOMS 10; 6 double, 4 twin, 9 with bath, 1 with shower; all rooms have phone
FACILITIES sitting room, dining room, bar, terrace, garden
CREDIT CARDS MC, V **CHILDREN** accepted
DISABLED not suitable **PETS** accepted
CLOSED early Nov to Mar; restaurant lunch Tue to Fri, Oct to May Wed, lunch Tue and Thurs
MANAGERS Michèle Cadillon and Rémi Chapotin

PROVENCE-COTE D'AZUR

LE CLOS DES AROMES
~ TOWN HOTEL ~

10 rue Paul Mouton, 13260 Cassis (Bouches-du-Rhône)
TEL 04 42 01 71 84 **FAX** 04 42 01 31 76

THIS IS A VERY PRETTY SMALL HOTEL, in a quiet street near the old port and run and completely redecorated by the young, friendly and informal Bonnets, who took over from the previous owners seven years ago. The hotel's history goes back 50 years and in the dining room there is a little oil painting of it as it was.

It is a bright, sunny place, entered either off the street into a large, attractive dining room or through the delightful paved garden. The dining room has old terracotta tiles on the floor, stripped wooden panelling on the walls, a big stone fireplace at one end, little tables with blue and yellow cloths and painted blue chairs.

Bedrooms are on the two floors above, up steep stairs. Behind simple white-painted doors, the rooms are small, but very pretty. Each one has a different colour scheme: fabrics, wallpapers and paintwork are carefully co-ordinated. Furniture is quality country-style reproduction. Bathrooms are smallish, but spotlessly clean and sparkling white. There are two tiny rooms, with double beds, but usually let as singles. They offer hardly any room to move, but are nonetheless very appealing. The Provençal menu here is very reasonably priced.

~

NEARBY Marseille (20 km); Aix-en-Provence (35 km).
LOCATION in a quiet side-street in the old town, near the port; car parking
FOOD breakfast, lunch, dinner
PRICE €
ROOMS 8; 5 double, 2 single, 1 family, 3 with bath, 5 with shower; all rooms have phone
FACILITIES dining room, terrace, garden
CREDIT CARDS AE, MC, V **CHILDREN** accepted
DISABLED not suitable
PETS accepted
CLOSED Oct to late Dec, Jan to mid-Feb
PROPRIETOR M. Fabrice Bonnet

PROVENCE-COTE D'AZUR

LA BONNE ETAPE

~ TOWN INN ~

chemin du Lac, 04160 Château-Arnoux (Alpes-de-Haute-Provence)
TEL 04 92 64 00 09 **FAX** 04 92 64 37 36 **E-MAIL** bonneetape@relaischateaux.com
WEBSITE www.bonneetape.com

'EXCEPTIONAL FOOD, impeccable service, beautiful pool and rooms,' says a recent customer of this 'good stopover' – a former coaching inn in an unremarkable small town. Outside, it gives little hint of what lies within – one of the most satisfactory blends of refinement and hospitality to be found in the region. Although the kitchen lost its second Michelin star, we would re-award it if we could. Chefs Pierre and Jany Gleize (father and son) make innovative and stylish use of largely home-grown ingredients. A house speciality is Sisteron lamb (raised on mountain pastures): try it with a deep-red Vacqueyras Côtes du Rhone. Tables in the formal dining room have fresh flowers; Bach plays in the background. There are serious eaters here, many alone. The atmosphere is slightly hushed, but the waiters are helpful and friendly. There is a charming bar with painted beams. But this is no restaurant-with-rooms. Bedrooms are luxuriously comfortable – beautifully decorated with a tasteful mix of modern and antique pieces. Some have marble bathrooms. The Gleize family are warmly welcoming hosts, happily committed to their work; they also own a simpler restaurant nearby.

~

NEARBY Eglise St Donat; Sisteron (14 km).
LOCATION just off main RN85, 14 km SE of Sisteron (motorway 3 km); car parking and garage
FOOD breakfast, lunch, dinner; room service
PRICE €€€
ROOMS 19 double and twin, all with bath; all rooms have phone, TV, air conditioning, minibar, hairdrier
FACILITIES sitting room, dining room, terrace, garden, swimming pool
CREDIT CARDS AE, DC, MC, V **CHILDREN** accepted
DISABLED access possible **PETS** accepted
CLOSED mid-Nov to mid-Dec, Jan to mid-Feb; restaurant closed Tue lunch and Mon Oct to Mar
PROPRIETORS Gleize family

PROVENCE-COTE D'AZUR

CRILLON-LE-BRAVE

✳ HOSTELLERIE DE CRILLON LE BRAVE ✳

∼ VILLAGE HOTEL ∼

place de l'Eglise, 84410 Crillon-le-Brave (Vaucluse)
TEL 04 90 65 61 61 **FAX** 04 90 65 62 86
E-MAIL crillonlebrave@relaischateaux.fr **WEBSITE** www.crillonlebrave.com

'DELIGHTFUL', ENTHUSES one satisfied visitor to this luxurious hotel occupying the old vicarage in a hilltop village. 'Very good restaurant, excellent service, a lovely setting and charming staff.' Another more recent guest is not so complimentary, sensing 'an air of complacency' in the housekeeping. He also finds the Provençal cooking 'disappointing, not in quality but in the absence of a menu change or a *plat du jour*.' However, he praises the wine list, which 'offered excellent value', and a recently opened summer bistro, gives guests an alternative choice for dinner.

The rambling 16thC stone-built house is solid and calm, but most of the credit for the resounding success of the hotel must go to the owner, Peter Chittick, a Canadian lawyer with clear ideas about hotelkeeping, although he is no longer there full-time. A considerable share goes also to the perched location, giving uninterrupted views of a heavenly landscape of olive groves and vineyards. The central trick that Mr Chittick and his collaborator Craig Miller have pulled off is to provide luxury without erasing character. Despite the designer fabrics, fitted carpets and smart bathrooms, the exposed beams, white walls and rustic furniture dominate both in the sitting rooms and the spacious bedrooms (13 of which have recently been added). You eat beneath stone vaults, or out on the pretty terrace.

∼

NEARBY Mont Ventoux; Orange (35 km); Avignon (35 km). **LOCATION** in village NE of Avignon, on D138 off D974; car parking **FOOD** breakfast, lunch (Sat and Sun only), dinner, snacks **PRICE** €€€€€ **ROOMS** 32 double, twin and suites, all with bath or shower; all rooms have phone, minibar, hairdrier **FACILITIES** 3 sitting rooms, dining room, terrace, garden, swimming pool **CREDIT CARDS** AE, DC, MC, V **CHILDREN** welcome **DISABLED** access difficult **PETS** accepted **CLOSED** Jan to Mar; restaurant lunch Mon to Fri; bistro Tue, lunch Mon to Fri **PROPRIETORS** Peter Chittick and Craig Miller

PROVENCE-COTE D'AZUR

ENTRECHAUX

LA MANESCALE
∿ COUNTRY HOTEL ∿

route de Faucon, Les Essareaux, 84340 Entrechaux (Vaucluse)
TEL 04 90 46 03 80 **FAX** 04 90 46 03 89

THE KING OF BELGIUM has slept here. No doubt, like so many others, he was charmed by all he found in this remote former sheperd's house up in the hills. The thoughtfulness of owners, M. and Mme Warland, permeates what could be described as a pocket-sized hotel with every comfort, and the emphasis on the privacy of guests. The smallest details are attended to here, from towels for the swimming pool to a small library for serious readers and helpfully labelled light switches.

The house is beautifully decorated with the Warlands' own books, paintings, *objets d'art* and furniture. Stone steps and pathways connect the main building to the garden rooms, each giving privacy and views of the forest and hillsides. Two rooms are named after M. Warland's favourite painters, Tiepolo and Dali. A place for lovers of quiet and of nature, there are numerous paths through the woods for long walks. Classical music plays on the terrace at aperitif time; the views across the vineyards and valleys to Mont Ventoux in the distance are superb.

It's a steep, if short, walk from the car park to the hotel; a luggage trolley is provided.

∿

NEARBY Vaison-la-Romaine (7 km); Côtes du Rhône vineyards.
LOCATION 3 km N of Entrechaux, signposted off D205 road to Faucon; car parking
FOOD breakfast
PRICE €€
ROOMS 5 double and twin, 2 with bath, 3 with shower; all rooms have phone, TV, minibar, hairdrier
FACILITIES sitting room, breakfast room, terrace, garden, swimming pool
CREDIT CARDS AE, DC, MC, V
CHILDREN accepted over 12
DISABLED not suitable
PETS accepted
CLOSED end Oct to Easter
PROPRIETORS M. and Mme Warland

PROVENCE-COTE D'AZUR

AUBERGE PROVENCALE
~ VILLAGE INN ~

place de la Mairie, 13810 Eygalières (Bouches-du-Rhône)
TEL 04 90 95 91 00

I N DELIGHTFUL EYGALIERES, this 18thC former coaching inn has a paved
courtyard with trees and potted plants and small marble-topped tables,
and is well known locally for its Provençal dishes. The horses' stone drink-
ing troughs remain and guests' cars are safely locked away for the night in
the magnificent coach house, which has a great arched gateway on to the
street. There is also a spacious bar, deliberately and charmingly evocative
of the 19th century.

Owner and chef Didier Pézeril and his young family extend their hospitality to rooms, some of which look out on to the courtyard, and all of
which are exceptional. There are just four: quantity has been sacrificed
for space and quality – simple and stylish in the best, least fussy Provençal
manner, some with huge bathrooms, some with huge bedrooms. Our
inspector's room had blue-washed walls, rough white cotton curtains and a
paisley cover on the bed, and a view out of the window of the lively
Progrès café opposite. Tiled floors are attractively uneven and some rooms
have traditional cupboards set in the walls. M. Pézeril's philosophy is cor-
respondingly down-to-earth: 'We're an *auberge*, we don't have pretensions
to being anything else'. The whole place oozes character.

~

NEARBY St-Remy-de-Provence (13 km); Les Baux (23 km); the Alpilles
LOCATION in village; car parking
FOOD breakfast, lunch, dinner
PRICE €€€
ROOMS 4 double and twin, all with bath; all rooms have phone, TV
FACILITIES bar, dining room, courtyard, terrace
CREDIT CARDS MC, V
CHILDREN welcome
DISABLED not suitable
PETS accepted
CLOSED mid-Nov to mid-Dec; restaurant closed Wed, Thur lunch
PROPRIETORS Pézeril family

PROVENCE-COTE D'AZUR

AUBERGE DU VIEUX FOX
~ VILLAGE INN ~

place de l'Eglise, Fox-Amphoux, 83670 Barjols (Var)
TEL 04 94 80 71 69 **FAX** 04 94 80 78 38

O UR MOST RECENT ATTEMPT to re-visit this old favourite ended in failure: it
was cut off by snow – in spring! Reports continue to be satisfactory,
however.

Fox-Amphoux, a charming little village, rich in history, has nothing to
do with foxes – the name comes from its Roman origins. The inn was once
a priory attached to the 12thC church, headquarters of the Knights
Templar. Where owner, M. Staudinger, now has his reception desk was a
sacristy, with a door leading directly into the church, the bells of which
ring out every half hour. M. Staudinger is normally to be found here in his
beamed reception area with his cat, and happy to talk about the life and
times of Fox-Amphoux and the surrounding area.

Bedrooms are carpeted and some renovation has been carried out
(satellite TVs have recently been installed); curtains and bedspreads are
in fresh, bright colours. Two small rooms in the tower were once monks'
cells. Bathrooms are spotless. There are comfortable leather armchairs in
the *salon*; there is also a library and a billiard table. The dining room is
full of character and the outside terraces have fine views over Aix and the
Alpes de Haute-Provence. Fish is delivered from Marseille and there is an
emphasis on fresh farm produce and country cooking, with huge helpings.

NEARBY Lac de Sainte-Croix; Gorges du Verdon; Thoronet Abbey.
LOCATION in centre of small perched village, 32 km N of Brignoles, 37 km W of
Draguignan; public car parking in square
FOOD breakfast, lunch, dinner
PRICE €€
ROOMS 8 double and twin, 6 with bath, 2 with shower; all rooms have phone, TV,
hairdrier
FACILITIES sitting room, dining room, library, billiards, 2 terraces
CREDIT CARDS AE, MC, V **CHILDREN** accepted but not encouraged
DISABLED no special facilities **PETS** accepted **CLOSED** never
PROPRIETORS Rudolph and Nicole Staudinger

PROVENCE-COTE D'AZUR

GEMENOS

RELAIS DE LA MAGDELEINE
~ COUNTRY HOTEL ~

13420 Gémenos (Bouches-du-Rhône)
TEL 04 42 32 20 16 **FAX** 04 42 32 02 26
WEBSITE www.relais-magdeleine.com

'WE SIMPLY COULD NOT FAULT IT; the atmosphere, welcome and service could not have been better and the food was excellent. Even though we had one of the more expensive rooms at the front, we felt it was very good value.' So begins the latest eulogy on this lovely old *bastide*, a sentiment strongly echoed by our most recent inspector. For those of us who can't or won't pay the prices (or don't like the style) of Relais & Châteaux places, a gracious country house like this is quite a find.

It is a family affair. Daniel Marignane's mother opened the hotel in 1932, and he and his wife have run it with great dedication, charm and good humour for many years. Now their three sons work alongside them, one as the (excellent) chef. Improvements are being made all the time. Many of the bedrooms have been (charmingly) redecorated and all – even the cheapest – are in elegant country taste, with delightful fabrics (often on the walls, too) and antiques and pictures collected by the Marignanes.

On the airy, spacious ground floor, one of the three dining rooms has been sandblasted to expose vaultings and beams in a lovely, light honey-coloured wood. In summer you eat on the romantic gravelled terrace. There's a pool – and a donkey – in the garden, and children will enjoy the giant chessboard and the ping-pong table. It is worth going miles out of one's way to be so warmly welcomed to such a beautiful house.

~

NEARBY Cassis (15 km); Marseille (23 km); Aix-en-Provence (25 km).
LOCATION on the edge of town; ample car parking
FOOD breakfast, lunch, dinner
PRICE €€€-€€€€
ROOMS 24 double, twin and family, all with bath or shower; all rooms have phone, TV
FACILITIES sitting rooms, dining room, lift, terrace, garden, swimming pool, table tennis **CREDIT CARDS** MC, V **CHILDREN** accepted
DISABLED no special facilities **PETS** accepted **CLOSED** Dec to mid-Mar
PROPRIETORS M. and Mme Marignane

PROVENCE-COTE D'AZUR

GIGONDAS

LES FLORETS

◁ COUNTRY INN ▷

route des Dentelles, 84190 Gigondas (Vaucluse)
TEL 04 90 65 85 01 **FAX** 04 90 65 83 80

FLOWERS ABOUND AT LES FLORETS: all around the hotel on the nearby hills in spring, in pots and vases on the terrace and in the dining room, on the curtains, the lampshades and the pretty hand-painted plates, each one different. The setting, alone in a fold of wooded hills east of Gigondas and facing the dramatic Dentelles de Montmirail, is delightful, and the ambience is loved by everyone who has a hankering for traditional, proud, family-run places. The Bernard family, who bought the hotel in 1960, have long been respected for their honest, straightforward approach, and for the good value food served in the animated dining room or on the lovely leafy terrace in summer. Now they have refurbished all the bedrooms and the once dim corridors, making this a very comfortable place in which to stay for a few days. The bedrooms remain appropriately sober but the bathrooms are a surprise – very opulent for a two-star establishment, with particularly comfortable baths, expensivley tiled walls, good towels and intelligent lighting. The rooms in the garden annexe are pleasantest, with little terraces in front for breakfast; one of them is perfect for a family.

The Bernards are also wine-growers; they keep an excellent cellar, or you can drink a bottle of their own Gigondas or Vacqueras for dinner. Good walking country.

◁

NEARBY Côtes-du-Rhône vineyards; Vaison-la-Romaine (15 km).
LOCATION in hills, 2 km E of Gigondas; car parking
FOOD breakfast, lunch, dinner
PRICE €€
ROOMS 15 double and twin, 1 family, all with bath; all rooms have phone, TV, hairdrier
FACILITIES sitting room, bar, dining room, terrace
CREDIT CARDS AE, DC, MC, V **CHILDREN** welcome
DISABLED access possible **PETS** accepted
CLOSED Jan, Feb; restaurant Wed
PROPRIETORS Bernard family

PROVENCE-COTE D'AZUR

LAGNES

LE MAS DES GRES

~ COUNTRY HOTEL ~

la route d'Apt, 84800 Lagnes (Vaucluse)
TEL 04 90 20 32 85 **FAX** 04 90 20 21 45
E-MAIL info@masdesgres.com **WEBSITE** www.masdesgres.com

NINA AND THIERRY CROVARA run their hotel in a restored farmhouse with such a friendly, relaxed attitude that parents bring their children here from far and wide on family holidays. For the very young, high chairs are provided in the dining room and cots in the bedrooms; and for older children, there's a video machine in one of the sitting rooms, table tennis and a pool outside. Bedrooms are functional – plainly decorated with rough plaster walls and Provençal fabrics – and hard to damage. There are two sets of connecting rooms, where Nina has thoughtfully added black-out blinds to prevent an interior dawn chorus.

Before dinner, guests sit outside on the vine-covered terrace and sip the delicious iced 'orange wine' made according to Thierry's own recipe. He is the chef, and though French, trained in Nina's native Switzerland. He takes his cooking seriously and, after consultations about allergies, likes and dislikes, produces a mainly regional no-choice menu six nights a week (the Crovaras take off one night to fit in with their guests). Menu planning also takes children into account. In between courses, Thierry emerges from his kitchen to introduce himself to new guests and chat to old ones.

There is some noise from the RN100 road but plans to declassify it should lighten the traffic considerably.

~

NEARBY L'Isle-sur-la-Sorgue (6 km); Avignon (28 km); golf.
LOCATION on RN100 outside village; car parking
FOOD breakfast, dinner; light lunch (in July and Aug)
PRICE €€€-€€€€
ROOMS 14 double, twin, triple and family, all with bath; all rooms have phone, CD; TV on request
FACILITIES sitting rooms, TV room, dining room, terrace, garden, swimming pool, table tennis **CREDIT CARDS** MC, V **CHILDREN** welcome
DISABLED 2 ground-floor rooms **PETS** not accepted **CLOSED** Dec to Mar
PROPRIETORS Nina and Thierry Crovara

PROVENCE-COTE D'AZUR

LA BASTIDE DE MOUSTIERS

~ COUNTRY HOUSE HOTEL ~

La Grisolière, 04360 Moustiers-Ste-Marie (Alpes-de-Haute-Provence)
TEL 04 92 70 47 47 **FAX** 04 92 70 47 48
E-MAIL bastide@i2m.fr **WEBSITE** www.bastide-moustiers.i2m.fr

THIS IS THE MADELEINE of chef and hotelier supremo Alain Ducasse. In a pale-pink restored 17thC *bastide* overlooking green meadows on the edge of a village near the dramatic Verdon gorge, he has created his own remembrance of times past. His country house for lovers of Provence is a resounding triumph; delicious smells of cooking come from the kitchen all day. Chefs, in their whites, can be seen collecting salad and fresh herbs from a vegetable garden which is a work of art in itself. The *bastide* and the discreet swimming pool are surrounded by beds of lavender and each of the 12 romantically decorated bedrooms evokes a colour or an image of Provence. To sit on the terrace in the morning air with a bowl of *café au lait*, fresh bread from the village bakery and home-made rhubarb jam among green glazed pots overflowing with white petunias is a moment to be treasured. Dinner is just as memorable; traditional dishes with plenty of olive oil and garden vegetables. You might find *millefeuille de blettes braisées au parfum de sauge* or *agneau de Beauregard piqué de sarriette et rôti à la broche*. Upstairs, the sheets are being turned down as you eat.

~

NEARBY Moustiers ceramics; Lac de Ste-Croix; gorges.
LOCATION within walking distance of Moustiers; car and garage parking
FOOD breakfast, lunch, dinner; room service
PRICE €€€€
ROOMS 12; 11 double and twin, 1 suite, all with bath; all rooms have phone, TV, air conditioning, minibar, hairdrier
FACILITIES sitting room, dining room, bar, terrace, garden, swimming pool, riding
CREDIT CARDS AE, DC, MC, V
CHILDREN welcome
DISABLED access possible
PETS not accepted
CLOSED never
PROPRIETOR Alain Ducasse

PROVENCE-COTE D'AZUR

NICE

LE GRIMALDI
~ TOWN HOTEL ~

15 rue Grimaud, 06000 Nice (Alpes-Maritimes)
TEL 04 93 16 00 24 **FAX** 04 93 87 00 24

NOT TO BE CONFUSED with the rather dreary-looking Nice Grimaldi just down the road, this upmarket and stylish little hotel was opened only in 1999. Englishwoman Joanna Zedde and her French husband gutted the fairly basic hotel that already occupied the elegant 1920s town house with its white shutters and wrought-iron balconies, aiming for something altogether smarter. The location – a lively area of stylish shops, bars and restaurants – is ideal, and the beach is only a ten-minute walk.

The ground floor is occupied by a large reception area decorated in bright reds and yellows which doubles as breakfast room, bar and sitting room; it is full of fresh flowers and leafy plants. The comfortable bedrooms are all tastefully (and not too fussily) decorated with co-ordinating Soleido fabrics and wallpapers set against cool white. Some are done out in vibrant sun colours, others are more restrained in shades of blue and green and the delicate wrought-iron furniture fits in well. There are two types of room; the 'Superiors' have sufficient space for an invitingly squashy sofa. Bright yellow towels make a splash in the immaculate all-white bathrooms. A classy B&B.

~

NEARBY Vieux Nice; Opéra; beach.
LOCATION on street just W of Vieux Nice; public car parking nearby (50 m)
FOOD breakfast
PRICE €€
ROOMS 23 double and twin, all with bath; all rooms have phone, TV, air conditioning, minibar, safe, hairdrier
FACILITIES bar/breakfast room/sitting room; lift
CREDIT CARDS AE, DC, MC, V
CHILDREN accepted
DISABLED no special facilities
PETS accepted
CLOSED 3 weeks Jan
PROPRIETOR Joanna Zedde

PROVENCE-COTE D'AZUR

PEILLON

AUBERGE DE LA MADONE
~ VILLAGE INN ~

06440 Peillon (Alpes-Maritimes)
TEL 04 93 79 91 17 **FAX** 04 93 79 99 36
E-MAIL madone@chateauxhotels.com **WEBSITE** www.chateauxhotels.com/madone

'**H**OW STUNNING', commented a recent visitor on seeing the setting for the first time. 'Delightful' was the one-word verdict offered by another on the top-of-the-range family-run *logis*, which happily combines a sense of special hospitality with affordable (though not low) prices. The Millos have now opened an annexe in the old part of the village – Auberge du Pourtail. Rooms here are less expensive and you eat at the Madone.

You may think that you have taken a wrong turning as you first spy Peillon, perched impossibly above, with little sign of any road leading up. Time stands still here. The medieval village consists of a few dark cobbled alleys leading up to the church, and tall stone houses looking out over rocky crests and distant forests.

The *auberge* is set just ouside the walled village itself. Behind, paths lead off into the hills, past the grazing sheep with their tinkling bells; in front is the village car park and *boules* area. Within, the rather small bedrooms (with equally small balconies) are attractive and comfortable with stylish all-white bathrooms. Meals are served on the sunny terrace, under a large awning, or in the welcoming Provençal-style dining room. Cooking is above average, using organic local ingredients. An all-weather tennis court is another of the hotel's attractions.

~

NEARBY Monaco – palace, museums, exotic gardens; Nice (19 km).
LOCATION on edge of perched village, 19 km NE of Nice; ample car parking
FOOD breakfast, lunch, dinner
PRICE €€€
ROOMS 19; 16 double and twin, 8 with bath, 8 with shower, 3 suites with bath; all rooms have phone, TV, 9 have hairdrier
FACILITIES sitting room, bar, TV room, 2 dining rooms, terrace, tennis
CREDIT CARDS MC, V **CHILDREN** welcome
DISABLED access difficult **PETS** not accepted **CLOSED** mid-Oct to mid-Dec, 2 weeks Jan; restaurant closed Wed
PROPRIETORS Millo family

PROVENCE-COTE D'AZUR

AUBERGE DE L'ORANGERIE
~ TOWN INN ~

4 rue de l'Ormeau, 84420 Piolenc (Vaucluse)
TEL 04 90 29 59 88 **FAX** 04 90 29 67 74
E-MAIL orangerie@wanadoo.fr **WEBSITE** www.orangerie.net

THIS CURIOUS LITTLE *auberge,* almost submerged by a jungle of greenery, is just off the main street of a small town that prides itself on its garlic festival. Owners Gérard and Micky Delarocque have given an original and imaginative 'retro' feeling to an 18thC house in a gated courtyard. The lively restaurant draws in local business people at lunchtime with dishes like *filets de rascasse à la provençale* and *noisettes de gigot d'agneau au basilic frais*. In the dining room, a collection of striking Georges de La Tour pictures are, in fact, painted by M. Delarocque, a talented copyist (and single-malt connoisseur). But the real fun starts upstairs, with Madame's evocative decoration and her charming written 'thoughts' on the theme of each room, which hang framed on the walls. The George Sand room has a portrait of the writer by Delacroix – or could it be a copy by M. Delarocque? The room named after Mme Récamier has a chaise-longue like the ones she made so fashionable. Behind the bohemianism, though, is a professional management, with orthodox ideas on things such as rules: no washing of clothes in bedrooms, for example.

Guests can also stay in 'La Mandarine' nearby, a Provençal farmhouse in its own grounds, with six bedrooms, a pool and a patio.

~

NEARBY Orange (5 km); Avignon (35 km).
LOCATION in a side-street off the main street; car parking
FOOD breakfast, lunch, dinner
PRICE (€); half-board obligatory in high season
ROOMS 5 double, 2 with bath, 3 with shower; all rooms have TV
FACILITIES dining room, terrace, garden
CREDIT CARDS MC, V
CHILDREN accepted
DISABLED no special facilities
PETS accepted
CLOSED never
PROPRIETORS M. and Mme Delarocque

PROVENCE-COTE D'AZUR

LE PONTET-AVIGNON

✳ AUBERGE DE CASSAGNE ✳

∼ SUBURBAN HOTEL ∼

450 allée de Cassagne, 84130 Le Pontet-Avignon (Vaucluse)
TEL 04 90 31 04 18 **FAX** 04 90 32 25 09
E-MAIL cassagne@wanadoo.fr **WEBSITE** www.valruges.cassagne.com

LE PONTET, A SUBURB OF AVIGNON with wide, busy roads and new housing developments, does not appear to be a place where anyone might find a hotel of any interest, let alone charm. However, behind a high wall is a former cottage of the nearby château which has been turned, with much hard work, into a remarkably comfortable and pleasant hotel, with a locally renowned one-Michelin-star kitchen, chef from Bocuse, and an abundant wine cellar. At dinner, our inspector counted 20 different cheeses on the tray and 45 Côtes du Rhône reds on the wine list. In somewhat confined grounds, the hotel also manages, with clever use of lawns, paths and landscaped gardens, to create an impression of space and even rusticity. Everything is immaculately well tended; the cypress trees look as if someone brushes and combs them every night.

Bedrooms in the garden bungalows are large and pretty, with fresh Provençal prints; each one has its own terrace, with table and chairs, where guests can have breakfast in dressing gowns – and do. Rooms 16 and 17 are almost in the swimming pool and delightfully secluded and quiet in the evenings, when the restaurant – a popular gathering place – buzzes with local custom as well as residents.

∼

NEARBY Avignon (4 km); Aix-en-Provence (82 km); Arles (36 km).
LOCATION in a quiet suburban side-road; car parking **FOOD** breakfast, lunch, dinner
PRICE ⓔⓔⓔ-ⓔⓔⓔⓔ **ROOMS** 30 double and twin, 28 with bath, 2 with shower; all rooms have phone, TV, air conditioning, minibar, hairdrier, safe
FACILITIES 2 sitting rooms, dining room, bar, gym, sauna, garden, swimming pool, tennis, table tennis, boules

CREDIT CARDS AE, DC, MC, V
CHILDREN welcome **DISABLED** 3 specially adapted rooms
PETS accepted **CLOSED** never
PROPRIETORS M. Gallon, M. Trestour and M. Boucher

PROVENCE-COTE D'AZUR

PORQUEROLLES (ILE DE)

AUBERGE DES GLYCINES

~ ISLAND HOTEL ~

place d'Armes, 83400 Ile de Porquerolles (Var)
TEL 04 94 58 30 36 **FAX** 04 9458 35 22
E-MAIL auberge.glycines@wanadoo.fr

THERE ARE NO CARS on the island of Porquerolles and when the daytrippers leave in the evening, peace prevails. This delightful small hotel is a fun, casual, bright and sunny place in the little port of Porquerolles, but within an easy walk there are rocky creeks for swimming and splendid diving spots.

Pale yellow with blue shutters, the hotel is built around an inner courtyard, which has lemon trees, wistaria (*glycines*) and a fig tree; food is served here on red Provençal tablecloths under white umbrellas. The entire hotel is decorated with bright, fresh colours and has a charming look of stylish simplicity. Downstairs, there are dried flowers and straw hats on the walls and terracotta tiles on the floor. Bedrooms are variations on a theme: clean, modern bathrooms have pale tiles and white fittings; bedrooms have matching Provençal print bedspreads and curtains. Rooms have little balconies or terraces looking into the courtyard or out towards pine and eucalyptus trees. The food, which includes plenty of fresh fish, is excellent value. Our inspector ate *loup de mer* flambéed at the table with fennel and grilled in a salt crust that was cracked open before being served. Young, friendly staff; laid-back atmosphere.

~

NEARBY beaches; diving; cycling and walking; national park.
LOCATION in Porquerolles village on car-free island, 5 minutes from beach; access 20 mins by ferry from La Tour Fondue (Hyères) or water taxi
FOOD breakfast, lunch, dinner
PRICE €€
ROOMS 13; 12 double and twin, 1 triple, 10 with bath, 3 with shower; all rooms have phone, TV, air conditioning
FACILITIES dining room, courtyard, terrace **CREDIT CARDS** DC, MC, V
CHILDREN welcome
DISABLED no special facilities **PETS** accepted
CLOSED mid- to end Jan
PROPRIETOR Florence Venture

PROVENCE-COTE D'AZUR

PORT-CROS (ILE DE)

LE MANOIR
~ SEASIDE HOTEL ~

Ile de Port-Cros, 83400 Hyères (Var)
TEL 04 94 05 90 52 **FAX** 04 94 05 90 89

PORT-CROS, THE MIDDLE OF THE THREE Iles d'Hyères, is a nature reserve on which no vehicles, not even bicycles, and no pet animals are allowed. With a resident population of no more than a handful, it is, therefore, entirely peaceful, and this large, green-shuttered 19thC manor house fits perfectly into its green and serene surroundings. Previously a private house, it has been run as a hotel since the late 1940s, and by its present owner, Pierre Buffet, since the 1960s. Set in lush, sub-tropical grounds by the sea, its seems much more than just a 20-minute ferry ride from the crowded coast. You feel you are in a gracious private house, and the hotel is run along house-party lines. There are several sitting rooms in which to relax, read or play cards, and the airy, comfortable white-walled bedrooms are simply but elegantly furnished with 19thC pieces of furniture; some have little terraces.

The grounds are extensive and lovely, full of palm, eucalyptus and oleander trees. There's a splendid swimming pool, beside which you can have lunch; or you can take a picnic and a ride in the hotel's motor launch to a nearby bay or cove. You must walk to the nearest sandy beach – about 25 minutes. The Provençal cooking is praised.

~

NEARBY nature trails in national park; Hyères; Toulon; Porquerolles.
LOCATION in own grounds by sea on car-free island
FOOD breakfast, lunch, dinner
PRICE €€; half board obligatory
ROOMS 22; 17 double and twin, 5 family, 15 with bath, 7 with shower; all rooms have phone, some have air conditioning
FACILITIES sitting rooms, dining room, garden, swimming pool
CREDIT CARDS MC, V
CHILDREN accepted **DISABLED** rooms on ground floor
PETS not accepted
CLOSED Oct to Apr
PROPRIETOR Pierre Buffet

PROVENCE-COTE D'AZUR

LA FERME D'HERMES
~ COUNTRY HOTEL ~

route de l'Escalet, 83350 Ramatuelle (Var)
TEL 04 94 79 27 80 **FAX** 04 94 79 26 86

MME VERRIER HAS NAMED her charming hotel after her much loved late Welsh terrier – there is now a junior version in his place. Our inspector's report is positively glowing. 'This is a gorgeous spot – exquisite.'

The hotel is a recently built *mas*, now softened by the weather and creepers and surrounded by a mass of trees, shrubs, plants and greenery. Vines come up to the pool. Inside, loving attention is given to detail. Rooms are all white, with terracotta tiles on the floor – burnished with beeswax – and co-ordinated Provençal fabrics. Furniture is old, stripped pine. Each bedroom has its own private terrace and little tiled kitchenette, with gas and electric rings, oven, sink and refrigerator. Tea towels are provided and changed every day. Madame returns from the market every Saturday morning with armfuls of fresh flowers. Breakfast is the only meal served – on each private terrace – with fresh bread and pastries and home-made jams. Guests are treated as if they were part of a circle of friends, and Mme Verrier has thought of everything: alarm clock, electric mosquito repellent, daily room service, iron and ironing board, hairdrier, and even toothbrush in case you forgot yours.

~

NEARBY Ramatuelle (2 km); St-Tropez (10 km).
LOCATION in own grounds down a narrow lane 2 km from beaches; car parking
FOOD breakfast
PRICE €€€
ROOMS 10 double and twin, all with bath; all rooms have phone, TV, kitchenette, terrace
FACILITIES sitting room, garden, swimming pool
CREDIT CARDS DC, MC, V **CHILDREN** not encouraged
DISABLED no special facilities
PETS accepted
CLOSED Nov to Apr
PROPRIETOR Mme Verrier

PROVENCE-COTE D'AZUR

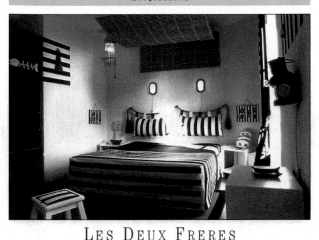

LES DEUX FRERES
~ VILLAGE RESTAURANT-WITH-ROOMS ~

06190 Roquebrune-Village Cap Martin (Alpes-Maritimes)
TEL 04 93 28 99 00 **FAX** 04 93 28 99 10
E-MAIL 2freres@webstore.fr **WEBSITE** www.lesdeuxfreres.com

THE BROTHERS IN QUESTION are the two large rocks which loom over this small hotel-restaurant; it stands on a little square in the unspoiled village of Roquebrune with a terrace that looks down over a tumble of villas and exotic gardens to the sea far below and, in the distance, the ghastliness of Monte Carlo.

Willem Bonestroo has a passion for large motorbikes, but that doesn't stop him running Les Deux Frères with infectious enthusiasm. The whitewashed building was a schoolhouse until 1965, and he has kept things refreshingly simple. The ground floor is mostly occupied by the bar-restaurant, a rustic room filled with tall plants, gorgeous fresh flowers and interesting modern art. Our inspector was most impressed with the food; Provençal and French cooking with a twist – the *gambas* were marinated in ginger and served with orange peel. The quirky bedrooms are simple but full of tongue-in-cheek humour; one is nautical with porthole mirrors and oars as curtain rails, another ('The 1001 Nights') is done out in gold and midnight blue with silk curtains (a video of Aladdin is supplied) while the tiny, white Bridal Room has a canopied bed and romantic views.

NEARBY Monte Carlo (5 km); beaches (5 km); Nice (22 km).
LOCATION in centre of village; free public parking nearby
FOOD breakfast, lunch, dinner
PRICE €€
ROOMS 10; 8 double and 2 single, 9 with bath; all rooms have phone, TV, video, hairdrier
FACILITIES dining room, bar, terrace
CREDIT CARDS AE, DC, MC, V
DISABLED 1 room on ground floor
PETS accepted
CLOSED never; restaurant closed mid-Nov to mid-Dec and Sun, Mon eve in winter
PROPRIETOR Willem Bonestroo

PROVENCE-COTE D'AZUR

MAS DE GARRIGON
~ COUNTRY VILLA ~

route de St-Saturnin d'Apt, Roussillon, 84220 Gordes (Vaucluse)
TEL 04 90 05 63 22 **FAX** 04 90 05 70 01 **E-MAIL** mas-de-garrigon@wanadoo.fr
WEBSITE www.avignon-et-provence.com/mas-garrigon

'WE ARRIVED WITHOUT RESERVATION and were willingly accommodated; the Provençal-style room was very comfortable, the bathroom large and well stocked; the pool was heavenly after a long drive, and the surrounding areas pleasant for strolling; dinner was wonderful.'

A long-time favourite of this guide, Mas de Garrigon continues to please both our readers and our inspectors, who appreciate its cosy yet sophisticated ambience. Purpose-built by Christiane Drouart in 1979, it has the feel of a traditional Provençal farmhouse, with a jumble of rough-tiled roofs facing this way and that, as if built at random over the years. The hotel stands isolated among pines and scrub, facing the Luberon hills. At the front is a sheltered pool sharing country views with the sunny private terraces of the bedrooms, which are bright and comfortable. The place is run more on house-party than conventional hotel lines. Guests are encouraged to browse in the well-stocked library or listen to classical music in the *salon* – before an open fire in winter. Dinner is often a convivial affair, with guests chatting between tables in the intimate dining room which overlooks the pool; the food, by well-regarded chef Jean-Paul Minery, is delicious, with the emphasis on local ingredients (truffles in winter).

~

NEARBY Roussillon (3 km) Gordes (7 km); Village des Bories (5 km).
LOCATION signposted, in countryside on D2, 3 km N of Roussillon, 7 km E of Gordes; car parking
FOOD breakfast, lunch, dinner
PRICE €€€; half board obligatory May-Oct
ROOMS 9; 7 double and twin, 2 family, all with bath; all rooms have phone, TV, minibar, terrace
FACILITIES sitting room, 3 dining rooms, bar, library, terrace, swimming pool
CREDIT CARDS AE, DC, MC, V **CHILDREN** accepted over 12
DISABLED ground-floor bedrooms **PETS** accepted
CLOSED mid-Nov to Mar; restaurant Mon
PROPRIETOR Christiane Druart

PROVENCE-COTE D'AZUR

AUBERGE DU PRESBYTERE

~ VILLAGE HOTEL ~

place de la Fontaine, 84400 Saignon (Vaucluse)
TEL 04 90 74 11 50 **FAX** 04 90 04 68 51 **E-MAIL** auberge.presbytere@provence-luberon.com **WEBSITE** www.provence-luberon.com

ON THE THRESHOLD OF the Luberon National Park – a relatively undiscovered area – Saignon is a hilltop village with a chequered history dating back to the 11th century. In the centre, overlooking the pretty square where the village fountain plays, this *auberge* occupies three houses, one almost completely submerged beneath an unstoppable creeper. The houses have been knocked together, to produce a quirky series of rooms downstairs, one leading off another, with those upstairs on different levels and connected by separate staircases and corridors. All have great charm, polished terracotta or wood floors, low vaulted or beamed ceilings and a combination of wicker furniture and antiques. The apparently effortless Provençal style has in fact been perfected over the past 14 years by the suavely charming half-American half-French owner.

The restaurant is split between a cosy wood-panelled room for non-smokers and a larger, airier one with glass doors leading to a little gravelled terrace. Traditional Provençal dishes are prominent on the daily changing menu and always include fish and a vegetarian option. There is no *carte*. After dinner you can sink into one of the cream sofas beside the fireplace in the civilized sitting room or have a nightcap in the small, atmospheric bar, a popular gathering place for the village.

~

NEARBY Apt (4 km); Bonnieux (12 km); Aix (56 km).
LOCATION in the village centre; car parking nearby
FOOD breakfast, lunch, dinner
PRICE €€€
ROOMS 10; 9 double and twin, 1 with single, all with bath; all rooms have phone, hairdrier
FACILITIES sitting room, dining room, bar **CREDIT CARDS** MC, V
CHILDREN accepted
DISABLED no special facilities **PETS** accepted
CLOSED early Nov to late Feb; restaurant Wed, lunch Thur
PROPRIETOR Jean Pierre de Lutz

PROVENCE-COTE D'AZUR

ST-PAUL-DE-VENCE

LA COLOMBE D'OR

~ VILLAGE HOTEL ~

06570 St-Paul-de-Vence (Alpes-Maritimes)
TEL 04 93 32 80 02 **FAX** 04 93 32 77 78
WEBSITE www.la-colombe-dor.com

WHEN PAUL ROUX (grandfather of the present owner) opened his modest inn in the 1930s, he would not have dreamed that La Colombe d'Or would become the famous and chic hotel that it is today. Many of his customers were the artists that lived and worked in St-Paul at the time, and they often paid their way with their work. It became a well-known meeting place for an arty, bohemian crowd who were joined by the emerging Riviera jet set. Today, many of the guests are well-heeled Americans, but it has not completely lost the feel of a laid-back country inn.

The art on the walls and the sculpture in the garden are extraordinary; you hardly need to visit the nearby Fondation Maeght. The wood-panelled dining rooms are hung with Picasso, Miro and Chagall, enough to take one's mind off the fairly mediocre food. The style throughout is rustic chic and refreshingly casual; old tiled floors, natural colours and fabrics, country antiques, spectacular ceramics, plenty of plants…and art everywhere. In summer, food is served on the delightful, flower-filled terrace in the shade of ancient trees. The pool is heated year-round; for chillier days, there is a cosy sunken sitting area with leather sofas grouped around an open fire.

~

NEARBY Fondation Maeght; Nice (15 km); Grasse (25 km).
LOCATION on edge of village; valet car parking
FOOD breakfast, lunch, dinner
PRICE €€€€
ROOMS 26; 15 double and twin, 11 suites all with bath or spa bath; all rooms have phone, TV, air conditioning, hairdrier
FACILITIES dining rooms, bar, sitting rooms, terraces, garden, swimming pool
CREDIT CARDS AE, DC, MC, V **CHILDREN** accepted
DISABLED access difficult
PETS accepted
CLOSED Nov, 2 weeks Jan
PROPRIETORS M. and Mme Roux

PROVENCE-COTE D'AZUR

ST-PAUL-DE-VENCE

LE HAMEAU
~ COUNTRY VILLA ~

528 route de la Colle, 06570 St-Paul-de-Vence (Alpes-Maritimes)
TEL 04 93 32 80 24 **FAX** 04 93 32 55 75
WEBSITE www.le-hameau.com

'**O**UR LAST REPORT did not do this place justice', says our most recent inspector to this collection of 18th and 19thC buildings that was once a farm. 'It's *very* nice, set in countryside outside Vence, with a lovely garden with orange and mandarin trees which give off a heady scent in season and produce the breakfast marmalade. Bedrooms are very stylish: elegant rustic with some gorgeous country antiques and attractive fabrics, and good bathrooms. Some are large, others small and cosy. A captivating place, and very good value for money.'

Le Hameau consists of a cluster of red-roofed Provençal villas, surrounded by fruit trees. Bedrooms have beams, dark-wood furniture and rugs on red-tiled floors; they vary considerably in price as well as size and many have their own terrace or balcony. There is a cool, neat breakfast room, but it's much more fun to have breakfast in the large terraced garden, which accommodates a small but smart pool.

Since 1999 Le Hameau has been owned by a young Italian couple, but the manager remains the same.

~

NEARBY Fondation Maeght; Cagnes-sur-Mer (5 km); Nice (15 km); Grasse (25 km).
LOCATION 1 km outside village, 15 km NW of Nice; car parking
FOOD breakfast
PRICE €€-€€€
ROOMS 17; 14 double and twin, 3 apartments, 15 with bath, 2 with shower; all rooms have phone, TV, air conditioning, minibar, hairdrier, safe
FACILITIES breakfast room, sitting room, terrace, garden, swimming pool
CREDIT CARDS AE, MC, V
CHILDREN accepted
DISABLED rooms on ground floor
PETS accepted
CLOSED mid-Nov to mid-Dec, mid-Jan to mid-Feb
MANAGER Xavier Huvelin

PROVENCE-COTE D'AZUR

ST-REMY-DE-PROVENCE

MAS DES CARASSINS
∽ CONVERTED FARMHOUSE ∽

1 chemin Gaulois, 13210 St-Rémy-de-Provence (Bouches-du-Rhône)
TEL 04 90 92 15 48 **FAX** 04 90 92 63 47
E-MAIL carassin@pacwan.fr

AFTER ALMOST 25 YEARS of running the Mas des Carassins in her family's farmhouse, M. and Mme Ripert – with great sadness – had to sell in December 2000. They put it on the market, but knew they wanted to wait until the right people came along, and in a touching letter in the book of comments, they say how privileged they were to hand over to Michel and Pierre. When our inspector arrived only a month after the reopening, and finishing touches were still being made, the Riperts had come to tea and to see the changes. They were as enchanted as we were.

The new owners (Michel is also manager) had more experience of being guests than hoteliers, but they knew what they liked and, with great style, they have created a stunning hotel, including seven bedrooms in soothing colours, with terracotta floors and smart fabrics. They have thought of everything (a strip of carpet set into the stair tiles to eliminate noise) and nothing is too much trouble: "It's a three-star hotel, but we like to give four-star service." Seven bedrooms are untouched: their project for next year. In the secluded gardens, they have made a gorgeous pool, where they will give you a light lunch. A *table d'hôte* is provided four nights a week.
∽

NEARBY Les Baux-de-Provence (7 km); Avignon (20 km).
LOCATION in quiet, residential lane on S edge of town; car parking
FOOD breakfast, light lunches (mid-Jun to mid-Sep), evening snacks (Mon, Wed, Fri, Sat)
PRICE €€
ROOMS 14 double, twin, triple and family, all with bath or shower; all rooms have phone, TV, minibar; 9 have air conditioning; 7 have safe
FACILITIES sitting room, dining room, terrace, garden, swimming pool
CREDIT CARDS MC, V **CHILDREN** accepted
DISABLED 1 specially adapted room
PETS accepted
CLOSED Jan to Apr
PROPRIETORS Michel Dimeux and Pierre Ticot

PROVENCE-COTE D'AZUR

ST-REMY-DE-PROVENCE

DOMAINE DE VALMOURIANE
~ COUNTRY HOTEL ~

petite route des Baux, 13210 St-Rémy-de-Provence (Bouches-du-Rhône)
TEL 04 90 92 44 62 **FAX** 04 90 92 37 32
E-MAIL domdeval@wanadoo.fr **WEBSITE** valmouriane.com

IF YOU WANT TO KNOW what *herbes de Provence* smell like, then take a room at Philippe and Martina Capel's Domaine de Valmouriane and simply open your window. Tucked away in a peaceful fold in the rocky hills of the Alpilles, this beautifully converted farmhouse is surrounded by pines, cypresses, rosemary, juniper and lavender – scents and flavours you will come across again in its dining room. Beyond a wide lawn are a sheltered swimming pool and a tennis court and if you want to go further afield a ten-minute drive will take you to Les Baux – but as cars are kept out you might prefer to walk there along the marked woodland trail.

The house has tiled floors and is tastefully decorated with Provençal fabrics and fine antique furniture. The old kitchen, with a huge fireplace, is a cosy winter sitting room and in summer there is a canopied terrace for open-air dining: the cooking is contemporary Provençal and the traditional staples are given stylish twists with fresh herbs and spices. There is also a well-informed selection of local wines to choose from. Two of the smartly comfortable bedrooms have their own private terraces and several others on the ground floor have doors opening directly outside.

~

NEARBY Les Baux-de-Provence (5 km); Avignon (24 km).
LOCATION 4 km W of town, on road to Baux; car parking
FOOD breakfast, lunch, dinner
PRICE ©©©-©©©©
ROOMS 14; 12 double and twin, 1 family, 1 apartment, all with bath; all rooms have phone, TV, air conditioning, minibar
FACILITIES sitting room, bar, dining rooms, terrace, garden, swimming pool, tennis
CREDIT CARDS AE, DC, MC, V
CHILDREN welcome
DISABLED 1 specially adapted room
PETS accepted
CLOSED never
PROPRIETORS Philippe and Martina Capel

PROVENCE-COTE D'AZUR

ST-TROPEZ

LA PONCHE
～ TOWN HOTEL ～

3 rue des Remparts, 83990 St-Tropez (Var)
TEL 04 94 97 02 53 **FAX** 04 94 97 78 61
E-MAIL laponche@nova.fr **WEBSITE** www. nova.fr/ponche

YOU MIGHT NOT THINK that St-Tropez would be our kind of town, but La Ponche is our kind of hotel, at least when we're feeling like a treat. Tucked away in a tiny square overlooking the small fishing port and tiny beach of La Ponche (where Vadim's *And God Created Woman* was filmed, starring Brigitte Bardot), this cluster of 17thC houses offers a compelling combination of sophistication and warmth. What began as a simple fishermen's bar in 1937, has been steadily transformed over the years by Simone Duckstein into a stylish, arty four-star hotel, full of personal touches. Paintings by Mme Duckstein's first husband cover the walls.

You can eat on a terrace, looking across a square to the sea, or in one of several areas indoors, including the main dining room – unpretentious but sophisticated. The food is memorable, particularly the seafood. Bedrooms are captivating and very comfortable. Many have been smartly revamped, with stylish colour schemes and slick bathrooms. A couple of noisier bedrooms facing the street may persuade you to sleep with the double-glazing windows closed and the air conditioning on.

～

NEARBY beaches: Les Graniers (100 m); La Bouillabaisse (1 km); Tahiti (4 km).
LOCATION in heart of old town, overlooking Port des Pêcheurs; car parking and garage
FOOD breakfast, lunch, dinner
PRICE €€€€
ROOMS 18; 11 double and twin, 2 family, 3 suites, 2 apartments, all with bath; all rooms have phone, TV, air conditioning, minibar, safe
FACILITIES bar, dining room, sitting room, lift
CREDIT CARDS AE, MC, V
CHILDREN accepted
DISABLED access difficult
PETS accepted
CLOSED mid-Nov to mid-Feb
PROPRIETOR Simone Duckstein

PROVENCE-COTE D'AZUR

LES STES-MARIES-DE-LA-MER

HOSTELLERIE DU MAS DE CACHAREL
～ COUNTRY HOTEL ～

route de Cacharel, 13460 Les Stes-Maries-de-la-Mer (Bouches-du-Rhône)
TEL 04 90 97 95 44 **FAX** 04 90 97 87 97
E-MAIL mail@hotel-cacharel.com **WEBSITE** www.hotel-cacharel.com

A KILOMETRE FROM THE ROAD and on a 70-hectare estate adjoining a nature reserve, this small hotel was built in the 1960s by film director and photographer Denys Colomb de Daunant, who made the beautiful slow-motion film, *The Dream of the Wild Horses*. Now run by his son, Florian, a former shipbroker, it has remained very simple and unpretentious. There's no television (much frowned on) and the ground-floor rooms – looking into a courtyard and out to the marshes – are basic, and charming, with white walls, and some contain huge grainy photographs of horses. There are also plenty of horses to ride; the family has about 60.

With no restaurant, there's a bar and tables in a huge beamed barn, decorated with mounted bulls' horns, cattle bells and farm implements. The centrepiece is a massive 18thC stone fireplace. An *assiette campagnarde* – of ham, goats' cheese and sausages – is served, with wine, from noon to 8 pm. The stables are close by, and can be visited any time. The bird life, all around, is a wonder; there's a constant parade of flamingos. The frenetic tourist activity in Les Stes-Marie-de-la-Mer, 5 km down the road, is in another world. The Colomb de Daunants are delightful hosts.

～

NEARBY Arles (39 km); Aigues-Mortes (31 km); Nîmes (54 km).
LOCATION in the marshes of the Camargue; car parking
FOOD breakfast, light meal (noon to 8 pm)
PRICE €€
ROOMS 15; 12 with bath, 3 with shower; all with phone and heating
FACILITIES bar, barn, garden, swimming pool, riding
CREDIT CARDS MC, V
CHILDREN welcome
DISABLED 1 suitable room
PETS accepted
CLOSED never
PROPRIETORS Colomb de Daunant family

PROVENCE-COTE D'AZUR

MAS DE LA FOUQUE
~ COUNTRY HOTEL ~

route du Petit-Rhône, 13460 Les Stes-Marie-de-la-Mer (Bouches-du-Rhône)
TEL 04 90 97 81 02 **FAX** 04 90 97 94 84
E-MAIL masdelafouque@francemarket.com **WEBSITE** www.masdelafouque.com

O VER A CANDLELIT DINNER, a young woman was confiding to her companion how much she loved him. But his eyes were elsewhere: a large grey
heron was wading through the pond. The evening floor show, as seen
through the picture windows here, is extraordinary: white horses and the
little black bulls of the Camargue wander through the reeds and grasses of
the marshes and squadrons of pink flamingos fly overhead. This Spanish-
style whitewashed hotel, on the water's edge, resembles a kind of
Southfork with saddles in the hall. It is, however, a four-star luxury ranch
with a helicopter pad, exotic bathrooms, whirlpool baths and where they
like you to dress for dinner.

Many of the smartly-decorated rooms – well protected against mosqui-
toes and with fans – have private terraces built over the lagoon for sunbathing and birdwatching. (Take binoculars.) Plenty of white wicker
chairs give a light and airy feel to the *salon*. There's a comfortable bar
decorated with illustrations from a turn-of-the century harness catalogue.
Food is excellent, with elegantly presented regional dishes; many vegetables and herbs are home grown. The Mas has recently changed hands, so
we would welcome reports.

~

NEARBY Arles (35 km); Aigues-Mortes (26 km); Nîmes (50 km).
LOCATION in the Camargue, 4 km NW of the town; car parking
FOOD breakfast, lunch, dinner
PRICE €€€; half-board obligatory in high season
ROOMS 13; 6 double, 4 twin, 1 family, 2 suites, all with bath; all rooms have phone,
TV, air conditioning, minibar, hairdrier; 4 have whirlpool baths
FACILITIES 2 sitting rooms, bar, dining room, terraces, garden, swimming pool,
fishing, putting, helipad
CREDIT CARDS AE, DC, MC, V **CHILDREN** accepted
DISABLED 1 specially adapted room **PETS** accepted
CLOSED early Nov to late Mar; restaurant Sep to mid-Jul Mon lunch and Tue
PROPRIETOR Didier Rivière

PROVENCE-COTE D'AZUR

LE SAMBUC

MAS DE PEINT

~ COUNTRY HOTEL ~

Le Sambuc, 13200 Arles (Bouches-du-Rhône)
TEL 04 90 97 20 62 **FAX** 04 90 97 22 20
E-MAIL hotel@masdepeint.net **WEBSITE** www.masdepeint.com

THIS IS CAMARGUE CHIC, achieved at lavish expense by the owners, the Bons, whose cattle-branding mark appears on the crisp, white linen in an exquisite little hotel created out of an 18thC stable attached to their own house. Mme Bon, an architect and interior designer, has considerably altered the building to make lovely, spacious rooms with wooden beamed ceilings, sandstone floors, paintwork the colour of sugared almonds and enviable antiques. The whole ensemble feels like a wing for private guests rather than a hotel, which is the way it's meant to be. Everyone eats – sometimes a little awkwardly – in the old-fashioned kitchen, which emanates inviting smells before dinner; vegetables and herbs come from the garden. A harness hangs in the hall, shelves are filled with books, there's a quiet little reading room, and a newspaper for the breakfast table. Jacques Bon, who breeds bulls and horses, is often in and out, inviting visitors to come and see his stock and his farm, on which he grows rice. The bedrooms are in classic country-house style; some have cast-iron baths and little wooden staircases up to a galleried bathroom. There's a discreet swimming pool hidden from the house.

~

NEARBY Arles (20 km); Avignon (36 km); Nîmes (31 km).
LOCATION in open countryside; car parking
FOOD breakfast, lunch, dinner
PRICE €€€€
ROOMS 11; 8 double and twin, 3 suites, all with bath; all rooms have phone, TV, air conditioning, minibar, safe
FACILITIES sitting rooms, dining room, garden, swimming pool, riding
CREDIT CARDS AE, DC, MC, V
CHILDREN welcome
DISABLED no special facilities
PETS accepted
CLOSED early Jan to mid-Mar
PROPRIETORS M. and Mme Bon

PROVENCE-COTE D'AZUR

HOTEL DES DEUX ROCS
~ VILLAGE HOTEL ~

place Font d'Amont, 83440 Seillans (Var)
TEL 04 94 76 87 32 **FAX** 04 94 76 88 68

THIS CAPTIVATING BLUE-SHUTTERED HOTEL in a charming protected medieval hill village has long been one of our favourites. Nothing changes at the Deux Rocs, which is one of the secrets of its enduring appeal. It conforms to what everyone *expects* of a small unspoiled hotel in Provence, from the pleasures of breakfast by the fountain in the little cobbled square in front, to the brilliant restrained decorating style of Mme Hirsch, whose touch is evident everywhere. 'Came for one night, stayed for six,' says a typical entry in the visitors' book. Did that guest, like so many others, fall in love with the wide 18thC staircase, or the bedroom so dashingly decorated in red-and-white checks, or the room with *toile de Jouy* on the walls, or the little downstairs *salon* with the open fireplace and the gigantic TV (none in the rooms here, of course)? Mme Hirsch and her assistant Mme Francine came to Seillans years ago when it was an artists' colony – Max Ernst lived here at the end of his life – and together they give the hotel its gentle civilized air which is so alluring. Bathrooms are old fashioned – a little too much so in some cases; but towels are thick, and the food is traditional and excellent. Parking, though, requires patience.

NEARBY Lac de St-Cassien (15 km); Grasse (32 km); St-Raphael (33 km); Cannes (47 km); Gorges du Verdon (40 km).
LOCATION at top of small village; limited car parking, or street parking
FOOD breakfast, lunch, dinner
PRICE €€
ROOMS 14 double and twin, 6 with bath, 8 with shower; all rooms have phone
FACILITIES sitting room, bar, dining room, terrace
CREDIT CARDS MC, V
CHILDREN accepted
DISABLED access difficult
PETS accepted
CLOSED Nov to mid-Mar
PROPRIETOR Mme Hirsch

PROVENCE-COTE D'AZUR

AUBERGE ST PIERRE

~ COUNTRY HOTEL ~

Tourtour, 83690 Salernes (Var)
TEL 04 94 70 57 17 **FAX** 04 90 70 59 04
WEBSITE www.guide.provence.com/hotel/saint.pierre/

A THIRD GENERATION OF MARCELLINS is now running this hotel which, on a 70-hectare agricultural estate, is surrounded by lush green fields and has its own farm. (The approach, though, through a development of holiday villas gives a mildly worrying first impression.) Little of the old 16thC house can be recognized, but adaptations have been done fairly sympathetically; the TV room was once a chapel. However, it is the setting (rather than the bedrooms, found along utilitarian corridors) which gives this place its charm. There is nothing to be seen for miles except meadows and woods, and a deep calm prevails. Eight of the newer bedrooms have terraces and furniture made from estate-grown oak and elm. Furnishings are plain and the style is modest yet comfortable (with an abundance of plastic rather than fresh flowers) as befits the low prices. But with swimming pool, long walks, archery, tennis courts and fishing in the lake, the Saint Pierre provides everything needed for a complete retreat at affordable prices. It is also a good base for visiting delightful Tourtour – with its sensational views. M. Marcellin, a disciple of Escoffier, is the chef, and his cuisine uses a wide variety of produce from the family farm.

~

NEARBY Tourtour; Lac de Sainte Croix; Verdon Gorges.
LOCATION in countryside near Tourtour, off road to Ampus; car parking
FOOD breakfast, lunch, dinner
PRICE €
ROOMS 16; 6 double, 7 twin, 3 triple, all with bath or shower; all rooms have phone
FACILITIES sitting room, dining room, breakfast room, sauna, fitness room, terraces, swimming pool, tennis, cycling, archery, fishing
CREDIT CARDS MC, V
CHILDREN accepted
DISABLED no special facilities
PETS accepted
CLOSED Oct to Apr; restaurant Wed
PROPRIETORS M. and Mme Marcellin

PROVENCE-COTE D'AZUR

TRIGANCE

CHATEAU DE TRIGANCE
~ CONVERTED CASTLE ~

83840 Trigance (Var)
TEL 04 94 76 91 18 **FAX** 04 94 85 68 99
E-MAIL trigance@relaischateaux.com **WEBSITE** relaischateaux.com/trigance

FOR MORE THAN 30 YEARS, Jean-Claude Thomas and his wife have run this characterful and comfortable hotel near the dramatic Gorges du Verdon. Nowadays their son, William, is involved. Trigance remains a welcome port of call in a region of rough terrain and few villages. On arrival, you might be taken aback. Is this fortress, perched high on a rocky peak, really your hotel? (Yes.) And if it is, how are you to penetrate its defences? (By climbing a steep flight of 100 steps – don't worry, your bags will be carried up.) Once inside, you are in the Middle Ages. M. Thomas has painstakingly rebuilt his 11thC castle stone by stone (villagers had stolen many of them to build their own houses); if you ask, you can see photographs of the various stages of his amazing project. The impressive stone-vaulted, candlelit dining room (with a knight in armour at the entrance), and the sitting room below, are windowless and highly atmospheric, furnished in medieval style. Most of the bedrooms (cut into the hill) are similar, with canopied beds, antique furniture, tapestries and banners – and stunning views from their windows. You can have breakfast on the battlements. The cooking is surprisingly good, considering the remote location.

~

NEARBY Gorges du Verdon (10 km); Castellane (20 km).
LOCATION at 750 m, overlooking tiny village, 10 km NW of Comps-sur-Artuby; car parking
FOOD breakfast, lunch, dinner; room service
PRICE €€€-€€€€
ROOMS 10 double and twin, all with bath; all rooms have phone, TV, hairdrier
CREDIT CARDS AE, DC, MC, V
CHILDREN accepted
DISABLED not suitable
PETS accepted
CLOSED Nov to mid-Mar
PROPRIETORS Thomas family -

PROVENCE-COTE D'AZUR

VACQUERAS

DOMAINE DE LA PONCHE

~ COUNTRY HOTEL ~

84190 Vacqueras (Vaucluse)
TEL 04 90 65 85 21 **FAX** 04 90 65 85 23
E-MAIL domaine.laponche@wanadoo.fr **WEBSITE** www.hotel-laponche.com

'WHAT A FIND', wrote the reader who told us about this new hotel in wine country near the jagged Dentelles de Montmirail. 'Admittedly we were tired, hungry and in need of a bed for the night when we called in here, but we couldn't believe our luck. Our room was enormous, with a fabulous bathroom, and dinner was excellent.'

Enormous is the word: lofty ceilings striped by vast beams and bedrooms which are like prairies compared to most hotel rooms. They are decorated à la mode with spartan good taste involving pastel colours for the walls, wrought-iron beds, one or two good pieces of country furniture; the more expensive have sitting areas, and the bathrooms are, as reported, huge and excellent. The public rooms are also large-scale; the laid-back sitting room made cosy by a huge open hearth.

The fine, old, blue-shuttered 17thC bastide, surrounded by its own vines, olive and cypress trees, was converted into a hotel four years ago by two Swiss sisters and the French husband of one of them. They are good cooks, making their own fresh pasta to add to their repertoire of tasty Provençal dishes. Light lunches are served around the lovely flowery pool.

~

NEARBY Côtes-du-Rhône vineyards; Vaison-la-Romaine (20 km).
LOCATION signposted 2 km N of Vacqueras, on D8 to Cairanne; car parking
FOOD breakfast, lunch, dinner
PRICE €€€
ROOMS 6; 4 double and twin, 2 suites, all with bath; all rooms have phone, hairdrier
FACILITIES sitting room, dining room, terrace, garden, swimming pool
CREDIT CARDS MC, V
CHILDREN accepted
DISABLED access difficult
PETS accepted
CLOSED never
PROPRIETORS Ruth Spahn, Madeleine Frauenknecht, Jean-Pierre Onimus

PROVENCE-COTE D'AZUR

VAISON-LA-ROMAINE

HOSTELLERIE LE BEFFROI

~ TOWN HOTEL ~

rue de l'Evêché Haute Ville, 84110 Vaison-la-Romaine (Vaucluse)
TEL 04 90 36 04 71 **FAX** 04 90 36 24 78

THE HOTEL OCCUPIES two beautiful houses in the same street of this medieval hilltop town – one was built in the 16th century for the Comte de Saint Véran, the other, built in the 17th century, was the home of the Marquis de Taulignan. There are plenty of beams, old stone, and polished red-tiled floors in both and views from the terraces look down to the new town below, which is built around two sites of Roman excavations. (Some of the houses in the old town were built of stone from the ruins.) The Beffroi is above it all – even in the hottest weather there's a fresh breeze.

The friendly, young, and often very busy, proprietor, Yann Christiansen (the hotel has been in the family for three generations now) and his wife, Christine, constantly strive to come up with ways of making the hotel even more comfortable and convenient for their guests. Not all the rooms have baths, however. Serving lunchtime salads on the terrace has proved a great success. At dinner, the cooking is traditional Provençal. A swimming pool with fine views of the rooftops below and an ingenious mini-golf course nearby are added attractions in summer.

~

NEARBY Orange (25 km); Avignon (40 km).
LOCATION in the old town, up a steep hill; car parking
FOOD breakfast, lunch, dinner
PRICE €€
ROOMS 22; 8 double, 13 twin, 1 single, 10 with bath, 12 with shower; all rooms have phone, TV, minibar, hairdrier
FACILITIES sitting room, dining room, terraces, garden, swimming pool, mini-golf (summer only)
CREDIT CARDS AE, DC, MC , V
CHILDREN welcome
DISABLED not suitable
PETS accepted
CLOSED Feb to late Mar; restaurant mid-Nov to Apr
PROPRIETORS M. and Mme Christiansen

PROVENCE-COTE D'AZUR

VENCE

LA ROSERAIE
~ TOWN VILLA ~

avenue Henri Giraud, 06140 Vence (Alpes-Maritimes)
TEL 04 93 58 02 20 **FAX** 04 93 58 99 31

THE WHOLE FEELING of this pale pink *belle époque* villa is of a rambling family house – straw hats and little bunches of dried flowers hang on the walls and there are old photographs and prints. The ownership has recently changed and some updating has taken place since our last visit: smart, wrought-iron garden furniture and wooden, colonial-style sunbeds have replaced white plastic, for example. The mature garden is full of exotic plants and trees – a banana palm, a 100-year-old giant magnolia, orange trees and oleander. The reception area/sitting room is immediately inviting, with low beamed ceiling, little stone fireplace, Provençal fabrics and pleasing objects. A smell of lavender lingers in the air.

The bedrooms have remained largely the same: bright and sunny. One particularly pretty room is in an attic under the eaves, with heavy beams, rough brick walls and arched window under the roof, with a beautiful carved wrought-iron bed. Another room has a clawfoot bath; others have handmade ceramic tiles from Salernes. All are spotless and well-equipped. The hotel is not in a pretty part of Vence, though.

~

NEARBY Matisse chapel; Vence old town; Cannes (5 km).
LOCATION on outskirts of town, 10 km N of Cagnes-sur-Mer; car parking
FOOD breakfast
PRICE ⓔⓔ
ROOMS 13 double and twin, 11 with bath, 2 with shower; all rooms have phone, TV, minibar, hairdrier, some have safe, 1 has air conditioning
FACILITIES sitting room, breakfast room, terrace, garden, swimming pool
CREDIT CARDS AE, DC, MC, V
CHILDREN accepted
DISABLED 4 rooms on ground floor
PETS accepted
CLOSED mid-Nov to mid-Feb
PROPRIETOR M. Marteton

PROVENCE-COTE D'AZUR

AUBERGE DES SEIGNEURS ET DU LION D'OR

~ TOWN HOTEL ~

place du Frêne, 06140 Vence (Alpes-Maritimes)
TEL 04 93 58 04 24 **FAX** 04 93 24 08 01

FIND THE HUGE ASH TREE, and you will find this elegant town house, which has been a hotel since 1895 and in the family since 1936. The only thing that has changed over the years is the faces of the guests, who once numbered artists such as Renoir and Modigliani. Once inside, you'll find a large, rather gloomy reception hall with old tiled foors, lumbering country antiques, bits of olive press, a spinning wheel, a huge shaggy dog, nooks, crannies and curiosities. Off this is the restaurant, where Mme Rodi prepares delicious rack of lamb or chicken on the ancient spit over the open fire. There is also a fabulous *soupe de poissons* and *le tourton des patres*, a kind of cheese pie. Breakfast is simple, but particularly good, with stewed fruit, fromage frais, cheeses, breads and home-made jams. Bedrooms are quite spartan, but not without charm. There are some superb antique pieces, and many rooms have their original terracotta tiled floors, with fresh Provençal fabrics and bowls of fresh fruit. They vary widely in shape and size; bathrooms are gradually being renovated. So, nothing modern here, and God forbid there should be any suggestion of televisions, a website, or even a brochure. Perhaps some modernity will creep in when Madame (a character) finally hands over to her daughter, but not too much, we hope.

~

NEARBY Matisse chapel; Vence old town; Cannes (5 km).
LOCATION on square near town centre; public car parking nearby
FOOD breakfast, lunch, dinner
PRICE €
ROOMS 10 double and twin, all with shower
FACILITIES sitting room, dining room, bar
CREDIT CARDS AE, DC, MC, V **CHILDREN** accepted
DISABLED access difficult
PETS accepted
CLOSED mid-Nov to mid-Mar; restaurant closed Mon, Tue lunch
PROPRIETOR Daniele Rodi

The Rhone Valley

La Santoline
~ CONVERTED HUNTING LODGE ~

07460 Beaulieu (Ardèche)
Tel 04 75 39 01 91 **Fax** 04 75 39 38 79
E-MAIL contacts@santoline.com **WEBSITE** www.lasantoline.com

RESIDENTS OF NEARBY VILLAGES still speak of the big, old, stone Santoline as *'le château'* – a reference to its 15thC origins. As time passed, it was used as a hunting lodge and remains a secluded place well off the beaten track. With no television or other disruptions, there is little to disturb except birdsong and the occasional braying of a donkey. It is difficult to imagine a more relaxed setting. In the evenings, guests dine outside on the flower-filled terrace and watch the sun set behind the Cévennes.

Since opening their hotel in 1991, the Espenels have gathered a very loyal clientele by striking the right balance between easy-going conviviality and discreet attentiveness. Outsiders use the restaurant, which provides a menu of regional fare that changes daily, and affordable wines of the Ardèche. (The inside dining room has a fine stone-vaulted ceiling and tiled floor.) Bedrooms are pretty and simple in design, with much use of natural, rustic textures – tiled or pine floors, wicker furniture, some iron bedsteads, and white plastered walls. There are thick towels in the bathrooms. Most have exhilarating views of mountains.

~

NEARBY Vallon-Pont-d'Arc (22 km); Gorges de l'Ardèche.
LOCATION off the D104 at La Croisée de Jalès, then the D225, 2 km from Beaulieu; car parking
FOOD breakfast, lunch, dinner
PRICE €€; half-board obligatory Jul to Sep
ROOMS 8; 7 double, 1 suite, all with bath; all rooms have phone, minibar; 2 have air conditioning
FACILITIES sitting room, dining room, terrace, garden, swimming pool
CREDIT CARDS MC, V **CHILDREN** accepted
DISABLED no special facilities **PETS** accepted
CLOSED Oct to late Apr
PROPRIETORS M. and Mme Espenel

THE RHONE VALLEY

LA TOUR ROSE

~ TOWN HOTEL ~

22 rue du Boeuf, 69005 Lyon (Rhône)
TEL 04 78 37 25 90 **FAX** 04 78 42 26 02
E-MAIL chavent@asi.fr

PHILIPPE CHAVENT is a Lyon chef with a Michelin star – and something of a Renaissance man. In St-Jean, the old quarter, he has recreated the atmosphere of the residences of the great Florentine bankers and merchants by turning a 17thC building into something extraordinary. There are 12 spectacular bedrooms, each designed to illustrate a period in the long history of Lyon's silk industry. One is decorated with Fortuny pleats, another with Art Deco patterns designed by Dufy, and all are draped, from floor to ceiling, in silk, taffeta, velvet and other textiles. (Bathrooms are modern, with stone floors and walls, and are fitted with shiny stainless steel washbasins.)

The heart of the hotel is a pink tower and there are balustraded galleries, ornamental ponds with waterfalls, and terraced gardens. The fireplace in the bar was rescued from a condemned château and there is an original 13thC wall of a *jeu de paume* (real tennis) court. Panelling in the bar comes from the law courts at Chambéry. The dining room is in the 13thC chapel of what used to be a convent, with a cobbled terrace and a fabulous glass extension which opens to the sky in the summer.

~

NEARBY Vieux Lyon.
LOCATION in the heart of Vieux Lyon, with car parking; ask hotel for details of car access
FOOD breakfast, lunch, dinner
PRICE €€€€€
ROOMS 12; 6 double and twin, 6 suites, all with bath; all rooms have phone, TV, minibar, hairdrier
FACILITIES 3 sitting rooms, bar, restaurant, lift, terraces
CREDIT CARDS AE, DC, MC, V
CHILDREN accepted
DISABLED no special facilities **PETS** accepted
CLOSED never
PROPRIETOR Philippe Chavent

THE RHONE VALLEY

MALATAVERNE

DOMAINE DU COLOMBIER

~ OLD COACHING INN ~

route de Donzère, 26780 Malataverne (Drôme)
TEL 04 75 90 86 86 **FAX** 04 75 90 79 40
E-MAIL domainecolombier@voila.fr **WEBSITE** www.domaine-colombier.com

METICULOUSLY RESTORED and full of flowers and colour, this pleasing 14thC stone building, once a stopover for pilgrims on the road to Santiago de Compostela, remains an ideal base for travellers (largely due to its position near the *autoroute* yet in the countryside). With its vine-clad façade, stone staircases, tiled roof, wrought-iron railings and penchant for flowers, this hotel really feels it is on the road to the South.

Wild flowers, gathered in the grounds, brighten every table and service is efficient and professional. When the weather is favourable (and the infamous mistral is not blowing) guests dine on the terrace, which is, again, packed with flowers and absolutely enchanting in the evening glow of lamplight. There is a large restaurant with a vaulted ceiling. Flowers appear everywhere, on the tablecloths, on curtains and bedspreads and wallpaper (floral fabrics and cane furniture are on sale in the hotel shop).

There has been a change of ownership since our last visit. M. and Mme Chochois are now in charge, and we would welcome reports.

~

NEARBY Montélimar (20 km); Valence (50 km).
LOCATION on private estate, off D144a from A7 to Donzère; car parking
FOOD breakfast, lunch, dinner
PRICE €€€
ROOMS 25; 22 double and twin, 3 suites, 24 with bath, 1 with shower; all rooms have phone, TV, minibar; some rooms have hairdrier
FACILITIES sitting room, dining room, terrace, garden, swimming pool, pétanque
CREDIT CARDS AE, DC, MC, V
CHILDREN welcome
DISABLED no special facilities
PETS accepted
CLOSED never
PROPRIETORS M. and Mme Chochois

THE RHONE VALLEY

LES HOSPITALIERS

~ CONVERTED CASTLE ~

Le Poët-Laval, 26160 La Bégude-de-Mazenc (Drôme)
TEL 04 75 46 22 32 **FAX** 04 75 46 49 99
E-MAIL hotel.hospitaliers@wanadoo.fr

READERS CONTINUE TO BE IMPRESSED by this distinctive hotel, within the ramparts of a 13thC castle and in a dominating position above the perched medieval village of Le Poët-Laval (400 m). So do we.

The attractive old stone buildings were formerly part of a stronghold of the Knights of Malta. (The Maltese cross is the hotel's emblem.) From the pool and the terrace – where meals are served in fine weather – the views across wooded countryside to hills beyond are spectacular. The very comfortable sitting room is – unusually – on the top floor and makes the most of this feature. Owner Bernard Morin's father was an art dealer and there are many original paintings in the bedrooms, as well as antique, carved hardwood furniture. The restaurant also has an interesting collection of pictures. Tables are laid with fine china, white linen, and candles; service is hard to fault and the food is excellent. The menu changes daily. The welcome from the charming Morin family is warm and genuine. The eldest son, Bernard, has recently taken over the hotel from his father; he also cooks, using the freshest produce available. His younger brother is the *sommelier;* there's a comprehensive cellar. A delightful hotel that makes a lasting impression on all its guests.

~

NEARBY Montélimar (20 km); Viviers (30 km).
LOCATION at the top of the old village, 5 km W of Dieulefit; car parking nearby
FOOD breakfast, lunch, dinner
PRICE €€€
ROOMS 24; 13 double, 8 twin, 20 with bath, 1 with shower, 3 family with bath; all rooms have phone
FACILITIES 2 sitting rooms, 2 dining rooms, bar, terrace, swimming pool
CREDIT CARDS AE, DC, MC, V **CHILDREN** accepted
DISABLED no special facilities **PETS** accepted
CLOSED mid-Nov to Feb
PROPRIETOR Bernard Morin

THE RHONE VALLEY

MAISON PIC
~ TOWN HOTEL ~

285 avenue Victor Hugo, 26001 Valence (Drôme)
TEL 04 75 44 15 32 **FAX** 04 75 40 96 03
E-MAIL pic@relaischateaux.fr **WEBSITE** www.pic-valence.com

THE FOOD'S THE THING HERE. Despite the death in 1992 of Jacques Pic, this remains (under his daughter Anne) one of the best restaurants in the country with, at the last count, two Michelin stars – yet it is still delightfully modest. The good news *chez* Pic, however, has little to do with caviar and sea bass. It is that the small hotel that Anne's grandfather opened so many years ago was expanded in 1997 and transformed into the Hôtel des Senteurs (the name Pic remains outside), and another small restaurant, Auberge du Pin.

The existing five bedrooms have been updated with a smart new Provençal look and ten large rooms have been added. And very attractive and stylish they are, too: damask upholstery, antique rugs, bathrooms in marble. Rooms vary in size, yet even the 'small' doubles are reasonably spacious. Some are very pretty: one has blue-and-white gingham wallpaper. The present generation of Pics devotes greater attention to the hotel, and it shows. What hasn't changed is the lovely terrace, pool and flower-filled garden. The few rooms at Pic were rarely vacant. Now there's more of a chance for those who wish to follow up their delicious – and expensive – Pic dinner with a copious Pic breakfast served in the room.

~

NEARBY Vercors mountains; the Rhône.
LOCATION in town centre; car parking
FOOD breakfast, lunch, dinner
PRICE €€€€
ROOMS 15 double with bath; all rooms have phone, TV, air conditioning, minibar, hairdrier, safe
FACILITIES sitting room, restaurant, terrace, swimming pool, French billiards
CREDIT CARDS AE, DC, MC, V
CHILDREN accepted **DISABLED** 1 specially adapted room
PETS accepted
CLOSED never; restaurant Sun dinner, Mon, 3 weeks Jan
PROPRIETOR Anne Pic

THE ALPS

AUBERGE DU BOIS PRIN
~ CHALET HOTEL ~

69 chemin de l'Hermine, Les Moussoux, 74400 Chamonix (Haute-Savoie)
TEL 04 50 53 33 51 **FAX** 04 50 53 48 75 **E-MAIL** boisprin@relaischateaux.fr
WEBSITE www.boisprin.com

DESPITE INCREASING COMPETITION, the Bois Prin remains our favourite spot in, or at least near, Chamonix. This is partly because of the stunning views – the kind that would have driven the19thC Romantics crazy – across the valley to the spires and glaciers of Mont Blanc, but also because (as recent visits attest) it is a deeply cossetting place to stay.

The Bois Prin is a traditional, dark-wood chalet, in a pretty, flowery garden close to the foot of the Brévent cable car, on the north side of the deep, steep-sided Chamonix valley. The Carriers have run the hotel since it was built (by Denis Carrier's parents) in 1976. The first impression may be of a surprising degree of formality, with crisply dressed staff. But in fact you quickly find that the informal and friendly approach of the young owners sets the tone. Bedrooms face Mont Blanc, and are lavishly furnished, with rich fabrics and carved woodwork (much of it Denis's own work) and a sprinkling of antiques; the best have private terraces. Food is excellent, with a good choice of menus and a 'wonderful' cheeseboard. 'Luxurious...yet at the same time homely and cosy', praises a recent guest.

~

NEARBY Mont Blanc and Le Brévent.
LOCATION on hillside, NW of town; ample car parking and garages
FOOD breakfast, lunch, dinner; room service
PRICE €€€
ROOMS 11; 9 double and twin, 2 family, all with bath; all rooms have phone, TV, minibar, hairdrier
FACILITIES dining room, lift, sauna, spa, terrace, garden
CREDIT CARDS AE, DC, MC, V
CHILDREN welcome
DISABLED no special facilities
PETS accepted
CLOSED mid-Apr to early May, Nov
PROPRIETORS Denis and Monique Carrier

THE ALPS

MANIGOD

CHALET HOTEL DE LA CROIX-FRY

~ CHALET HOTEL ~

rue du Col de la Croix-Fry, Manigod, 74230 Thônes (Haute-Savoie)
TEL 04 50 44 90 16 **FAX** 04 50 44 94 87
WEBSITE www.hotelchaletcroixfry.com

'ABSOLUTELY GORGEOUS' was the verdict of one of our reporters, and a recent visit confirms the star rating of this wooden mountain chalet at the highest point of an alpine *col*, with a terrace overflowing with flowers. Run, with great pride, by a third generation of Veyrats – the chalet was once shared in the summer by the family and their cows – the hotel is cosy and welcoming. A wood fire burns on cool evenings and the sofas and armchairs gathered around the hearth are covered in sheepskin. The bedrooms are attractively rustic – even in the modern annexe-chalets, which provide adaptable family accommodation with kitchenettes. But what really impresses us is the evident pride of the family and their endless efforts to maximize a guest's stay. The Veyrats love running their hotel and the pleasure shows.

The restaurant, serving nourishing mountain food, has spectacular views of peaks and valleys. Mme Guelpa-Veyrat's brother, Marc, is one of Savoy's culinary celebrities, but the *tarte aux myrtilles* has many admirers. In summer the Veyrat's invite their guests to picnic in the pastures with their cows; in winter the invitation is to ski.

~

NEARBY Vallée de Manigod; Thônes (10 km); Annecy (26 km).
LOCATION on the *col*, 5 km NE of Manigod, on D16, 6 km S of La Clusaz; car parking
FOOD breakfast, lunch, dinner
PRICE €€€
ROOMS 10; 5 double, 4 one bedroom suites, 1 two bedroom suite, all with bath (suites with Jacuzzi bath); all rooms have phone, TV, terrace or balcony
FACILITIES sitting room, dining room, bar, gym, terrace, garden
CREDIT CARDS AE, MC, V **CHILDREN** accepted
DISABLED no special facilities
PETS not accepted
CLOSED mid-Sep to mid-Dec, mid-Apr to mid-Jun
PROPRIETOR Marie-Ange Guelpa-Veyrat

BORDEAUX AND THE DORDOGNE

BONNET

THIS SLIGHTLY FADED beauty is one of a dying breed of affordable and old-fashioned roadside hotels. Decoration is a throwback to earlier times, but rooms are clean and comfortable and there's a pleasing veranda and terrace for meals. Rooms have views of the Dordogne and four châteaux. Very friendly, helpful staff.

24220 Beynac (Dordogne) **TEL** 05 53 29 50 01 **FAX** 05 53 29 83 74
FOOD breakfast, lunch, dinner **PRICE** ⓔ **ROOMS** 20
CREDIT CARDS AE, DC, MC, V **CLOSED** never

LE CHATENET

ONE OF OUR FAVOURITES, a noble stone *gentilhommière* (with yards of walnut panelling and a *pigeonnier*) whose owners of 20 years, the Laxtons, after thinking of selling, have happily for us decided to stay on. They thought of everything: heated swimming pool; barbecue and garden room, laundry room, antique-filled bedrooms.

24310 Brântôme (Dordogne) **TEL** 05 53 05 81 08 **FAX** 05 53 05 85 52
E-MAIL chatenet@wanadoo.fr **FOOD** breakfast **PRICE** ⓔⓔ **ROOMS** 10
CREDIT CARDS MC, V **CLOSED** Nov to Easter

AUBERGE DU NOYER

AN ENORMOUS WALNUT TREE gives this formerly ruined 18thC stone farmhouse its name. New proprietors took over from the Dyers, English emigrés, who turned the ruins into a winningly attractive, relaxed and tranquil inn, with rustic rooms, beams, and exposed stone walls.

Le Reclaud de Bouny Bas, 24260 Le Bugue (Dordogne) **TEL** 05 53 07 11 73
FAX 05 53 54 57 44 **E-MAIL** aubergedunoyer@perigord.com
WEBSITE www.perigord.com/aubergedunoyer **FOOD** breakfast **PRICE** ⓔ **ROOMS** 10
CREDIT CARDS DC, MC, V **CLOSED** Nov to Apr

MANOIR DE BELLERIVE

INCLUDED BECAUSE this is one of the few places open out of season, this is a fine Napoleon III manor house with 'magnificent rooms, spectacular grounds, friendly staff' to quote a reader. A recent guest is less enthusiastic: 'soulless; stripped of character', he says.

route de Siorac, 24480 Le Buisson-de-Cadouin (Dordogne) **TEL** 05 53 22 16 16
FAX 05 53 22 09 05 **E-MAIL** manoir.bellerive@wanadoo.fr
WEBSITE www.manoir-bellerive.com **FOOD** breakfast, lunch, dinner
PRICE ⓔⓔⓔ **ROOMS** 22
CREDIT CARDS AE, DC, MC, V **CLOSED** Jan to Mar

BORDEAUX AND THE DORDOGNE

CHATEAU DE FOULON

THE ENGAGING VICOMTE and Vicomtesse de Baritault du Carpia have opened up their elegant home in the heart of the Médoc for bed-and-breakfast guests. Bedrooms have beautiful antiques and the grounds are magnificent; there are swans on the lake and peacocks on the lawn.

33480 Castelnau-de-Médoc (Gironde) **TEL** 05 56 58 20 18 **FAX** 05 56 58 23 43
FOOD breakfast **PRICES** ©©© **ROOMS** 5 **CREDIT CARDS** not accepted
CLOSED never

AUBERGE SANS FRONTIERE

A MODEST LITTLE *AUBERGE* in a quiet town, about which we hear very little from readers. Rooms are smallish, but bright and tidy, with showers and loos located in the hallway. The restaurant provides good, no-nonsense food at reasonable prices. A modest but fair option, we think, but we would welcome your opinions.

Dégagnac, 46340 Salviac (Lot) **TEL** 05 65 41 52 88 **FOOD** breakfast, lunch, dinner
PRICE © **ROOMS** 8 **CREDIT CARDS** MC, V **CLOSED** never

L'ESPLANADE

UNFORTUNATELY OUR INSPECTOR reported a 'sour reception' at this hotel in a busy tourist village with splendid views over the Dordogne. Housekeeping, however, is immaculate, service is efficient, and the terrace and some rooms have superb views. Michelin star for the cooking. Difficult parking.

24250 Domme (Dordogne) **TEL** 05 53 28 31 41 **FAX** 05 53 28 49 92
FOOD breakfast, lunch, dinner **PRICE** ©© **ROOMS** 25
CREDIT CARDS AE, DC, MC, V **CLOSED** Nov to mid-Feb; restaurant only, Mon lunch;
Mon in winter

MOULIN DE LA BEUNE

THIS CHARMING OLD MILL is set beside a stream and far removed from the village bustle. Rooms are prettily furnished; bathrooms are spotless. There is a simple breakfast room, and an inviting restaurant in a separate building in the garden. Budget prices, a sublime setting and easy parking make this a perfect base.

24620 Les Eyzies-de-Tayac (Dordogne) **TEL** 05 53 06 94 33
FAX 05 53 06 98 06 **FOOD** breakfast, lunch, dinner **PRICE** © **ROOMS** 20
CREDIT CARDS AE, DC, MC, V **CLOSED** Nov to Mar; Tue and Wed lunch

BORDEAUX AND THE DORDOGNE

LA DAILLE

THIS PLACE, IN DEEP COUNTRYSIDE, combines the best of France and Britain if you can find it (check directions in advance). The Browns have been in their stone farmhouse set amid very English gardens for more than 25 years now, and own 18 hectares of woods and fields (with orchids) for visitors to enjoy. Rooms, in a modern outbuilding, are unfussy, clean and comfortable. Perfect for walkers. Good teas.

Florimont-Gaumiers, 24250 Domme (Dordogne) **TEL** 05 53 28 40 71
FOOD breakfast **PRICE** €€
ROOMS 3 **CREDIT CARDS** MC, V **CLOSED** Oct to May

MOULIN DE ST-AVIT

THE WINNING FEATURES of this former mill are the relaxed family atmosphere and the exceptionally warm welcome; it is the sort of place whose hidden charms grow on you. With its large pool and shady garden it is particularly suitable for children; there are also 12 donkeys which can be hired as pack animals on country hikes.

St-Avit, 47150 Gavaudun (Lot-et-Garonne) **TEL** 05 53 40 86 80
FAX 05 53 40 98 20 **E-MAIL** moulin.st.avit@wanadoo.fr
WEBSITE www.perso.wanadoo.fr/moulin.st.avit **FOOD** breakfast, dinner **PRICE** €
ROOMS 5 **CREDIT CARDS** MC, V **CLOSED** never

LE CHATEAU

SQUEEZED ON THE EDGE of the Dordogne, the setting of this odd little turreted castle is spectacular. The decoration is quirky and modernistic; rooms are comfortable, some with balconies overlooking the fast-flowing river. M. Gensou, the *patron,* rides a motorbike and stuffs snails with *foie gras* and walnut butter. For those who like water and something with a difference.

24150 Lalinde (Dordogne) **TEL** 05 53 61 01 82 **FAX** 05 53 24 74 60
FOOD breakfast, lunch, dinner **PRICE** €€ **ROOMS** 7 **CREDIT CARDS** MC, V
CLOSED mid-Dec to mid-Feb

DOMAINE DE SAINT-GÉRY

FROM THE MOMENT you are welcomed into the Duler's captivating *maison d'hôte* you know this is going to be a special experience. Formerly a working farm, the Domaine now produces top quality *foie gras*, cured hams and other produce served at the communal dining table. Walks, pool.

Domaine de St-Géry, 46800 Lascabanes (Lot) **TEL** 05 65 31 82 51
FAX 05 65 22 92 89 **E-MAIL** duler@st-gery.com **WEBSITE** www.st-gery.com
FOOD breakfast, dinner **PRICE** €€; half-board obligatory **ROOMS** 5
CREDIT CARDS MC, V **CLOSED** Oct to May, except New Year

BORDEAUX AND THE DORDOGNE

CHATEAU DE GAMOT

M. AND MME BELLIERS, a Parisian couple, have opened their attractive summer residence, dating from the 16th century, as a charming bed-and-breakfast. Set on a 50-hectare wooded estate, there's a pool and private parking. Rooms are well appointed, but simple, with few creature comforts.

46130 Loubressac (Lot) **TEL** 05 65 38 58 50 **FOOD** breakfast **PRICE** (€) **ROOMS** 4
CREDIT CARDS not accepted **CLOSED** Nov to May

RELAIS SAINTE-ANNE

SET IN AN FORMER GIRL'S CONVENT SCHOOL marked only by a discreet sign. Inside the arched entrance is a delightfully shaded and flower-filled courtyard with specimen trees and neatly clipped box hedges. The same attention to detail is echoed in the attractive, thoughtfully equipped bedrooms. Good breakfasts.

rue de Pourtanel, 46600 Martel (Lot) **TEL** 05 65 37 40 56 **FAX** 05 65 37 42 82
E-MAIL Relais.Sainteanne@wanadoo.fr **WEBSITE** www.relais-ste-anne.com
FOOD breakfast **PRICE** (€)(€) **ROOMS** 15
CREDIT CARDS AE, DC, MC, V **CLOSED** mid-Nov to Apr

LA TERRASSE

ONCE A RESIDENCE of the bishops of Tulle, set high above the Dordogne with impressive views, this is a characterful family-run hotel, some of whose bedrooms are impressively large, with beamed ceilings. M. Liebus produces good regional food, served in the vaulted dining room or on the riverside terrace.

46200 Meyronne (Lot) **TEL** 05 65 32 21 60 **FAX** 05 65 32 26 93
E-MAIL terrasse.liebus@wanadoo.fr **WEBSITE** www.hotel-la-terrasse.com
FOOD breakfast, lunch, dinner **PRICE** (€) **ROOMS** 17
CREDIT CARDS AE, DC, MC, V **CLOSED** mid-Nov to mid-Mar

HOTEL DE FRANCE

A CLASSIC TWO-FIREPLACE Logis de France – an old flower-decked inn at the heart of a bustling market town, with a pretty and warmly inviting restaurant serving regional dishes with modern touches; outdoor dining in fine weather. Modest bedrooms which can accommodate families. Excellent value.

3 rue Marc Dufraisse, 24600 Ribérac (Dordogne) **TEL** 05 53 90 00 61 **FAX** 05 53
91 06 05 **E-MAIL** hdfr@club-internet.fr **FOOD** breakfast, lunch, dinner **PRICE** (€)
ROOMS 12 **CREDIT CARDS** MC, V **CLOSED** mid-Nov to mid-Dec; restaurant closed Tues
lunch, Sat lunch, Mon Sep-Jun

BORDEAUX AND THE DORDOGNE

LES VIEILLES TOURS

EVEN THE SMALLEST ROOMS in this beautifully restored stone building, dating from the 13th century and 17th century, are spacious and bright. The sitting-room is in a turret wing. Views across open countryside are uninterrupted. The proprietor's paintings (for sale) adorn the walls. Excellent cooking. Pool with valley vistas.

Lafage, 46500 Rocamadour (Lot) **TEL** 05 65 33 68 01 **FAX** 05 65 33 68 59
E-MAIL lesvieillestours@wanadoo.fr **WEBSITE** www.rocamadour.com/ fr/hotels/
VieillesTours **FOOD** breakfast, lunch (by arrangement), dinner **PRICE** €
ROOMS 17 **CREDIT CARDS** AE, DC, MC, V **CLOSED** mid-Nov to Apr

AUBERGE DU SOMBRAL

MADAME HAS BEEN KNOWN to give a cool reception, but there is much to like about this beautifully restored house in the heart of a lovely – but much visited – medieval village. Food and housekeeping are excellent. There's a small terrace. But there is no car parking within the town walls; heavy baggage is a problem.

St-Cirq-Lapopie, 46330 Cabrerets (Lot) **TEL** 05 65 31 26 08
FAX 05 65 30 26 37 **FOOD** breakfast, lunch, dinner **PRICE** € **ROOMS** 8
CREDIT CARDS DC, MC, V **CLOSED** mid-Nov to mid-Apr

L'ABBAYE

THIS UNPRETENTIOUS, friendly place has a captivating atmosphere. In the rustic, stone-flagged sitting room you can see the old pastry oven. The best bedrooms (first floor of annexe) are spacious and attractive, with antique French beds. Terrace, pool, car parking.

rue de l'Abbaye, 24220 St-Cyprien (Dordogne) **TEL** 05 53 29 20 48
FAX 05 53 29 15 85 **E-MAIL** hotel@abbaye-dordogne.com
WEBSITE www.abbaye-dordogne.com **FOOD** breakfast, dinner **PRICE** €€
ROOMS 23 **CREDIT CARDS** AE, MC, V **CLOSED** Oct to mid-Apr

HOSTELLERIE DE PLAISANCE

A NEWLY RENOVATED, creamy stone hotel in this immaculately preserved wine village.The setting is a little square with terrace and garden, and inside the china alone – all Limoges – makes this luxurious little place worthy of note. Smart bedrooms and bathrooms: glossy taps, fluffy towels, fresh freesias.
place du Clocher, 33330 St-Emilion (Gironde) **TEL** 05 57 55 07 55
FAX 05 57 74 41 11 **E-MAIL** hostelliere.plaisance@wanadoo.frt
WEBSITE www.saint.emilion.org **FOOD** breakfast, dinner **PRICE** €€ **ROOMS** 23
CREDIT CARDS AE, MC, V **CLOSED** Oct to mid-Apr

Bordeaux and the Dordogne

Hostellerie les Aiguillons

A LITTLE *LOGIS* BUILT IN 1993 on the ruins of a farmhouse set among the woods and fields of Périgord Blanc. Christophe Beeuwsaert is a dedicated patron and there are many tributes to him – and his cooking – in the visitors' book. Comfy rooms, large bathrooms; pool; breakfast on the terrace to the sound of birdsong. High standards, and tranquillity.

Le Beuil, 24320 St-Martial-Vivyrols (Dordogne) **TEL** 05 53 91 07 55 **FAX** 05 53 90 40 97 **E-MAIL** aiguillons@aol.com **WEBSITE** www.hostellerie.les.aiguillons.com **FOOD** breakfast, dinner **PRICE** € **ROOMS** 8 **CREDIT CARDS** MC, V **CLOSED** Dec to Apr

Au Rendez-Vous des Pecheurs

L OST DEEP IN THE WOODS along a particularly isolated stretch of the Dordogne, this fishing lodge serves up excellent fresh fish and *foie gras* in the surprisingly elegant dining room and offers inexpensive, comfortable rooms. Friendly welcome; car parking.

Pont du Chambon, 19320 St-Merd-de-Lapleau (Corrèze) **TEL** 05 55 27 88 39 **FAX** 05 55 27 83 19 **FOOD** breakfast, lunch, dinner **PRICE** € **ROOMS** 8 **CREDIT CARDS** MC, V **CLOSED** mid-Nov to mid-Feb; restaurant closed Fri dinner, Sat lunch

Hostellerie de Meysset

'S PLENDID ROOM, very good food, pleasant owners, good views,' runs a reader's report on this creeper-covered, typical Périgord country house. Its style is traditional and unpretentious, though not without floral excesses. The food leans towards traditional regional elements, too.

Route des Eyzies, 24299 Sarlat (Dordogne) **TEL** 05 53 59 08 29 **FAX** 05 53 28 47 61 **FOOD** breakfast, lunch, dinner **PRICE** € **ROOMS** 26 **CREDIT CARDS** AE, DC, MC, V **CLOSED** mid Oct to mid-Apr

Manoir de Rochecourbe

T HIS OLD FAVOURITE has passed from one generation of the Roger family to another. A round tower housing the staircase gives the house a touch of grandeur. Large bedrooms have beams and enormous fireplaces; many have a view of the nearby château. A swimming pool adds to its appeal.

24220 Vézac (Dordogne) **TEL** 05 53 31 09 84 **FAX** 05 53 28 59 07 **FOOD** breakfast **PRICE** €€ **ROOMS** 6 **CREDIT CARDS** AE, DC, MC, V **CLOSED** mid-Oct to May

THE SOUTH-WEST

TOWN INN, ARGELES-GAZOST

BEAU SITE

THREE MAJOR PLUSSES for this modest inn: value for money; delightful hosts; and the only hotel in our guide where fluent English, Italian and Burmese is spoken. Grand views from the fine terrace and delightful garden created by Mme Taik-Colpi. Best rooms, with *bateaux lits* and antique cupboards, overlook the valley.

10 rue Capitaine-Digoy, 65400 Argelès-Gazost (Hautes-Pyrénées) **TEL** 05 62 97 08 63 **FAX** 05 62 97 06 01 **E-MAIL** hotel.beausite@wanadoo.fr **WEBSITE** www.hotel-beausite-argeles.com **FOOD** breakfast, lunch, dinner **PRICE** ⑤ **ROOMS** 15 **CREDIT CARDS** DC, MC, V **CLOSED** Nov

TOWN GUESTHOUSE, BIARRITZ

MAISON GARNIER

CLOSE TO THE BEACHES, yet in an old part of the town which belongs to the locals, a neglected family hotel has been transformed into the pleasantest place to stay in Biarritz at a reasonable price. Here you will find everything you need and nothing you don't. Stylish public rooms; uncluttered, practical bedrooms and bathrooms.

29 rue Gambetta, 64200 Biarritz (Pyrénées-Atlantiques) **TEL** 05 59 01 60 70 **FAX** 05 59 01 60 80 **E-MAIL** maison-garnier@hotel-biarritz.com **WEBSITE** www.hotel-biarritz.com **FOOD** breakfast **PRICE** ⑤-⑤⑤ **ROOMS** 7 **CREDIT CARDS** AE, DC, MC, V **CLOSED** never

SPA TOWN HOTEL, CAUTERETS

LE LION D'OR

NOTHING SPECIAL OR FANCY, but a good-hearted establishment on the edge of this spa town which, in its heyday, attracted the good and the great, from Rabelais to Edward VII. Jolly decoration; bedrooms varying in size; bar/*salon* and terrace; *cuisine familiale*.

12 rue Richelieu, 1a avenue du Dr Domer, 65110 Cauterets (Hautes-Pyrénées) **TEL** 05 62 92 52 87 **FAX** 05 62 92 03 67 **E-MAIL** hotel.lion.dor@wanadoo.fr **WEBSITE** www.cauterets.com/ hotel-liondor **FOOD** breakfast, lunch, dinner **PRICE** ⑤ **ROOMS** 25 **CREDIT CARDS** AE, DC, MC, V **CLOSED** Oct to Dec

MEDIEVAL INN, CORDES

HOSTELLERIE DU VIEUX CORDES

A GENUINELY MEDIEVAL BUILDING in a popular 13thC fortified village, this comfortable hotel has a delightful open courtyard, shaded by a twisted wisteria. Bedrooms are modern and the quietest look out over open countryside. Part of the Yves Thuriès domain.

rue St-Michel, 81170 Cordes-sur-Ciel (Tarn) **TEL** 05 63 53 79 20 **FAX** 05 63 56 02 47 **E-MAIL** vieux.cordes@thuries.fr **WEBSITE** www.thuries.fr/hostellerie **FOOD** breakfast, lunch, dinner **PRICE** ⑤ **ROOMS** 21 **CREDIT CARDS** AE, MC, V **CLOSED** Jan

THE SOUTH-WEST

LA FERME AUX GRIVES

Michel Guerard runs no less than four establishments in this elegant little spa town: the triple Michelin star restaurant and hotel Les Prés d'Eugénie; the charming, luxurious Couvent aux Herbes; the more modestly priced Maison Rose; and this luxurious, characterful village *auberge*, with just four gorgeous rooms.

40320 Eugénie-les-Bains (Landes) **Tel** 05 58 05 05 06 **Fax** 05 58 51 10 10
E-mail guerard@relaischateaux.fr **Website** www.relaischateaux.guerard.com
Food breakfast, lunch, dinner **Price** ©©©©© **Rooms** 4
Credit cards AE, DC, MC, V **Closed** Jan

AUBERGE LES MYRTILLES

Some 19 km west of Foix, at an altitude of 1000 m, stands this timbered inn, near the road but blending naturally with the wooded landscape. In this wild setting you find a pool, Jacuzzi and sauna, plus a cluster of separate chalets. It's rustic, friendly, and immaculately kept. Good food by a fire in winter, terrace in summer.

Col des Marrous, 09000 Foix (Ariège) **Tel** 05 61 65 16 46 **Fax** 05 61 65 16 46
E-mail aubergelesmyrtilles@wanadoo.fr **Website** www.perso.wanadoo.fr/
auberge.les.myrtilles **Food** breakfast, lunch, dinner **Price** © **Rooms** 7
Credit cards MC, V **Closed** Nov to Jan

LES HUITRIERES DU LAC

Primarily a restaurant, specializing (as you might expect) in fish and seafood – though there are alternatives. The larger dining room and the best bedrooms share a view over the adjacent lake. Bedrooms are plain but spacious; some have balconies. Pleasant setting; value for money.

1187 avenue du Touring Club, 40150 Hossegor (Landes)
Tel 05 58 43 51 48 **Fax** 05 58 41 73 11 **E-mail** hotel.huitrieres @aol.com
Website www.thuries.fr/hostellerie **Food** breakfast, lunch, dinner **Price** ©
Rooms 21 **Credit cards** AE, MC, V **Closed** Jan

BIDEGAIN

An old family hotel, with many original features intact – Basque panelling and furnishing, moulded ceilings, period wallpaper, cobbled entrance – is now in the capable hands of Martine and Pierre Chilo from nearby Barcus (see page 55). Bedrooms have been updated and brightened; good, straightforward menus.

13 rue de la Navarre, 64130 Mauléon (Pyrénées-Atlantiques)
Tel 05 59 228 16 05 **Fax** 05 59 19 10 26 **E-mail** bidegain-hotel@wanadoo.fr.
Food breakfast, lunch, dinner **Price** © **Rooms** 20 **Credit cards** AE, DC, MC, V
Closed mid-Jan to Feb

THE SOUTH-WEST

TOWN HOTEL, MIREPOIX

LA MAISON DES CONSULS

MIREPOIX IS WONDERFULLY WELL PRESERVED (the original *bastide* was completed in 1304) and one of the finest surviving 15thC houses is this, decorated with carvings of heads and strange animals. The interior has been restored with care, and rooms are distinctive. Our favourite is Chambre du Marquis, overlooking the square and furnished in the style of Louis XV. Good breakfasts.

6 place Maréchal Leclerc, 09500 Mirepoix (Ariège) **TEL** 05 61 68 81 81
FAX 05 61 68 81 15 **E-MAIL** pyrene@afarvoyages.fr **FOOD** breakfast
PRICE €€ **ROOMS** 8 **CREDIT CARDS** AE, DC, MC, V **CLOSED** never

COUNTRY HOTEL, MONTFORT-EN-CHALOSSE

AUX TAUZINS

A SOLID *logis* in its third generation of family ownership, this is a very comfortable, pleasant hotel with white walls and green shutters and excellent views over the countryside. Rooms are bright and fair value for family use. Wisteria-shaded terrace and pool; good food (Michelin Bib Gourmand).

route d'Hagetmau, 40380 Montfort-en-Chalosse (Landes)
TEL 05 58 98 60 22 **FAX** 05 58 98 45 79 **FOOD** breakfast, lunch, dinner **PRICE** €
ROOMS 16 **CREDIT CARDS** MC, V **CLOSED** early to mid-Oct, Jan; restaurant closed Sun dinner Mon, except Jul, Aug

VILLAGE HOTEL, PLAISANCE

LE RIPA ALTA

A COMFORTABLE, UNFUSSY village hotel whose reputation rests on veteran owner Maurice Coscuella, who trained alongside Bocuse at Troisgros. Bedrooms are adequate (one with balcony) and quiet, except Saturday nights when the nearby disco is on.

3 place de l'Eglise, 32160 Plaisance (Gers) **TEL** 05 62 69 30 43
FAX 05 62 69 36 99 **E-MAIL** ripaalta@aol.com **FOOD** breakfast, lunch, dinner
PRICE € **ROOMS** 15 **CREDIT CARDS** AE, MC, V
CLOSED never; restaurant closed Mon in winter

FARMHOUSE HOTEL, PONT-DE-L'ARN

LA METAIRIE NEUVE

THE METAIRIE IS a tastefully renovated old farm with its heritage properly respected – exposed beams, stone walls, polished tiled floors – and a relaxed atmosphere. Mme Tournier is a charming hostess who keeps the antique-furnished public areas looking immaculate. Large grounds, covered terrace.

Pont-de-l'Arn, 81660 Mazamet (Tarn) **TEL** 05 63 97 73 50
FAX 05 63 61 94 75 **FOOD** breakfast, lunch, dinner **PRICE** €
ROOMS 14 **CREDIT CARDS** DC, MC, V **CLOSED** mid-Dec to mid-Jan; restaurant closed Sun

THE SOUTH-WEST

AUBERGE DES PINS

AN EXCELLENT EXAMPLE of unpretentious French hotelkeeping – a three-fireplace *logis*, which is being steadily improved, in a chalet-style building offering satisfactory accommodation and food in well-cared-for surroundings at moderate prices. The restaurant caters as much to locals as to travellers.

route de la Piscine, 40630 Sabres (Landes) **TEL** 05 58 08 30 00
FAX 05 58 07 56 74 **FOOD** breakfast, lunch, dinner **PRICE** €-€€ **ROOMS** 25
CREDIT CARDS AE, V **CLOSED** Jan -

EYCHENNE

'**D**ELIGHTFUL AND PROFESSIONAL,' comments our reporter on this sixth-generation, family-run hotel. Every year entails a new project, resulting in smart, richly decorated public rooms, very comfortable bedrooms, excellent food and wine, an attractive courtyard set with tables under pollarded trees, a swimming pool and children's play area.

8 avenue Paul-Laffont, 09200 St-Girons (Ariège) **TEL** 05 61 04 04 50
FAX 05 61 96 07 20 **FOOD** breakfast, lunch, dinner **PRICE** €-€€€ **ROOMS** 45
CREDIT CARDS AE, DC, MC, V **CLOSED** Dec to Feb

PARC VICTORIA

THE PREDOMINANT FEELING here is of space, light and colour, both inside and out. The park has neat lawns, formal flower beds and magnificent specimen trees, while the owner, M. Larralde, has filled the house with charming furnishings, including an elegant Napoleon III style *salon*. Lovely bedrooms; delightful restaurant.

5 rue Cepé, 64500 St Jean-de-Luz (Pyrénées-Atlantiques) **TEL** 05 59 26 78 78
FAX 05 59 26 78 08 **WEBSITE** www.relaischateaux.com/parcvictoria
FOOD breakfast, lunch, dinner; room service **PRICE** €€€€€ **ROOMS** 12
CREDIT CARDS AE, DC, MC, V **CLOSED** mid-Nov to mid-Mar

LES BAINS DE SECOURS

UNCOMPROMISINGLY RUSTIC *logis* – a renovated old farm with rustic wooden wall panelling, paved floors and no frills. Good country cuisine is served and complete peace and calm is assured. Nearby is a small private spa with sulphur springs and steam bath dating back to the 18th century.

64260 Sévignacq-Meyracq (Pyrénées-Atlantiques) **TEL** 05 59 05 62 11
FAX 05 59 05 76 56 **FOOD** breakfast, lunch, dinner **PRICE** € **ROOMS** 7
CREDIT CARDS AE, DC, MC, V **CLOSED** Jan; restaurant **CLOSED** Thur lunch, Sun dinner;
Mon Nov to Apr

THE SOUTH-WEST

COUNTRY VILLA, SOUSTONS

LA BERGERIE

MME CLAVIER HAS MADE her immaculate whitewashed house – built in southern single-storey style – a calm and civilized haven where the slow pace of life is infectious. The (obligatory) set dinner is based on whatever is fresh and good at the time. The bedrooms look on to satisfyingly neat gardens.

avenue du Lac, 40140 Soustons (Landes) **TEL** 05 58 41 11 43 **FAX** 05 58 41 21 61 **FOOD** breakfast, dinner **PRICE** € **ROOMS** 12 **CREDIT CARDS** DC, MC, V **CLOSED** Nov to Mar

TOWN HOTEL, TOULOUSE

BEAUX-ARTS

POSITIVE FEEDBACK from readers for this elegant listed 18thC building on the banks of the Garonne, close to the Ecole des Beaux-Arts. A hotel for over 100 years, it has been completely – and smartly – renovated. Car parking. At street level is the separately owned *Brasserie des Beaux-Arts*, a lively, very French, eating place.

1 place du Pont Neuf, 31000 Toulouse (Haute-Garonne) **TEL** 05 34 45 42 42 **FAX** 05 34 45 42 43 **E-MAIL** contact@hoteldesbeauxarts.com **FOOD** breakfast **PRICE** €€ **ROOMS** 19 **CREDIT CARDS** DC, MC, V **CLOSED** never

COUNTRY HOTEL, VALENCE-SUR-BAISE

LA FERME DE FLARAN

A DECENT PIT STOP on a convenient road for travellers. Typial farmhouse architecture; decoration executed with a smart touch. The farm once belonged to the community of Cistercians in the adjacent abbey, now a venue for concerts and art exhibitions. Busy, good-value restaurant; unpretentious bedrooms.

92310 Valence-sur-Baise (Gers) **TEL** 05 62 28 58 22 **FAX** 05 62 28 56 89 **E-MAIL** fermedeflaran@minitel.com **WEBSITE** www.gascogne.com /guide.hotels/fermeflaran.htm **FOOD** breakfast, lunch, dinner **PRICE** € **ROOMS** 15 **CREDIT CARDS** MC, V **CLOSED** mid-Nov to mid-Dec, Jan

MOUNTAIN VILLAGE HOTEL, VISCOS

LES CAMPANULES/LA GRANGE AUX MARMOTTES

TWO HOTELS, one simple, the other smarter, with a shared restaurant. Viscos is a delightful mountain village, and these make a wonderful base for nature lovers and ornithologists. Les Campanules was created out of an original sheepcote, and has preserved its charm; the Marmot Barn is a new, but strictly traditional, building. Mme Sénac is a caring hostess.

65120 Viscos (Hautes-Pyrénées) **TEL** 05 62 92 88 88 **FAX** 05 62 92 93 75 **FOOD** breakfast, lunch, dinner **PRICE** € **ROOMS** 15 **CREDIT CARDS** MC, V **CLOSED** mid-Nov to mid-Dec

LANGUEDOC-ROUSSILON

TOWN HOTEL, AIGUES-MORTES

LES ARCADES

IN THIS ARCHITECTURAL gem of a little town, a handsome listed 16thC house owned by the obliging Merquiol family offers beamed and chandeliered rooms over their restaurant. The original stone staircase leads up to marble fireplaces and gilt mirrors. A small terrace and pool have been added.

23 boulevard Gambetta, 30220 Aigues-Mortes (Gard) TEL 04 66 53 81 13 FAX 04 66 53 75 46 E-MAIL info@les-arcades.fr WEBSITE www.les-arcades.fr FOOD breakfast, lunch, dinner PRICE ⓔ-ⓔⓔ ROOMS 9 CREDIT CARDS AE, DC, MC, V CLOSED first 2 weeks Mar

TOWN HOTEL, AIGUES-MORTES

LES TEMPLIERS

THIS 17THC TOWN HOUSE in a peaceful corner of the old fortified town was rescued from ruin and lovingly restored to become this smart little hotel. Painted furniture and Provençal fabrics abound. Regional food is served in the restaurant. A pretty paved garden to the rear and a secure garage (there is a small daily charge) are additional perks.

23 rue de la République, 30220 Aigues-Mortes (Gard) TEL 04 66 53 66 56 FAX 04 66 53 69 61 FOOD breakfast; light meals PRICE ⓔⓔ ROOMS 11 CREDIT CARDS AE, DC, MC, V CLOSED Nov to Feb

SEASIDE HOTEL, ARGELES-SUR-MER

LE COTTAGE

THIS BRIGHT, MODERN holiday hotel, with a young, charming *patronne* is in a quiet, residential part of town, with views south towards the mountains and a large pool and garden. Very comfortable, with cheerful rooms and an excellent Mediterranean restaurant, L'Orangeraie. Substantial buffet breakfasts.

21 rue Arthur-Rimbaud, 66703 Argelès-sur-Mer (Pyrénées-Orientales) TEL 04 68 81 07 33 FAX 04 68 81 59 69 E-MAIL hotel.lecottage@wanadoo.fr WEBSITE www.hotel-lecottage.com FOOD breakfast, lunch, dinner PRICE ⓔⓔ ROOMS 34 CREDIT CARDS AE, MC, V CLOSED mid-Oct to Apr

COUNTRY HOUSE HOTEL, CARCASSONNE

LE DOMAINE D'AURIAC

A RELAXING COUNTRY house where the attractions are mainly outdoors: golf and tennis on the doorstep, a pool surrounded by beautifully manicured gardens, and a dining terrace with serene and verdant views. Comfortable inside, too. A Relais et Châteaux.

Route de St-Hilaire, 11009 Carcassonne (Aude) TEL 04 68 25 72 22 FAX 04 68 47 35 54 E-MAIL auriac@relaischateaux.fr WEBSITE www.relaischateaux.fr FOOD breakfast, lunch, dinner PRICE ⓔⓔⓔ-ⓔⓔⓔⓔ ROOMS 26 CREDIT CARDS AE, DC, MC, V CLOSED early Jan to early Feb; restaurant Sun dinner, Mon lunch, Mon dinner low season, Wed lunch and Fri lunch high season

LANGUEDOC-ROUSSILON

LE VIEUX CASTILLON

THIS IS A CONVENTIONAL, expensive Michelin-starred Relais et Châteaux, offering comfort and a surprise: it is a cluster of houses in a restored medieval village. A street runs through it. Sleep in a vaulted bedroom, and dine in a beamed restaurant across the bridge. Gardens and a pool.

rue Turion Sabatier, 30210 Castillon-du-Gard (Gard) **TEL** 04 66 37 61 61
FAX 04 66 37 28 17 **E-MAIL** vieux.castillon@wanadoo.fr **WEBSITE**
www.relaischateaux.fr/vieuxcastillon **FOOD** breakfast, lunch, dinner **PRICE**
€€€€ **ROOMS** 35 **CREDIT CARDS** AE, DC, MC, V **CLOSED** early Jan to late Feb

LA FERME DE LA SAUZETTE

GUESTS TO THIS old stone farmhouse near Carcassonne receive a warm welcome from British owners, Chris and Diana Gibson. Surrounded by vineyards, the five well-decorated and comfortable (no smoking) beamed bedrooms are above the old winery. Breakfast and dinner (both excellent) are taken house party-style round a single large table. Spacious grounds.

route de Villefloure, 11570 Cazilhac (Aude) **TEL** 04 68 79 81 32
FAX 04 68 79 65 99 **FOOD** breakfast, lunch, dinner **PRICE** € **ROOMS** 5 **CREDIT CARDS**
not accepted **CLOSED** Nov, Christmas to Feb

AUBERGE CEVENOLE

ALTHOUGH THE APPROACH through an industrialized valley is disagreeable, this small hotel has an above-average garden with a decent-sized (unheated) pool, fine views of the surrounding hills, and is a haven of peace and calm. Bedrooms, many decorated with *toile de Jouy* wallpaper, and bathrooms range from adequate to very comfortable.

La Favède, 30110 Les-Salles-du-Gardon (Gard) **TEL** 04 66 34 12 13
FAX 04 66 34 50 50 **FOOD** breakfast, lunch, dinner **PRICE** €-€€ **ROOMS** 19
CREDIT CARDS MC, V **CLOSED** mid-Oct to Mar

CHATEAU DE FLOURE

THE CHARMING ASSOUS run this handsome manor house built on the remains of a 12thC abbey in an engagingly friendly style. The informal atmosphere, large rooms and extensive grounds, including a swimming pool, make it a popular choice with families.

1 allée Gaston Bonheur, 11800 Floure (Aude) **TEL** 04 68 79 11 29 **FAX** 04 68 79 04
61 **E-MAIL** contact@chateau_de_floure.com **WEBSITE** www.chateau_de_floure.com
FOOD breakfast, lunch, dinner **PRICE** €€ **ROOMS** 17 **CREDIT CARDS** AE, DC, MC, V
CLOSED Nov to mid-Dec, mid-Jan to Apr; restaurant Nov to mid-Mar

Languedoc-Roussilon

Auberge Atalaya

Iℕ UNSPOILED mountain country, the Atalaya has been ingeniously built from the ruins of a stone *mas*, entirely in harmony with its craggy surroundings. Inside, antiques and tasteful fabrics give the natural feel of a home, with a distinguished cultured atmosphere that emanates from the personality and taste of the owner, Mme Toussaint. There has been criticism of some staff; reports please.

66800 Llo (Pyrénées-Orientales) **Tel** 04 68 04 70 04 **Fax** 04 68 04 01 29
Food breakfast, lunch, dinner **Price** €€€€ **Rooms** 13 **Credit cards** MC, V
Closed mid-Jan to Easter, early Nov to late Dec

Le Guilhem

Tᴜᴄᴋᴇᴅ ᴀᴡᴀʏ in the heart of the old city, a stone's throw from the cathedral (the bells don't ring at night), this delightful B&B occupies a fine 16thC building. Most of the bedrooms overlook the peaceful garden, and are simply but attractively decorated: painted white with colourful fabrics and antique furniture. There is a lovely balustraded terrace where summer breakfasts are served.

18 rue Jean-Jacques Rousseau, 34000 Montpellier (Hérault) **Tel** 04 67 52 90 90
Fax 04 67 60 67 67 **Food** breakfast; brunch **Price** €€€€ **Rooms** 33
Credit cards AE, DC, MC, V **Closed** never

Ostaria Cardabela

Tʜɪs ᴇʟᴇɢᴀɴᴛ ʜᴏᴛᴇʟ has been added as another string to the bow of the Mimosa, a superb restaurant down the road at St-Guiraud (tel 04 67 96 67 96), where Bridget Pugh, a former ballerina, pursues her present career as a top-flight *cuisinière*. The bedrooms are large and stylish, and there is a kitchen for guests to use.

10 place Fontaine, 34725 St-Saturnin-de-Lucian (Hérault) **Tel** 04 67 88 62 62
Fax 04 67 88 62 82 **Food** breakfast; lunch and dinner (at Mimosa)
Price €€-€€€€ **Rooms** 7 **Credit cards** DC, MC, V **Closed** late Oct to mid-Mar;
restaurant Mon, Sep to Jun Sun dinner

Demeures du Ranquet

Tʜᴇ ᴍᴀɪɴ ʙᴜɪʟᴅɪɴɢ is a long, low, well-restored farmhouse, principally devoted to the restaurant, with the comfortable bedrooms in chalets scattered amongst pines and scrub oak on a slope above the swimming pool. The *cuisine* is a real treat: inventive, original and fresh, and supported by an excellent wine list.

route St-Hippolyte-du-Fort, Tornac, 30140 Anduze (Gard) **Tel** 04 66 77 51 63
Fax 04 66 77 55 62 **e-mail** ranquet@mnet.fr **Food** breakfast, lunch, dinner
Price €€€-€€€€ **Rooms** 10 **Credit cards** DC, MC, V **Closed** Oct to Apr;
restaurant mid-Sep to mid-Jun Tue dinner and Wed

AUVERGNE & MASSIF CENTRAL

COUNTRY HOUSE HOTEL, BOISSET

AUBERGE DE CONCASTY

WITH ROOMS NAMED after wild flowers and the cattle of *le patron* in the pasture, this remote, pretty *auberge* radiates country charm. Madame (Martine Causse) cooks unpretentious Franco-Auvergnat dishes. Improvements include a gym, sauna, whirlpool bath and swimming pool. Set in splendid hiking country.

15600 Boisset (Cantal) **TEL** 04 71 62 21 16 **FAX** 04 71 62 22 22
E-MAIL info@auberge-concasty.com **WEBSITE** www.auberge-concasty.com **FOOD** breakfast, lunch, dinner **PRICE** € **ROOMS** 15 **CREDIT CARDS** AE, DC, MC, V **CLOSED** mid-Nov to Dec, Jan

RIVERSIDE HOTEL, COULANDON

LE CHALET

IN THE SECLUDED, wooded garden surrounding this traditional hotel, there is a large fish pond which is perfect for strolling around, drink in hand, before dinner. Bedrooms are in the chalet-style main building and in converted outbuildings. They vary in style and size; none is notably stylish, but the best are cheerfully comfortable with exposed beams and bright wallpaper.

03000 Coulandon (Allier) **TEL** 04 70 44 50 08 **FAX** 04 70 44 07 09
E-MAIL hotelchalet@cs3i.fr **FOOD** breakfast, lunch, dinner **PRICE** € **ROOMS** 28 **CREDIT CARDS** AE, DC, MC, V **CLOSED** mid-Dec to Feb

CHATEAU HOTEL, LA MALENE

CHATEAU DE LA CAZE

THIS 15THC CASTLE, complete with turrets, massive doors and a dramatic position above the Tarn, is just as impressive inside, where tapestries decorate vast frescoed and vaulted rooms. The friendly owners, the Lecroqs, ensure that it is anything but intimidating.

route des Gorges du Tarn, 48210 La Malène (Lozère) **TEL** 04 66 48 51 01 **FAX** 04 66 48 55 75 **E-MAIL** chateau.de.la.caze@wanadoo.fr
WEBSITE www.chateauxhotels.com/lacaze **FOOD** breakfast, lunch, dinner **PRICE** €€€ **ROOMS** 19 **CREDIT CARDS** AE, DC, MC, V **CLOSED** mid-Nov to mid-Mar; restaurant Wed, Thur lunch low season

VILLAGE INN, MONTSALVY

L'AUBERGE FLEURIE

THE TWO ATTRACTIVE DINING ROOMS – polished wood dressers, gleaming copper, red-check tablecloths – are the focal point of this delightful creeper-covered *auberge*. Newly decorated, the bedrooms have a fresh, contemporary look, but face on to a main road. Half the hotel is taken up by a busy *café tabac*.

place du Barry, 15120 Montsalvy (Cantal) **TEL** 04 71 49 20 02 **E-MAIL** info@auberge-fleurie.com **WEBSITE** www.auberge-fleurie.com **FOOD** breakfast, lunch, dinner **PRICE** € **ROOMS** 11 **CREDIT CARDS** AE, DC, MC, V **CLOSED** never; restaurant mid-Jan to mid-Feb

Auvergne & Massif Central

Hostellerie de la Maronne

WITH ITS POOL and tennis court surrounded by lovely gardens and sweeping country, this elegantly furnished 19thC *hostellerie* makes a fine retreat. There have been many improvements since Alain de Cock took over, including revamped bedrooms and a smart new dining room. Food is taken seriously with 'excellent' results.

Le Theil, 15140 St-Martin-Valmeroux (Cantal) **TEL** 04 71 69 20 33
FAX 04 71 69 28 22 **E-MAIL** hotelmaronne@cfi15.fr
WEBSITE www.cfi15.fr/hotelmaronne **FOOD** breakfast, lunch, dinner **PRICE** €€
ROOMS 21 **CREDIT CARDS** AE, DC, MC, V **CLOSED** Nov to Mar

Carayon

THE CARAYONS HAVE BECOME almost too successful for our guide – their hotel now has 60 bedrooms and a terrace to take 250 covers. But the professionalism and quality remain the same. Excellent food from Pierre Carayon's kitchen, and despite outdoor and indoor pools, tennis, sauna and gym, prices represent good value.

place du Fort, 12380 St-Sernin-sur-Rance (Aveyron) **Tel** 05 65 98 19 19
Fax 05 65 99 69 26 **e-mail** carayon.hotel@wanadoo.fr **website** www.hotel-caray-on.com
Food breakfast, lunch, dinner **Price** € **Rooms** 60 **Credit cards** AE, DC, MC, V
Closed 4 weeks in Nov

Hostellerie Placide

IN A SLEEPY VILLAGE in the lush Velay region, this former post house has been in the Placide family for four generations. Pierre-Marie and Véronique are currently in charge. He is a first-class chef who has raised the reputation of the restaurant. The decoration is traditional; leather furniture complementing beams and panelling.

1 route d'Annonay, 43190 Tence (Haute-Loire) **TEL** 04 71 59 82 76 **FAX** 04 71 65 44 46 **E-MAIL** placide@hostellerie-placide.fr **WEBSITE** www.hostellerie-placide.com
FOOD breakfast, lunch, dinner **PRICE** €€€ **ROOMS** 13 **CREDIT CARDS** AE, MC, V
CLOSED mid-Nov to mid-Mar, Mon and Tue Oct to May

Chateau de Trancis

THIS ORIGINALLY quite ordinary Auvergnat *maison de maître*. was transformed a century ago into an Italian Renaissance château, bristling with turrets. Its former English owners brought great panache to the decoration, with plenty of gilded mirrors, ornate chandeliers and a grand Louis XIV *salon*. It is now run by a Dutch couple, the van Beymas, who have won awards for their food.

15210 Ydes (Cantal) **TEL** 04 71 40 60 40 **FAX** 04 71 40 62 13
E-MAIL trancis@wanadoo.fr **WEBSITE** www.trancis.com **FOOD** breakfast, dinner
PRICE €€€ **ROOMS** 9 **CREDIT CARDS** AE, MC, V **CLOSED** Jan; restaurant Tue

PROVENCE-COTE D'AZUR

LE PIGONNET

IF YOU'RE LUCKY, your room might have a view of Mont Ste-Victoire, made famous by Cézanne. If not, there are wonderful paintings by local artists throughout this pretty villa. It stands in a park, is decorated like a home, and run by the charming Swellen family.

5 avenue Pigonnet, 13090 Aix-en-Provence (Bouches-du-Rhône)
TEL 04 42 59 02 90 **FAX** 04 42 59 47 77 **E-MAIL** reservation@hotelpigonnet.com
WEBSITE www.hotelpigonnet.com **FOOD** breakfast, lunch, dinner **PRICE** €€€€
ROOMS 52 **CREDIT CARDS** AE, DC, MC, V **CLOSED** never; restaurant lunch Sat and Sun

HOTEL DES QUATRE DAUPHINS

THERE ARE STILL some original features in this simple, charming *maison bourgeoise*, such as the lovely tiled terracotta floors. It is decorated in a plain and pleasing style: walls are painted in pastel shades; bedspreads and curtains are Provençal prints; the furniture is antique – handsome big mirrors, little tables – or painted wood. Perfect for visiting Aix on a budget.

54 rue Roux Alphéron, 13100 Aix-en-Provence (Bouches-du-Rhône)
TEL 04 42 38 16 39 **FAX** 04 42 38 60 19 **FOOD** breakfast **PRICE** € **ROOMS** 13
CREDIT CARDS DC, MC, V **CLOSED** never

LES GERANIUMS

AT THE ENTRANCE to a small, medieval village, M. Roux's ever-expanding hotel has rather boring, uniform bedrooms – some in a block over the road – but continues to bring in compliments from readers. Large terrace; locked parking. Often busy with functions and groups.

84330 Le Barroux (Vaucluse) **TEL** 04 90 62 41 08 **FAX** 04 90 62 56 48
FOOD breakfast, lunch, dinner **PRICE** € **ROOMS** 22 **CREDIT CARDS** AE, DC, MC, V
CLOSED mid-Nov to Apr

AUBERGE DE LA BENVENGUDO

THE BEAUPIED FAMILY'S creeper-clad hotel just outside the village has the style of a private country house: cosy beamed sitting room, intimate dining room, and delightful garden. Young Bocuse-trained chef Sebastien has come home to manage the hotel for his parents – and, of course, to cook. Affordable prices.

Vallon de l'Arcoule, 13520 Les Baux-de-Provence (Bouches-du-Rhône)
TEL 04 90 54 32 54 **FAX** 04 90 54 42 58 **FOOD** breakfast, lunch, dinner
PRICE €€-€€€ **ROOMS** 20 **CREDIT CARDS** AE, MC, V **CLOSED** Nov to early Mar;
restaurant Sun and Mon Oct to Jun

PROVENCE-COTE D'AZUR

COUNTRY HOTEL, LES BAUX-DE-PROVENCE

MAS D'AIGRET

THE APPEAL of this simple hotel just below the vertiginous village lies in its secluded enclosed pool and tranquil surrounding gardens, a world away from the tourist hub. Go for one of the special bedrooms: No. 16 has a private terrace and bathroom incorporating the rock face into which the *mas* has been built.

13520 Les Baux-de-Provence (Bouches-du-Rhône) TEL 04 90 54 20 00
FAX 04 90 54 44 00 E-MAIL masdaigret@aol.com WEBSITE www.masdaigret.com
FOOD breakfast, lunch, dinner PRICE ©©© ROOMS 17 CREDIT CARDS MC, V
CLOSED 2 weeks Jan

RIVERSIDE HOTEL, CALLAS

HOSTELLERIE LES GORGES DE PENNAFORT

AT NIGHT, the lights of this elegant one-Michelin-star hotel illuminate the dramatic crags of the Pennafort gorges; there's a constant sound of running water. Chef Philippe da Silva is meticulous about the quality of his ingredients. Specialities include *carré d'agneau* and *langoustine*. Bedrooms are modern and luxurious.

83830 Callas (Var) TEL 04 94 76 66 51 FAX 04 94 76 67 23 FOOD breakfast, lunch,
dinner PRICE ©©© ROOMS 16 CREDIT CARDS AE, MC CLOSED mid-Jan to mid-
Mar; restaurant Mon lunch, Mon dinner Sep to Jun, Sun dinner in low season

TOWN HOTEL, CAP D'ANTIBES

LA GARDIOLE

COMPLETELY RENOVATED in 1999, in Provençal style, this modest, pink-washed small hotel in one of the famous 'jet set' Riviera resorts has a charming terrace, bargain prices for the area, and a friendly feel. Some rooms have their own little terraces. Parking is on the street outside. It is now affiliated to the Hôtel Garoupe, down the road at No. 60 (tel 04 92 93 33 33).

74 chemin de la Garoupe, 06160 Cap d'Antibes (Alpes Maritimes)
TEL 04 93 61 35 03 FAX 04 93 67 61 87 FOOD breakfast, lunch, dinner PRICE ©©
ROOMS 17 CREDIT CARDS AE, MC, V CLOSED Nov to Apr

COUNTRY HOTEL, EYGALIERES

LA BASTIDE

WHAT MAKES THIS TYPICAL blue-shuttered Provençal *bastide* special is its remarkable garden. Cross the cavernous marble hall to a profusion of flowers, olive trees, lavender, rosemary and thyme at the back. Nestled among the shrubs is a glorious curved swimming pool, surrounded by sun loungers and parasols. Although technically a B&B, light lunches can be served by the pool on request.

chemin de Pestelade, 13810 Eygalières (Bouches-du-Rhône) TEL 04 90 95 90 06
FAX 04 90 95 99 77 FOOD breakfast; light lunch May to Sep PRICE © ROOMS 12
CREDIT CARDS MC, V CLOSED Jan

PROVENCE-COTE D'AZUR

MAS DE LA BRUNE

IT'S A PRIVILEGE to stay in this *monument historique*, a rare example of a Renaissance mansion in the country rather than a town. Here you will find luxury accommodation with plenty of character. The owners are charming; bedrooms are decorated in perfect country house taste; and the atmosphere is one of calm privacy.

13810 Eygalières (Bouches-du-Rhône) **TEL** 04 90 90 67 67 **FAX** 04 90 95 99 21
E-MAIL MasBrune@Francemarket.com **WEBSITE** www.Francemarket.com/brune/
FOOD breakfast **PRICE** €€€€ **ROOMS** 10 **CREDIT CARDS** MC, V
CLOSED Nov to Jan

CHATEAU EZA

WHEN THE AMERICAN Giles took over this hotel, once the private home of Prince William of Sweden, they redecorated from top to toe, with a medieval look in mind, which can be a little kitsch. Some of the rooms have private terraces and four-posters, all have views, antiques and wood-burning stoves. Fabulous food.

rue de la Pise, 06360 Eze (Alpes-Maritimes) **TEL** 04 93 41 12 24
FAX 04 93 41 16 64 **E-MAIL** chateza@webstore.com **WEBSITE** www.slh.com/chateza
FOOD breakfast, lunch, dinner; room service **PRICE** €€€€€ **ROOMS** 10
CREDIT CARDS AE, DC, MC, V **CLOSED** Nov to Apr

LA VIEILLE BASTIDE

SINCE A DYNAMIC, young husband-and-wife team came from Paris a few years ago to take over this old *bastide*, there has been a new spirit about the place. Mme d'Aubreby's chic blue and yellow dining room and simple country-style bedrooms set the tone. There's a large terrace and a pool. Prices remain very reasonable.

83780 Flayosc (Var) **TEL** 04 98 10 62 62 **FAX** 04 94 84 61 23
E-MAIL lavieillebastide@provence-verdon.com **WEBSITE** www.provence-verdon.com
FOOD breakfast, lunch, dinner **PRICE** € **ROOMS** 7 **CREDIT CARDS** MC, V **CLOSED** never;
restaurant last 3 weeks Jan, Sun dinner, Mon

LA REGALIDO

THIS CONVERTED 19THC oil mill manages to remain informal and friendly despite its elegant furnishings, pricey boutique and high rates – largely thanks to the presence of the welcoming chef-proprietor Jean-Pierre Michel. Excellent food. Pretty, flowery garden.

rue Frédéric-Mistral, 13990 Fontvieille (Bouches-du-Rhône) **TEL** 04 90 54 60 22
FAX 04 90 54 64 29 **E-MAIL** regalido@avignon.pacwan.net
WEBSITE www.relaischateaux.fr/ regalido **FOOD** breakfast, lunch, dinner
PRICE €€€€ **ROOMS** 15 **CREDIT CARDS** AE, DC, MC, V
CLOSED Jan to mid-Feb; restaurant Mon, Tue, Sat lunch

PROVENCE-COTE D'AZUR

AUBERGE CHAREMBEAU

THE BERGERS' 18THC FARMHOUSE, set among fields and trees, has been attractively adapted to retain its original character and provide modern amenities. Bedrooms are in the old stables; the attics are suites. A drystone wall surrounds the pool, and free-range hens supply eggs for breakfast. Some rooms have small kitchens.

route de Niozelles, 04300 Forcalquier (Alpes-de-Haute-Provence)
TEL 04 92 70 91 70 **FAX** 04 92 70 91 83 **E-MAIL** contact@charembeau.com
WEBSITE www.provenceweb.fr/ 04/charembeau **FOOD** breakfast, light lunch
PRICE €€ **ROOMS** 23 **CREDIT CARDS** AE, MC, V **CLOSED** Dec to Feb

LA FERME DE LA HUPPE

'LOVED THE SCALE of this dear little group of converted farm buildings' wrote one of our readers. Reception was the cartshed; bedrooms are in the stables. Classical music plays at dinner in the dining room decorated with farm implements. Bedrooms are similarly rustic. Swimming pool.

RD156, Les Porquiers, 84220 Gordes (Vaucluse) **TEL** 04 90 72 12 25
FAX 04 90 72 01 83 **E-MAIL** gerald.konings@wanadoo.fr
WEBSITE www.laprovence.com/lahuppe **FOOD** breakfast, dinner **PRICE** €€
ROOMS 9 **CREDIT CARDS** MC, V **CLOSED** Nov to Apr

LE GORDOS

NO RESTAURANT, but few other drawbacks to this *mas de pierre sèche*, just outside Gordes – especially if the Provençal sun shines. Most of the rooms are in outbuildings opening on to some part of the garden. Tennis, and an attractive, small pool. 'Very good' service.

route de Cavaillon, 84220 Gordes (Vaucluse) **TEL** 04 90 72 00 75
FAX 04 90 72 07 00 **E-MAIL** hotellegordos@pacwan.fr
WEBSITE www.provenceguide.com **FOOD** breakfast, snacks **PRICE** €€€-€€€€
ROOMS 19 Credit cards AE, MC, V **Closed** Nov to mid-Mar

LES ROMARINS

BRISKLY RUN by Mme Charles, this is a spotless, old-fashioned breakfast-only hotel with polished tiled floors and a spectacular view from the terrace, and the wide, bay windows, of the terracotta roofs and ochre walls of the pretty – and much visited – village of Gordes. Swimming pool and secure parking are bonuses.

route de Sénanque, 84220 Gordes (Vaucluse) **TEL** 04 90 72 12 13
FAX 04 90 72 13 13 **FOOD** breakfast **PRICE** €€ **ROOMS** 10 **CREDIT CARDS** AE, MC, V
CLOSED mid-Dec to mid-Feb

PROVENCE-COTE D'AZUR

COUNTRY HOTEL, GRIMAUD

LA BOULANGERIE

IN A SECLUDED pale-pink house – approached up a steep drive – with quiet garden and lovely swimming pool, this small hotel has country-style furniture, modern paintings and is comfortable, if somewhat cluttered. Lunch is served by the pool, with views of the distant hills. Mme Piget is most welcoming.

route de Collobrières, 83310 Grimaud (Var) **TEL** 04 94 43 23 16
FAX 04 94 43 38 27 **FOOD** breakfast, lunch **PRICE** €€ **ROOMS** 11
CREDIT CARDS AE, MC, V **CLOSED** mid-Oct to Easter

COUNTRY HOTEL, GRIMAUD

LE VERGER

A VERY UNPRETENTIOUS, relaxed, informal and quiet hotel in a typically Provençal building, Le Verger is a haven of peace and green, with smooth lawns, mature walnut trees and hydrangeas. Inside, the decoration is simple: white walls, local fabrics, antique country furniture and big beds. Anne Zachary is a delightful hostess; her husband is an experienced chef with quite a following.

route de Collobrières, 83310 Grimaud (Var) **TEL** 04 94 43 25 93
FAX 04 94 43 33 92 **FOOD** breakfast, lunch, dinner **PRICE** €€-€€€ **ROOMS** 9
CREDIT CARDS DC, MC, V **CLOSED** Nov to Easter

MEDIEVAL INN, HAUT-DE-CAGNES

LE CAGNARD

S ENSITIVELY CONVERTED from a series of medieval houses, most with separate street entrances, Le Cagnard has a dining room with an elaborately painted ceiling which slides away at the touch of a button, Michelin-starred food and stylish bedrooms.

rue Pontis-Long, Haut-de-Cagnes, 06800 Cagnes-sur-Mer (Alpes-Maritimes)
TEL 04 93 20 73 21 **FAX** 04 93 22 06 39 **E-MAIL** cagnard@relaischateaux.com
WEBSITE www.le-cagnard.com **FOOD** breakfast, lunch, dinner; room service
PRICE €€€€ **ROOMS** 25 **CREDIT CARDS** AE, DC, MC, V **CLOSED** never; restaurant
Thur lunch and Nov to mid-Dec

COUNTRY HOTEL, ISLE-SUR-LA-SORGUE

MAS DE CURE BOURSE

T HE CHIEF ATTRACTIONS of this 18thC *relais de poste* are the setting – in a big garden with orchards beyond – and the outstanding food. The kitchen's reputation, established under the previous owner, has continued to grow since Nadine and Jean-Noël Pomarède took over the hotel. Rooms are twee but comfortable. Pool.

route de Caumont-sur-Durance, 84800 Isle-sur-la-Sorgue (Vaucluse) **TEL** 04 90
38 16 58 **FAX** 04 90 38 52 31 **FOOD** breakfast, lunch, dinner **PRICE** €€
ROOMS 13 **CREDIT CARDS** MC, V **CLOSED** never; restaurant Mon, Tue

PROVENCE-COTE D'AZUR

SEASIDE HOTEL, LE LAVANDOU

AUBERGE DE LA CALANQUE

THIS ARCADED HOTEL overlooking the marina of Le Lavandou comes strongly recommended by a reader, despite its size – not only for the 'fantastic' sea view but also for the 'very comfortable, airy' rooms and 'very helpful' manager. L'Algue Bleue restaurant is in the hotel, and there are plenty of others nearby.

62 avenue du Général de Gaulle, 83980 Le Lavandou (Var) **TEL** 04 94 71 05 96
FAX 04 94 71 20 12 **FOOD** breakfast, lunch, dinner **PRICE** €€€ **ROOMS** 32
CREDIT CARDS AE, DC, MC, V **CLOSED** Nov to Apr

RESTAURANT-WITH-ROOMS, LOURMARIN

AUBERGE LA FENIERE

IF YOU FANCY A GOURMET dinner and a bed on the premises in the Luberon we would recommend this Michelin-starred restaurant, where the chef is a talented, self-taught and charming lady, Reine Sammut. Bedrooms, with little terraces, overlooking the inviting pool, are smart-modern if a little anodyne.

route de Cadenet, 84160 Lourmarin (Vaucluse) **TEL** 04 90 68 11 79
FAX 04 90 68 18 60 **E-MAIL** Reine@wanadoo.fr **website** www.tabledereine.com
FOOD breakfast, lunch, dinner **PRICE** €€€ **ROOMS** 9 **CREDIT CARDS** AE, DC, MC, V
CLOSED mid-Nov to Feb

VILLAGE HOTEL, MAUSSANE-LES-ALPILLES

L'OUSTALOUN

WE INCLUDE THIS traditional *auberge* as an antidote to the more expensive places around Les Baux. Once part of a 16thC abbey, it is right on the main square, and in summer puts its tables out under the plane trees beside the charming fountain. Rooms are simple with rough white-painted walls and smart bedcovers.

place de l'Eglise, 13520 Maussane-les-Alpilles (Bouches-du-Rhône)
TEL 04 90 54 32 19 **FAX** 04 90 54 45 58 **FOOD** breakfast, lunch, dinner **PRICE** €
ROOMS 8 **CREDIT CARDS** AE, MC, V **CLOSED** 3 weeks Nov, 3 weeks Feb; restaurant
Wed dinner, Thur lunch

COUNTRY HOTEL, MENERBES

LA BASTIDE DE MARIE

THIS VERY SMART, comfortable hotel is also very mannered and *Côte Sud* in style. The bedrooms of the old *mas* are now photo-shoot perfect in shades of grey and cream. However, the food is faultless; staff are friendly; and the all-inclusive price is not bad value at all.

route de Bonnieux, Quartier de la Verrerie, 84560 Ménerbes (Vaucluse)
TEL 04 90 72 30 20 **FAX** 04 90 72 54 20 **E-MAIL** Bastide@c-h-m.com
WEBSITE www.c-h-m.com **FOOD** breakfast, lunch, dinner; room service **PRICE**
€€€€ **ROOMS** 14 **CREDIT CARDS** AE, DC, MC, V **CLOSED** mid-Nov to mid-Mar

PROVENCE-COTE D'AZUR

MOUNTAIN HOTEL, LES MOLANES

AUBERGE DU CLOS SOREL

MME MERCIER GIVES a warm welcome at her old stone converted farmhouse in a little mountain village of wooden chalets, with spectacular views, pure, fresh air, and every comfort. Swimming pool; log fires; terrace; mountain walks and *pistes* on the doorstep. Dinner by candlelight.

Les Molanès, 04400 Pra-Loup (Alpes-de-Haute-Provence) TEL 04 92 84 10 74
FAX 04 92 84 09 14 E-MAIL info@seolan.com WEBSITE www.seolan.com/clos-sorel
FOOD breakfast, lunch, dinner PRICE ©©-©©©© ROOMS 11 CREDIT CARDS MC, V
CLOSED Sep to mid-Dec, mid-Apr to late Jun

RESTAURANT-WITH-ROOMS, MONDRAGON

LA BEAUGRAVIERE

A SPECIALIST IN TRUFFLES, Guy Jullien cooks memorable meals, served on a shady terrace in summer or in the dining room decorated with illustrations of vine species. His cellar boasts an excellent selection of Côtes du Rhône. Modest, clean rooms upstairs are double-glazed to keep out road noise. For more about the restaurant, see page 203.

RN7, 84430 Mondragon (Vaucluse) TEL 04 90 40 82 54 FAX 04 90 40 91 01
FOOD breakfast, lunch, dinner PRICE © ROOMS 3 CREDIT CARDS MC, V
CLOSED last 2 weeks Sep; restaurant Sun dinner, Mon

SUBURBAN VILLA, MONTFAVET

LES FRENES

THE FOUR-STAR Relais et Châteaux family-run Les Frênes looks like an iced cake, with pale-pink walls and pale-green shutters. Set in a neat park, its rooms are luxuriously furnished and chef Antoine Biancone's tempting dishes are served on Limoges china. Set in parkland with a handsome swimming pool.

avenue Vertes Rives, 84140 Montfavet (Vaucluse) TEL 04 90 31 17 93
FAX 04 90 23 95 03 E-MAIL contact@hostellerie-les-frenes WEBSITE
www.relaischateaux.fr/lesfrenes FOOD breakfast, lunch, dinner PRICE
©©©©© ROOMS 19 CREDIT CARDS AE, DC, MC, V CLOSED Nov to late Mar

COUNTRY MANOR HOUSE, MOUGINS

MANOIR DE L'ETANG

'THE OVERALL FEEL to this place', writes our inspector, 'is expensive and discreet'. The comfortable and extremely pretty, vine-clad, white-shuttered manor house has a large, beautiful garden – and lily-filled pond. It is a quiet, orderly, elegant retreat from the bustle of fashionable Mougins. The decoration is fresh and colourful and rooms are furnished with country pieces. Pool and terrace.

66 allée du Manoir, 06250 Mougins (Alpes-Maritimes) TEL 04 93 90 01 07
FAX 04 92 92 20 70 FOOD breakfast, lunch, dinner PRICE ©©©© ROOMS 21 CREDIT
CARDS AE, DC, MC, V CLOSED Nov to Mar

PROVENCE-COTE D'AZUR

CONVERTED FARMHOUSE, MOUGINS

LE MAS CANDILLE

THIS 18THC FARMHOUSE near fashionable Mougins has been a hotel for the past 30 years. It's a solid building the colour of honey, with wrought-iron balconies and heavy shutters. Inside, the decoration is elegantly rustic: terracotta floors, white walls, low ceilings and heavy oak beams. Superb views towards Grasse. Expensive.

boulevard Rebuffel, 06250 Mougins (Alpes-Maritimes) TEL 04 92 28 43 43
FAX 04 92 28 43 40 E-MAIL candille@chateauxhotels.com
WEBSITE www.chateauxhotels.com/candille Food breakfast, lunch, dinner
PRICE €€€€€ ROOMS 23 CREDIT CARDS AE, DC, MC, V CLOSED never

CONVERTED FARMHOUSE, MOUGINS

HOTEL DE MOUGINS

HERE IS A FOUR-STAR HOTEL with all the usual trappings plus a gloriously peaceful and scented Mediterranean garden of mimosa, lavender, rosemary and fig trees, and a courteous, caring staff. The bright bedrooms have large windows, balconies and excellent bathrooms. There's a romantic terrace for summer dining.

205 avenue du Golf, 06250 Mougins (Alpes-Maritimes) TEL 04 92 92 17 07
FAX 04 92 92 17 08 E-MAIL info@hotel-de-mougins.com
WEBSITE www.hotel-de-mougins.com Food breakfast, lunch, dinner PRICE FFFF
Rooms 51 CREDIT CARDS AE, DC, MC, V Closed never; restaurant late Nov to late Dec

COUNTRY HOTEL, MOUSTIERS-STE-MARIE

AUBERGE DE LA FERME ROSE

BASIC BEDROOMS are on the top floor of this small isolated hotel at the end of a rough track outside the pretty village of Moustiers. Downstairs reflects the owner's retro taste: a 1950s juke-box, the bar from the old Brasserie Noailles in Marseilles.

04360 Moustiers-Ste-Marie (Alpes-de-Haute-Provence) TEL 04 92 74 69 47
FAX 04 92 74 60 76 Food breakfast PRICE € ROOMS 6 Credit cards MC, V
CLOSED mid-Nov to mid-Mar

COUNTRY HOUSE HOTEL, NANS-LES-PINS

DOMAINE DE CHATEAUNEUF

ONCE A STOPOVER for pilgims en route to the Holy Land, and now a luxuriously comfortable four-star hotel with an 18-hole golf course, two tennis courts, and a pool in the grounds – and ducks. Hard to imagine that Napoleon slept here. Has recently changed hands; reports please.

83860 Nans-les-Pins (Var) TEL 04 94 78 90 06 FAX 04 94 78 63 30
E-MAIL chateauneufhotel@opengolfclub.com website www.opengolfclub.com/ch9
Food breakfast, lunch, dinner Price €€€€€ Rooms 30
Credit cards AE, DC, MC, V Closed mid-Jan to Mar, Nov to late Dec

PROVENCE-COTE D'AZUR

LA PEROUSE

THE RECEPTION AREA – a welcoming little space done out in country fabrics and rustic furniture – sets the tone for this friendly hotel at the eastern end of the seafront, right beneath Nice's château. All rooms have a balcony or terrace; ones on the top floor are huge. Small heated pool; outdoor Jacuzzi; fitness suite and sauna.

11 quai Rauba-Capeu, 06300 Nice (Alpes-Maritimes) TEL 04 93 62 34 63
FAX 04 93 62 59 41 E-MAIL lp@hroy.com WEBSITE www.hotel-la-perouse.com/lp
FOOD breakfast; lunch and dinner mid-May to mid-Sep PRICE €€€€
ROOMS 63 CREDIT CARDS AE, DC, MC, V CLOSED never

WINDSOR

BEHIND AN UNASSUMING turn-of-the-century façade the Windsor is definitely different and very *à la mode*. A Thai shrine takes centre stage in the hall, Indonesian hangings adorn the walls. Some bedrooms have been decorated by contemporary artists, mostly along clean, simple lines. One has a graffiti-covered wall. Garden; pool.

11 rue Dalpozzo, 06300 Nice (Alpes-Maritimes) TEL 04 93 88 59 35
FAX 04 93 88 94 57 E-MAIL contact@hotelwindsornice.com
WEBSITE www.hotelwindsornice.com FOOD breakfast, lunch in summer, dinner
PRICE €€€ ROOMS 58 CREDIT CARDS AE, DC, MC, V CLOSED never

MAS DES CAPELANS

A RESTORED 18THC SILK-BREEDER's residence, set among vineyards, this is a relaxed and welcoming place, where the Poiri family give complimentary cocktails and serve dinner under mulberry trees. Beamed sitting room; country bedrooms; heated pool.

84580 Oppède (Vaucluse) TEL 04 90 76 99 04 FAX 04 90 76 90 29
E-MAIL capelans@chateauxhotels.com WEBSITE www.chateauxhotels.com/capelans
FOOD breakfast, dinner PRICE €€€-€€€€ ROOMS 9 CREDIT CARDS AE, MC, V
CLOSED mid-Nov to Mar

LE BOSQUET

SET BETWEEN CANNES and Grasse in a plain modern (1960s) building, with large shady grounds which include fruit trees, a swimming pool and a tennis court, this is the sort of unpretentious yet beguiling family-run hotel beloved of this guide. As well as the simple, spotless bedrooms, there are seven useful studios with kitchenettes and private terraces. A warm welcome.

74 chemin des Périssols, 06580 Pégomas (Alpes-Maritimes) TEL 04 92 60 21 20
FAX 04 92 60 21 49 FOOD breakfast PRICE €-€€€ ROOMS 16 CREDIT CARDS AE,
MC, V CLOSED Feb

Provence-Cote d'A

MAS DES BRUGASSIERE

'An excellent place to unwind after the long drive south,' is the verdict of one visitor to this modern (1974) 'farmhouse', set in lush gardens surrounded by vineyards. Bedrooms are basic but cheerful; some open directly on to the garden. Breakfast is informal, served from 8 am onwards, or you can have brunch by the pool.

Plan-de-la-Tour, 83120 Ste-Maxime (Var) **Tel** 04 94 55 50 55 **Fax** 04 94 55 50 51
E-mail mas.brugassieres@free.fr **website** www.mas-des-brugassieres.com **Food**
breakfast **Price** €-€€ **Rooms** 14 **Credit cards** MC, V **Closed** mid-Oct to mid-Mar

LA FERME D'AUGUSTIN

In a large garden, near Tahiti Beach and five minutes from the centre of St-Tropez, this is a relaxed, friendly hotel, filled with old country furniture. Bedrooms are in various buildings; terraces; heated pool with hydromassage. Breakfast served until midday.

plage de Tahiti, 83350 Ramatuelle (Var) **Tel** 04 94 55 97 00 **Fax** 04 94 97 40 30
E-mail vallet.ferme.augustin@wanadoo.fr **website** www.fermeaugustin.com
Food breakfast, snacks **Price** €€€€-€€€€€ **Rooms** 46
Credit cards AE, MC, V **Closed** late Oct to late Mar

LA FIGUIERE

This old farmhouse, with various wings and annexes, is set back from the busy road, the only access to popular Tahiti beach. Rather than braving the beach, the temptation is to stay put by the inviting pool in the large garden, with its fig and oleander trees. Many of the modest rooms are in outbuildings. The rustic-style restaurant is run by different management.

route de Tahiti, 83350 Ramatuelle (Var) **Tel** 04 94 97 18 21 **Fax** 04 94 97 68 48
Food breakfast, lunch, dinner **Price** €€-€€€€ **Rooms** 40 **Credit cards** AE,
DC, MC, V **Closed** Oct to Apr

AUBERGE DU COLOMBIER

The chief attraction of this low, white *mas* is its setting – amid tall, shady trees, with views over wooded hills towards the sea. It also has a wonderful terrace for summer eating, and, in its lush garden, a swimming pool and tennis court. Rooms are clean and comfortable, and prices, way down the scale.

06330 Roquefort-les-Pins (Alpes-Maritimes) **Tel** 04 92 60 33 00
Fax 04 93 77 07 03 **e-mail** info@auberge-du-colombier.com **Food** breakfast, lunch,
dinner **Price** €-€€€ **Rooms** 20 **Credit cards** AE, DC, MC, V **Closed** Jan

PROVENCE-COTE D'AZUR

LE BERGER DES ABEILLES

NICOLE GRENIER, a celebrated cook, was born in this shuttered farmhouse that now caters for her large circle of admirers. Rooms upstairs are newly decorated in bright colours; but the action is downstairs in the beamed dining room or out on the shaded terrace. Mme Grenier puts her heart into her *cuisine provençale*.

RD74E, 13670 St-Andiol (Bouches-du-Rhône) **TEL** 04 90 95 01 91 **FAX** 04 90 95 48 26 **E-MAIL** abeilles13@aol.com **FOOD** breakfast, lunch, dinner **PRICE** € **ROOMS** 9 **CREDIT CARDS** AE, MC, V **CLOSED** Jan to mid-Feb

BELLE-VUE

THIS INFORMAL SEASIDE Relais du Silence in lush, colourful gardens lives up to its name, with a wonderful view across the bay. It offers unpretentious but comfortable accommodation: bedrooms vary – the best are bright and spacious, with big modern bathrooms; some have sea views. Reports welcome.

boulevard du Four des Maures, St-Clair, 83980 Le Lavandou (Var) **TEL** 04 94 00 45 00 **FAX** 04 94 00 45 25 **WEBSITE** www.relais-du-silence.com/belle-vue **FOOD** breakfast, lunch, dinner **PRICE** €€ **ROOMS** 19 **CREDIT CARDS** AE, DC, MC, V **CLOSED** Nov to Mar

CLAIR LOGIS

IT IS NOT EASY TO FIND a reasonably priced hotel in such an exclusive area, let alone one which has the charm of a private villa and is set in lush, secluded gardens. Bedrooms are simple (those in the annexe are not particularly spacious) and four can accommodate families. No restaurant.

12 avenue Centrale, 06230 St-Jean-Cap-Ferrat (Alpes-Maritimes) **TEL** 04 93 76 04 57 **FAX** 04 93 76 11 85 **WEBSITE** www.hotel-clair-logis.fr **FOOD** breakfast **PRICE** €€ **ROOMS** 18 **CREDIT CARDS** AE, DC, MC, V **CLOSED** mid-Nov to mid-Dec, early Jan to Mar

LE MOULIN DU CHATEAU

SWISS-FRENCH NICOLAS STAMPFLI and his Swiss-Italian wife Edith took four years to convert their old mill into an utterly peaceful retreat with colourful, modern bedrooms and delicious 'Mediterranean' food. The restaurant is only open to residents, and there is no pool, so that guests can enjoy absolute peace and quiet.

04500 St-Laurent-du-Verdon (Var) **TEL** 04 92 74 02 47 **FAX** 04 92 74 02 97 **E-MAIL** LMDCH@club-internet.fr **website** www.provenceweb.fr/04/moulin-du-chateau **FOOD** breakfast, dinner **PRICE** €-€€ **ROOMS** 10 **CREDIT CARDS** MC, V **CLOSED** mid-Oct to mid-Feb

LA GRANDE BASTIDE

O N THE HILLSIDE one kilometre from the village, La Grande Bastide is a solid, painted stone building in an oasis-like garden of flowers and palm trees. The interior is a version of 'country chic' though it doesn't always come off. Most rooms have their own terrace. Try for a superior room: quieter than the rest with splendid views.

350 route de la Colle, 06570 St-Paul-de-Vence (Alpes-Maritimes)
TEL 04 93 32 50 30 **FAX** 04 93 32 50 59 **E-MAIL** stpaullgb@lemel.fr
WEBSITE www.la-grande-bastide.com **FOOD** breakfast **PRICE** ⓔⓔⓔ **Rooms** 14
CREDIT CARDS AE, DC, MC, V **CLOSED** late Nov to late Dec, mid-Jan to mid-Feb

LE SAINT-PAUL

I F YOU CAN AFFORD IT, here is another exceptionally captivating place to stay in pricey St-Paul, in a beautifully restored 16thC house. Bedrooms are done out with real panache, and the public areas are equally welcoming; there is a romantic dining terrace.

86 rue Grande, 06570 St-Paul-de-Vence (Alpes-Maritimes) **Tel** 04 93 32 65 25
Fax 04 93 32 52 94 **e-mail** stpaul@relaischateaux.fr
website www.relaischateaux.com/stpaul **Food** breakfast, lunch, dinner
Price ⓔⓔⓔⓔ **Rooms** 19 **Credit cards** AE, DC, MC, V
Closed 3 weeks before Christmas, 3 weeks after New Year

CHATEAU DES ALPILLES

A N ELEGANT, UPRIGHT 19thC manor house where the atmosphere of gracious living is combined with the facilities of a modern luxury hotel. Bedrooms are spacious and furnished with antiques. Lunch is served around the pool; dinner on the terrace, in summer.

RD31, 13210 St-Rémy-de-Provence (Bouches-du-Rhône) **TEL** 04 90 92 03 33
FAX 04 90 92 45 17**E-MAIL** chateau.alpilles@wanadoo.fr
website www.chateauxhotels.com/alpilles **FOOD** breakfast, lunch, dinner l
PRICE ⓔⓔⓔⓔ **ROOMS** 20 **CREDIT CARDS** AE, DC, MC, V
CLOSED mid-Nov to mid-Feb; restaurant Wed

LE YACA

T HIS SMART LITTLE HOTEL occupies several old town houses (one of which was home to Colette), which have been knocked together. Discreet and casually chic, Le Yaca is the antithesis of St-Trop flash (apart, that is, from its prices). Bedrooms are individually decorated with great flair. Excellent Italian food. Garden; pool.

1 boulevard d'Aumale, 83990 St-Tropez (Var) **TEL** 04 94 55 81 00
FAX 04 94 97 58 50 **e-mail** hotel-le-yaca@wanadoo.fr **WEBSITE** www.hotel-le-yaca.fr
Food breakfast, light lunch on request, dinner **PRICE** ⓔⓔⓔⓔⓔ **Rooms** 27
CREDIT CARDS AE, DC, MC, V **CLOSED** mid-Oct to Apr

PROVENCE-COTE D'AZUR

CONVERTED ABBEY, SALON-DE-PROVENCE

ABBAYE DE SAINTE CROIX

SAVED FROM RUIN in 1969 and turned into a luxury, four-star Relais et Châteaux, this 12thC abbey on a hill has a warren of stone passages, rooms converted from monks' cells, and terrific views of the valley below. The vaulted dining room was the chapel. Pool.

Val de Cuech, 13300 Salon-de-Provence (Bouches-du-Rhône)
TEL 04 90 56 24 55 FAX 04 90 56 31 12 E-MAIL saintecroix@relaischateaux.fr
WEBSITE www.relaischateaux.com/saintecroix FOOD breakfast, lunch, dinner
PRICE ⓔⓔⓔⓔ-ⓔⓔⓔⓔⓔ CREDIT CARDS AE, DC, MC, V CLOSED Nov to mid-Mar; restaurant Mon lunch, Thur lunch

VILLAGE HOTEL, SEGURET

LA TABLE DU COMTAT

'SURELY THE MOST CHARMING small hotel in Provence', says one devotee of this eyrie at the top of one of the region's most captivating villages. After a tortuous drive, you are rewarded by magnificent views and by the delights of a much modernized, but essentially old-fashioned *auberge*. The food is not cheap, but it is good, if eclectic. The rooms are simple and comfortable. Terrace; pool.

Séguret, 84110 Vaison-la-Romaine (Vaucluse) TEL 04 90 46 91 49
FAX 04 90 46 94 27 FOOD breakfast, lunch, dinner PRICE ⓔⓔ ROOMS 8
CREDIT CARDS AE, DC, MC, V CLOSED Feb

COUNTRY HOTEL, SERIGNAN-DU-COMTAT

HOSTELLERIE DU VIEUX CHATEAU

THIS 18THC FARMHOUSE turned traditional *logis* won our inspector's heart, not because of its position in a pretty village, its highly regarded restaurant (Le Pré du Moulin, separately managed), its large rooms, or even its low prices, but because of its delightful owners, the Truchots. Half-board obligatory Apr to Oct. Pool.

route de Ste-Cécile-les-Vignes, 84830 Sérignan-du-Comtat (Vaucluse)
TEL 04 90 70 05 58 FAX 04 90 70 05 62 FOOD breakfast, lunch, dinner PRICE ⓔⓔ
ROOMS 8 CREDIT CARDS AE, MC, V CLOSED 2 weeks Feb, 1 week Nov, 2 weeks Dec

COUNTRY GUESTHOUSE, LE THOR

LA BASTIDE ROSE

ON A BANK OF THE SORGUE, this lovely old former paper mill, now the home of Poppy and Pierre Salinger (JFK's speech writer) is protected from the world by trees and lawns. Poppy used to be an antiques dealer, and it shows in the style and stunning pieces she has brought to the house. Book dinner 24 hours in advance.

99 chemin des Croupières, 84250 Le Thor (Vaucluse) TEL 04 90 02 14
33 FAX 04 90 02 19 38 E-MAIL poppynicole@yahoo.com
WEBSITE www.bastiderose.com FOOD breakfast; light lunch and dinner on request
PRICE ⓔⓔⓔ ROOMS 7
CREDIT CARDS AE, DC, MC, V CLOSED never

PROVENCE-COTE D'AZUR

AUBERGE DE TOURRETTES

TALENTED CHEF Christophe Dufau and his Danish wife Katrine opened their unassuming restaurant-with-rooms in the shell of a typical village inn overlooking wooded hillsides. Focal point is the airy restaurant occupying a glassed-in terrace with fabulous views. For more about the resaurant, see page 207.

11 route de Grasse, 06140 Tourrettes-sur-Loup (Alpes-Maritimes)
TEL 04 93 59 30 05 FAX 04 93 59 28 66 E-MAIL info@aubergedetourrettes.fr
WEBSITE www.aubergedetourrettes.fr FOOD breakfast, lunch, dinner PRICE €€€
ROOMS 6 Credit cards AE, DC, MC, V CLOSED 1 week end Nov, mid-Jan to mid-Feb

LA BASTIDE DE TOURTOUR

THIS MODERN BUT TRADITIONAL-STYLE hotel offers comfort and attentive service (it is in the Châteaux et Hôtels de France group), and the food is excellent, if not in the first rank. For many, the key attraction is the secluded setting, high up among pine forests, with terrific views and in excellent walking country. Pool.

route de Flayosc, Tourtour, 83690 Salernes (Var) TEL 04 98 10 54 20
FAX 04 94 70 54 90 E-MAIL bastide@verdon.net
WEBSITE www.chateauxhotels.com/tourtour FOOD breakfast, lunch, dinner
PRICE €€€€ ROOMS 25 CREDIT CARDS AE, DC, MC, V CLOSED never

AUBERGE DE LA FONTAINE

THIS PRETTY LITTLE 18thC hotel, in a village classed as one of the most beautiful in France, provides cleverly designed and comfortable suites of rooms, with kitchens, giving total privacy and independence. Downstairs is a bistro. The hotel hosts regular concerts, and cookery courses in low season.

place de la Fontaine, 84210 Vénasque (Vaucluse) TEL 04 90 66 02 96
FAX 04 90 66 13 14 E-MAIL fontvenasq@aol.com FOOD breakfast, lunch, dinner
PRICE €€€ ROOMS 5 CREDIT CARDS MC, V CLOSED never; restaurant Wed and mid-Nov to mid-Dec; bistro Sun dinner, Mon

HOTEL LA FLORE

NOT IN THE PRETTY old part of Villefranche, but with spectacular sea views, this pleasant *fin-de-siècle* villa has fresh, white Provençal-style bedrooms with terraces and sparkling bathrooms, a pool with space for sun-worshipping, and a considerate staff. Fresh flowers brighten the rooms. Good value for this area – 6 km from Nice.

5 boulevard Princesse Grace de Monaco, 06230 Villefranche-sur-Mer (Alpes-Maritimes) TEL 04 93 76 30 30 FAX 04 93 76 99 99
E-MAIL hotel-la-flore@wanadoo.fr WEBSITE www.hotel-la-flore.fr
FOOD breakfast, lunch, dinner PRICE €€€€ ROOMS 23
CREDIT CARDS AE, DC, MC, V CLOSED never

THE RHONE VALLEY

COUNTRY HOTEL, BAIX

LA CARDINALE ET SA RESIDENCE

THE BIRTHPLACE of the Relais et Châteaux chain, La Cardinale is a welcoming old house, with four beautiful bedrooms; the rest, along with a smart swimming-pool, are three kilometres away at the Résidence.

quai du Rhône, 07210 Baix (Ardèche) TEL 04 75 85 80 40
FAX 04 75 85 82 07 E-MAIL cardinale@relaischateau.com
WEBSITE www.relaischateau.com/cardinale FOOD breakfast, lunch, dinner; room service PRICE €€€€ ROOMS 14 CREDIT CARDS AE, DC, MC, V CLOSED Nov to mid-Dec, Jan to mid-Feb, Mar

RESTAURANT-WITH-ROOMS, BERZE-LA-VILLE

LE RELAIS DU MACONNAIS

PERFECTLY PLACED for visiting the circuit of Romanesque churches and the Mâconnais vineyards, this handsome stone village house has been drawn to our attention by a reader who praised the food, and recorded a comfortable, if unexceptional, night in a simple, old-fashioned room.

La Croix-Blanche, 71960 Berze-la-Ville (Saône-et-Loire) TEL 03 85 36 60 72
FAX 03 85 36 65 47 FOOD breakfast, lunch, dinner PRICE € ROOMS 10
CREDIT CARDS MC, V CLOSED Jan; Sun, Mon

CHATEAU HOTEL, BAGNOLS

CHATEAU DE BAGNOLS

CONFLICTING REPORTS on this astonishingly lavish hotel, created by Paul and Hélène Hamlyn in a superb medieval château. Some find it all a bit much, others relish in its over-the-top perfection. Silk, velvet and rare antiques co-exist with the latest in comfort and convenience. Michelin-starred cuisine. Relais et Châteaux.

69620 Bagnols (Rhône) TEL 04 74 71 40 00 FAX 04 74 71 40 49
E-MAIL chateaubagnols@compuserve.com WEBSITE www.bagnols.com
FOOD breakfast, lunch, dinner; room service PRICE €€€€€
ROOMS 20 CREDIT CARDS AE, DC, MC, V CLOSED Jan to Apr

CHATEAU HOTEL, CHATEAUNEUF-DU-PAPE

CHATEAU FINES ROCHES

IN A STUNNING SETTING, perched on the summit of a hill overlooking the famous vineyards, this crenellated, neo-Gothic former residence of a Provençal poet offers luxurious accommodation and a warm welcome. Elegant bedrooms; light, inventive cuisine.

Route d'Avignon, 84230 Châteauneuf-du-Pape (Drôme) TEL 04 90 83 70 23
FAX 04 90 83 78 42 E-MAIL finesroches@enprovence.com
WEBSITE www.chateau-neuf-du-pape.enprovence.com FOOD breakfast, lunch, dinner PRICE €€€ ROOMS 6 CREDIT CARDS AE, DC, MC, V CLOSED Jan

THE RHONE VALLEY

LE MARAIS SAINT-JEAN

O WNED BY THE GIRARDONS of nearby Domaine de Clairefontaine (see our Restaurant section, page 209) this neat farmhouse conversion has all modern comforts and original timbered ceilings, beams and floor tiles. Excellent Girardon food is served in the beamed dining room or on the terrace.

38121 Chonas-l'Amballan (Isère) **TEL** 04 74 58 83 28
FAX 04 74 58 81 96 **FOOD** breakfast, lunch, dinner **Price** €€ **ROOMS** 10
CREDIT CARDS AE, DC, MC, V **CLOSED** Feb

LA TREILLE MUSCATE

T HIS CHARMING, ivy-covered inn, in a small perched village, has sunny, ochre walls, stencilling, tiled floors, dried flowers, wrought-iron furnishings and cheerful Provençal fabrics. The shaded terrace and many of the bedrooms have expansive views of the Rhône valley. Home-made, seasonal cooking.

26270 Cliousclat (Drôme) **TEL** 04 75 63 13 10 **FAX** 04 75 63 10 79
E-MAIL latreillemuscate@wanadoo.fr **FOOD** breakfast, lunch, dinner
Price € **ROOMS** 12 **CREDIT CARDS** MC, V **CLOSED** mid-Dec to Mar; restaurant
CLOSED Wed

HOTELLERIE BEAU RIVAGE

W ITH CONDRIEU'S FAMOUS VINEYARDS on the hill behind and the Rhône on the front doorstep, this Relais et Châteaux hotel has a most pleasing position – and a Michelin star. Comfortable bedrooms are sometimes a little over-decorated and fussy, but the riverside terrace is charming.

69420 Condrieu (Rhône) **TEL** 04 74 59 52 24 **FAX** 04 74 59 59 36
E-MAIL info@hotel-beaurivage.com **WEBSITE** www.relaischateau.com/beaurivage
FOOD breakfast, lunch, dinner; room service **Price** €€€-€€€€ **ROOMS** 25
CREDIT CARDS AE, DC, MC, V **CLOSED** never

MANOIR DE LA ROSERAIE

T HIS PRIVATE MANOR house was built by the Mayor of Grignan in 1853 and has more than 350 rose bushes in the large garden, which is also planted with cedars. Bedrooms are stylishly decorated and one has a circular bath. There's a heated swimming pool.

route de Valréas, 26230 Grignan (Drôme) **TEL** 04 75 46 58 15
FAX 04 75 46 91 55 **E-MAIL** roseraie.hotel@wanadoo.fr **FOOD** breakfast, lunch, dinner
Price €€€ **ROOMS** 15 **CREDIT CARDS** AE, DC, MC, V
CLOSED early to mid-Dec, mid-Jan to mid-Feb, Tue, Wed in winter

THE RHONE VALLEY

CHATEAU D'URBILHAC

T HIS FAIRY-TALE CHATEAU – 19th century but in Renaissance style, with round tower and a steep roof – has a peaceful, elevated setting in a large park, with a pleasant pool. The interior is rather ponderous, but does not lack character or comfort. 'Good food,' but 'atmosphere a little stilted,' comments a visitor.

07270 Lamastre (Ardèche) **TEL** 04 75 06 42 11 **FAX** 04 75 06 52 75
FOOD breakfast, dinner **Price** €€ (half-board obligatory in season) **ROOMS** 11
CREDIT CARDS AE, DC, MC, V **CLOSED** Oct to May

HOTEL DU MIDI

T HE MICHELIN-STARRED restaurant is the heart of this hotel, serving a very successful blend of traditional and modern dishes. The dining rooms are rather plain, but intimate; service is helpful and friendly. Bedrooms, in a separate building a minute's walk away, are comfortably spacious and tastefully furnished.

place Seignobos, 07270 Lamastre (Ardèche) **TEL** 04 75 06 41 50
FAX 04 75 06 49 75 **FOOD** breakfast, lunch, dinner **PRICE** € **ROOMS** 12
CREDIT CARDS AE, DC, MC, V **CLOSED** mid Dec-Feb; restaurant closed Fri dinner, Sun dinner, Mon

LA CAPITELLE

A ROUGH STONE building in a backwater setting in a walled medieval village, yet only a few minutes' drive from the *autoroute*, La Capitelle makes an excellent stopover. It has an air of confident good taste, with a stylishly traditional feel to the individually and boldly decorated bedrooms, and the vaulted dining room.

Le Rempart, 25270 Mirmande (Drôme) **TEL** 04 75 63 02 72
FAX 04 75 63 02 50 **Food** breakfast, lunch, dinner **PRICE** € (half-board obligatory)
ROOMS 11 **CREDIT CARDS** AE, DC, MC, V **CLOSED** mid-Jan to mid-Feb, Tue and Wed lunch

COUR DES LOGES

I N THE HEART of the old city, an 'architectural masterpiece' fashioned out of four buildings that were once home to Claude de Beaumont, Lord of Burgundy. The memorable decoration is a stunning mix of old and new. Bedrooms are varied in size and type, some with open-plan bathrooms. Pool and sauna.

6 rue Boeuf, 69005 Lyon (Rhône) **TEL** 04 72 77 44 44
FAX 04 72 40 93 61 **E-MAIL** contact@courdesloges.com
WEBSITE www.courdesloges.com **FOOD** breakfast, lunch, dinner; room service **PRICE**
€€€-€€€€ **ROOMS** 52 **CREDIT CARDS** AE, DC, MC, V **CLOSED** never

THE RHONE VALLEY

HOSTELLERIE DU VIEUX PEROUGES

IN A PERFECTLY PRESERVED little medieval town, this timbered inn serves up local fare in a charming old-style restaurant. Spacious bedrooms in the two 14thC buildings are a copy of medieval sleeping quarters, right down to canopied beds. Simpler rooms in the 18thC annexe are less expensive. This is one of the oldest inns in France.

place du Tilleul, 01800 Pérouges (Ain) **TEL** 04 74 61 00 88
Fax 04 74 34 77 90 **E-MAIL** thibaut@hostellerie.com **FOOD** breakfast, lunch, dinner
PRICE €€€ **ROOMS** 28 **CREDIT CARDS** AE, MC, V **CLOSED** never

CHATEAU DE ROCHEGUDE

DESPITE THE HIGH COST of rooms here, we cannot resist including this sumptuous château because of its wonderful setting – overlooking the vineyards of the Rhône plain – and its equally wonderful food. Bedrooms are palatial. Relais et Châteaux.

26790 Rochegude (Drôme) **TEL** 04 75 97 21 10 **Fax** 04 75 04 89 87
E-MAIL rochegude@relaischateau.fr **WEBSITE** www.relaischateau.com/rochegude
FOOD breakfast, lunch, dinner; room service **PRICE** €€€€€-€€€€€€
ROOMS 26 **CREDIT CARDS** AE, DC, MC, V **CLOSED** mid-Nov to mid-Dec, Sun, Mon in winter

GRANGEON

THERE'S NO TV and no phone in the rooms in this remote place, four kilometres from the nearest village and reached by a winding road through hills and woods. Mme Valette, a writer, bakes her own bread and cooks with fresh vegetables from her *potager*. Strictly for escapists.

07800 St-Cierge-la-Serre (Ardèche) **TEL** 04 76 65 73 86 **FOOD** breakfast, dinner
PRICE € **ROOMS** 4 **CREDIT CARDS** not accepted **CLOSED** Oct-May

LE LIEVRE AMOUREUX

WE LACK RECENT feedback about this old *auberge de chasse*, set among corn fields and with a gabled overhung roof. There is a terrace, and a pool which is directly accessible from the pine-panelled rooms in the modern annexe. The older buildings have more traditional (and less expensive) rooms, which we prefer.

38840 St-Lattier (Isère) **TEL** 04 76 64 50 67 **Fax** 04 76 64 31 21
FOOD breakfast, lunch, dinner **PRICE** €€ **ROOMS** 12 **CREDIT CARDS** AE, DC, MC, V
CLOSED mid-Oct to Apr

THE RHONE VALLEY

VILLAGE INN, ST-RESTITUT

AUBERGE DES QUATRE SAISONS

THE VINE-CLAD *auberge* is a conversion of two Romanesque houses on the square of a medieval perched village that one of our readers says is so sleepy as to be comatose. Bedrooms are quiet, rather dark and cosy. Regional fare served in the restaurant. More reports would be welcome.

Place de l'Église, 26130 St-Restitut (Drôme) **TEL** 04 75 04 71 88
FAX 04 75 04 70 88 **FOOD** breakfast, lunch, dinner **PRICE** € **ROOMS** 10
CREDIT CARDS AE, DC, MC, V **CLOSED** Jan

CHATEAU HOTEL, ST-SAUVEUR-EN-RUE

AUBERGE DU CHATEAU DE BOBIGNEUX

THERE'S A WORKING FARM attached to this small, bargain-priced hotel in wine country: the family room overlooks the farmyard in order to amuse the children. Owners, the Labères, keep a relaxed, friendly house and provide meals using produce from the garden.

42200 St-Sauveur-en-Rue (Loire) **TEL** 04 77 39 24 33
FAX 04 77 39 25 74 **FOOD** breakfast, lunch, dinner **PRICE** € **ROOMS** 6
CREDIT CARDS AE, DC, MC, V **CLOSED** Jan to Mar

COUNTRY HOTEL, SOLERIEUX

LA FERME SAINT-MICHEL

THIS BEAUTIFUL STONE farmhouse, dating from the 16th century, is surrounded by fields of lavender and vineyards and is close to the château of the famous Mme de Sévigné. Very attractive, very comfortable, excellent value. Terrace, pool, private parking.

route La Baume, D341, 26130 Solerieux (Drôme) **TEL** 04 75 98 10 66
FAX 04 75 98 19 09 **FOOD** breakfast, lunch, dinner **PRICE** € **ROOMS** 14
CREDIT CARDS MC, V **CLOSED** never; restaurant closed mid-Dec to mid-Jan, Sun dinner, Mon lunch, Tue lunch

VILLAGE INN, VALLON-PONT D'ARC

MANOIR DU RAVEYRON

STANDING IN A GATED courtyard, this is the sort of rustic village inn that is the bedrock of French hotel-keeping – a two-fireplace *logis* offering simple but satisfactory accommodation, modest prices and wholesome food. We lack feedback since the Dierckx family took over – reports please.

rue Henri Barbusse, 07150 Vallon-Pont d'Arc (Ardèche) **TEL** 04 75 88 03 59
FAX 04 75 37 11 12 **FOOD** breakfast, lunch, dinner **PRICE** € **ROOMS** 14
CREDIT CARDS MC, V **CLOSED** mid-Oct to mid-Mar

THE ALPS

BEAUSOLEIL

AT THE FOOT of the Aiguille du Midi and Mont Blanc, this peaceful, family-run hotel with a delightful garden full of flowers, is surrounded by fields. Rooms are spruce and recently renovated. Recommended for family cooking.

Le Lavancher, 74400 Chamonix (Haute-Savoie) TEL 04 50 54 00 78
FAX 04 50 54 17 34 E-MAIL hotel.beausoleil@libertysurf.fr
FOOD breakfast, lunch, dinner PRICE €€ ROOMS 15 CREDIT CARDS MC, V
CLOSED mid-Sep to mid-Dec

JEU DE PAUME

THIS MODERN PASTICHE of a traditional wooden chalet has mounted stags' heads, leather 'club' armchairs, pine-panelled bedrooms and four-star comfort. Indoor and outdoor swimming pools and sauna. Sister hotel to the Jeu de Paume in Paris (so-named because it was once a real tennis court).

Le Lavancher, 74400 Chamonix (Haute-Savoie) TEL 04 50 54 03 76 FAX 04 50 54
10 75 E-MAIL jeu-de-paume-chamonix@wanadoo.fr FOOD breakfast, lunch, dinner;
room service PRICE €€€€ ROOMS 23 CREDIT CARDS AE, DC, MC, V
CLOSED mid-May to mid-Jun, mid-Oct to mid-Dec

LODGE NOGENTIL HOTEL

THE INTERIOR of this intimate, small chalet has a warm glow of polished wood and conviviality. The young owners (English, with a music-business background) began their venture with a flourish a few years back, and reports indicate that they are keeping standards high, just about justifying the prices. No restaurant.

rue Bellecôte, 73123 Courcheval (Savoie) TEL 04 79 08 32 32
FAX 04 79 08 03 15 E-MAIL lodgenogentil@wanadoo.fr FOOD breakfast
PRICE €€€€ ROOMS 10 CREDIT CARDS AE, DC, MC, V
CLOSED mid-Apr to mid-Dec

AUBERGE DES CHASSEURS

AT THE FOOT of the Jura mountains, facing the Alps, an attractive con-verted farmhouse which has been in the family of its owner, Dominique Lamy, since the mid-19th century. Thanks to the attentions of a Swedish decorator it now has a wealth of Scandinavian-inspired paint effects. Satisfying food, well-priced wine list. Lovely flowery terrace; pool.

Naz Dessus, 01170 Echenevex (Ain) TEL 04 50 41 54 07
FAX 04 50 41 90 61 FOOD breakfast, lunch, dinner PRICE €€ ROOMS 15
CREDIT CARDS MC, V CLOSED mid-Nov to mid-Apr

THE ALPS

AU GAY SEJOUR

A SIMPLE, HONEST INN in a secluded spot. The sturdy 17thC farmhouse has been in the Gay family for generations. Food is at the heart of the house, featuring local lake fish and truffles in season. Simple, spotless bedrooms; beautiful views from the terrace.

Le Tertenoz de Seythenex, 74210 Faverges (Haute-Savoie) **Tel** 04 50 44 52 52
Fax 04 50 44 49 52 **E-mail** gaysejour@chateauxhotels.com
Website www.chateauxhotels.com **Food** breakfast, lunch, dinner **Price** €
Rooms 12 **Credit cards** MC, V **Closed** mid-Nov to mid-Dec; restaurant closed Sun dinner, Mon

LA TOUR DE PACORET

T HERE ARE FINE mountain views from the upper windows of this old stone watchtower – built on the summit of a hill in the 13th century for the Dukes of Savoy. Bedrooms have fine views, and peace and quiet is ensured. Best feature is the vine-clad terrace, and the large garden with tempting swimming pool.

Montailleur, 73460 Gresy-sur-Isère (Savoie) **Tel** 04 79 37 91 59
Fax 04 79 37 93 84 **Food** breakfast, lunch, dinner **Price** €€ **Rooms** 9
Credit cards MC, V **Closed** Nov to May

CHALET REMY

I N SHARP CONTRAST to the glossy chalet hotels of nearby Megève, this chalet is as simple – and genuine – as you could hope to find. With breathtaking views across to Mont Blanc, it was a farmhouse in the 18thC and has all its original woodwork, indeed the interior seems frozen in time. The simple rooms are warm and have comfortable beds. Savoyard cooking.

Le Bettex, 74170 St-Gervais (Haute-Savoie) **Tel** 04 50 93 11 85
Fax 04 50 93 14 45 **Food** breakfast, lunch, dinner **Price** € **Rooms** 19
Credit cards MC, V **Closed** never

LA DEMEURE DE CHAVOIRE

T HIS IMPECCABLY-KEPT, charming hotel, in a pretty garden on the shores of Lake Annecy, has rooms named after famous writers – you may sleep in the Jean-Jacques Rousseau suite. Plenty of taste and calm – on the main road to the ski resorts.

route d'Annecy-Chavoire, 74290 Veyrier-du-Lac (Haute-Savoie)
Tel 04 50 60 04 38 **Fax** 04 50 60 05 36 **E-mail** demeure.chavoire @wanadoo.fr
Website www.demeuredechavoire.com **Food** breakfast, snacks **Price** €€€
Rooms 13 **Credit cards** AE, DC, MC, V **Closed** Nov

INTRODUCTION

I n the following pages we present, as a new departure for the *Charming Small Hotel Guides*, descriptions of 58 special restaurants in Southern France. They follow exactly the same order as the hotels: first Bordeaux and the Dordogne; then The South-West; Auvergne and the Massif Central; Provence-Côte d'Azur; The Rhône Valley; The Alps.

What's the criteria for this selection? Simple – they are all note-worthy addresses that we would like to pass on to our readers: places that we have particularly enjoyed, and places that we feel have the same quality of charm, individuality and value for money as the hotels that we recommend and which we know you appreci-ate. Some are restaurants which our London-based editors have come across on hotel inspection trips; most are the local favourites of our France-based inspectors. The majority are com-fortable rather than luxurious, pretty and atmospheric rather than formal, with an emphasis on good regional cooking. A few are smart and expensive, but in our opinion, worth it. We don't stray into the territory of *haute cuisine* and three Michelin stars – it's not our style. Instead, these are the kind of places you dream of finding round every bend in the road: honest and welcoming, serv-ing good food (it might be solidly traditional or subtly inventive) at fair prices.

The geographical distrubution of our recommendations is entirely random: inclusion is based on the merits of the restaurant rather than popularity of a location, and many are in towns and cities where we do not happen to have hotel recommendations. In addition to the separate restaurant descriptions, we have also list-ed all the hotels that feature in our guide which have exceptional-ly good restaurants themselves. Armed with the two, we hope you will eat in Southern France as contentedly and memorably as you will sleep there.

PRICES

As with our hotels, we have used price bands for the restaurants to indicate how much they cost. Restaurants vary widely in what they offer: some have just a couple of set menus; others offer menus ranging from cheap to expensive, plus an extensive *carte*. In devising our price bands we have calculated the cost of an aver-age three-course meal for one person, without wine. Very few of our recommendations will break the bank; several will leave your wallet hardly scathed.

The price bands are as follows:

The cost of an average three-course dinner for one without wine

15-30 Euros	€
30-45 Euros	€€
45 Euros and more	€€€

RESTAURANTS

HOTELS FEATURED IN THIS GUIDE WITH HIGHLY RECOMMENDED RESTAURANTS

BORDEAUX AND THE DORDOGNE

AGEN

MARIOTTAT

25 rue Louis-Vivent, 47000 Agen (Lot-et-Garonne)
TEL 05 53 77 99 77 **FAX** 05 53 77 99 79

AGEN'S TOP RESTAURANT occupies a lovely, elegant 19thC town house with high ceilings, chandeliers and large windows hidden in the back streets to the south of the town's Jacobin church. Part of the garden has been requisitioned for car parking, but there's still a pleasant gravelled terrace to one side for outdoor dining. As to the food, there's no mistaking the fact that you're in the heart of duck country; indeed, the speciality dish is *c'est tout un art d'être un canard* – a feast of duck in all its many guises. Other notable dishes include *croustillant de calamars à la biscaïenne* and *filet de limande-sole, sauce au fenouil*. The wine list is lovingly put together by *patronne* Christiane Mariottat (her husband Eric is the chef) and includes an unusually good selection of half-bottles.

PRICE €€€
CLOSED Sat lunch, Sun eve, Mon; first week Feb
CREDIT CARDS AE, MC, V

ARCINS-EN-MEDOC

LE LION D'OR

33460 Arcins-en-Médoc (Gironde)
TEL 05 56 58 96 79

HANDILY SITUATED on the D2 Bordeaux Route du Vin not far north of Margaux, the Lion d'Or is as popular with locals as it is with the passing tourist trade, particularly for its excellent-value lunchtime menu. The decoration is definitely a cut above the usual village restaurant, and there's even a small garden, but *patron* Jean-Paul Barbier's food remains traditional, unfussy *cuisine du terroir*: fish fresh from the Gironde, local lamb, tripe, lamprey, *tête de veau* or just a simple, perfectly cooked omelette. During the grape harvest pigeon, hare and other game feature strongly. One particularly pleasing innovation is that you can take along your own bottle of wine (the wine list concentrates on local reds). A well-deserved Bib Gourmand from Michelin.

PRICE €
CLOSED Sun, Mon; Jul, Christmas, New Year
CREDIT CARDS AE, MC, V

BORDEAUX AND THE DORDOGNE

FRANCESCAS

RELAIS DE LA HIRE

47600 Francescas (Lot-et-Garonne)
TEL 05 53 65 41 59 **FAX** 05 53 65 86 42

IT'S WELL WORTH DRIVING out of your way to eat at this fine, welcoming restaurant in a charming old 18thC house in the placid little village of Francescas, 10 km southeast of Nérac. The food – like the decoration – is a successful blend of modern and traditional, and the presentation truly memorable. The desserts in particular are works of art, though all the dishes come garnished with flowers or sprigs of aromatic plants from the restaurant's garden. On our most recent visit we ate a delectable soufflé of artichoke and *foie gras*, followed by sea bream roast with olives. The wine list is innovative and helpful, with suggestions for accompanying each dish on the menu. And you will be dazzled by the tremendous choice of armagnacs with which to finish.

PRICE €€€
CLOSED Sun eve, Mon
CREDIT CARDS AE, DC, MC, V

GRÉZELS

LA TERRASSE

46700 Grézels (Lot)
TEL 05 65 21 34 03

LA TERRASSE IS ONE of those wonderful old-style family restaurants which you won't find in the restaurant guides and where there's no menu – you just sit down and the food begins to appear. (If you phone ahead, however, the owners will be happy to cater for any particular dietary requirements.) You'll need a robust appetite to do justice to the no-nonsense country cooking of Mme Pignères. A typical dinner might consist of a hearty vegetable soup, followed by pâté, veal with fried potatoes and carrots in a cream sauce, cheese and salad, and, to finish, an irresistible *clafoutis* (similar to an upside-down cake, in this case made with local cherries). The cost for all this is miniscule – in fact it couldn't possibly be cheaper. Sadly, places offering such value for money and traditional home cooking are increasingly hard to find.

PRICE €
CLOSED every eve and Mon lunch, except Jul, Aug when closed Sat eve, Sun eve, Mon; 2 weeks Sep and 1 other week (not fixed)
CREDIT CARDS DC, MC, V

BORDEAUX AND THE DORDOGNE

LA TERRASSE

46200 Meyronne (Lot)
TEL 05 65 32 21 60 **FAX** 05 65 32 26 93

SET ON A LOW RISE overlooking the Dordogne, it is the vine-shaded terrace of this 11thC château, once the summer residence of the bishops of Tulle, that really appeals. In cooler weather, however, the main dining room of this hotel/restaurant is pleasant too, and in quiet periods food is served in another cosy, stone-vaulted room. In whichever setting, diners are regaled with beautifully presented regional fare: melt-in-the-mouth *foie gras*, lamb raised on the Quercy's uplands, earthy truffles, and *cabécou*, the smoky-sweet goats' cheese from nearby Rocamadour. There is also an interesting choice of fish dishes – perhaps an excellent filet of sea bass roasted on a bed of fennel – and a daily changing selection of desserts that are hard to resist.

PRICE €€
CLOSED late Nov to Mar
CREDIT CARDS AE, DC, MC, V

LA TOUR DES VENTS

Moulin de Malfourat, 24240 Monbazillac (Dordogne)
TEL 05 53 58 30 10 **FAX** 05 53 58 89 55

THE MODERN BUILDING in which this restaurant is located – part of a decommissioned windmill – may be nothing to shout about, but the menus at the Tour des Vents represent excellent value, the welcome is warm and the views are superb. You're perched high above the vine-clad Dordogne valley directly south of Bergerac; ask for a table on their pleasantly shaded terrace or, failing that, beside the dining room's big, picture windows. *Foie gras* and duck feature prominently, of course, on Marie Rougier's menu, as do the local Bergerac and sweet Monbazillac wines on the *carte des vins*, but there's also plenty of fresh fish and even a vegetarian menu. A perennial favourite is a dish of scallops sprinkled with balsamic vinegar and walnut oil – if you're feeling rich, you order it with truffles.

PRICE €€
CLOSED Sun eve, Mon Sep-Jun; Mon lunch only in Jul; Jan
CREDIT CARDS AE, DC, MC, V

BORDEAUX AND THE DORDOGNE

R E S T A U R A N T S

PERIGUEUX

LE CLOS ST-FRONT

5 rue de la Vertu, 24000 Périgueux (Dordogne)
TEL 05 53 46 78 58 **FAX** 05 53 46 78 20

THIS UP-AND-COMING RESTAURANT in central Périgueux has developed a well-deserved reputation for the excellent value and inventiveness of its food. The style tends towards *nouvelle*, but the flavours are rich and so beautifully balanced that you won't leave the table dissatisfied, however light the dishes. There is a limited menu – always a good sign – which changes monthly, plus a selection of speciality dishes, including an absolutely exquisite *foie gras* served warm with a spicy caramel sauce. The service is impeccable without being grand and the staff are exceptionally accommodating. Last but not least, in warm weather you can opt to eat in the haven of the restaurant's palm-filled courtyard. Take note: this place fills quickly – book your table well in advance.

PRICE €
CLOSED Sun, Mon; 2 weeks Jan, 1 week Jun, 1 week Sep
Credit cards AE, V

ST-LEON-SUR-VEZERE

LE PETIT LÉON

24290 St-Léon-sur-Vézère (Dordogne)
TEL & FAX 05 53 51 18 04

MIDWAY ALONG the lush Vézère valley with its world-famous prehistoric caves, the exquisite little riverside village of St-Léon (complete with elegant château and little Romanesque church) makes a perfect pit stop. The shaded and walled garden of Le Petit Léon looks out over one of the village's two châteaux, while in cooler weather you eat in an elegant, stone-vaulted dining room. On offer are four well-priced menus in addition to a limited *carte*: house specialities include mushroom-stuffed *magret de canard* (duck breast) topped with *foie gras*, and an unsual dish of *gésiers* (gizzards) fried with mushrooms – much better than it might sound. British visitors will no doubt be tempted to end with a generous slice of mouth-watering lemon meringue pie.

PRICE €
CLOSED Sun eve, Mon May-Jul & Sep; Nov to Apr
CREDIT CARDS AE, DC, MC, V

BORDEAUX AND THE DORDOGNE

ST-MACAIRE

L'ABRICOTIER

rue Bergoeing, 33490 St-Macaire (Gironde)
TEL 05 56 76 83 63 **FAX** 05 56 76 28 51

THE LOCATION OF THIS LITTLE RESTAURANT – on the main N113 as it skirts north of St-Macaire – may not appear too promising, but don't let that put you off. Once inside, you discover a pretty walled garden where, among the heady scents of roses and jasmine, all is peace and calm. Furthermore, as many locals will tell you, this is one of the best eating places in the area. The reason is simple: the young owners, Alain and Michèle Zanette, are sticklers for using only the freshest and highest quality ingredients. In doing so, they offer a limited menu, but one that changes almost every week, with a strong showing of fish – including delicacies such as lamprey, shad and eels from the nearby Garonne river – and plenty of game in season. The wine list is as well-judged as the food.

PRICE €€
CLOSED Mon eve, Tue eve; mid-Nov to mid-Dec
CREDIT CARDS V

ST-MEDARD

LE GINDREAU

46150 St-Médard (Lot)
TEL 05 65 36 22 27 **FAX** 05 65 36 24 54

LE GINDREAU, located in a former village school, isn't the sort of place you stumble across, but it's worth going out of your way to discover this superb restaurant which, over nearly 30 years, has been developed by Alexis and Martine Pélissou into one of the best in the region. (Prices, however, remain surprisingly affordable.) M. Pélissou's cuisine is anchored in authenticity and tradition, while at the same time creating fresh, light dishes which appeal to the modern palate. Each course is a work of art, and the desserts are so delectable they seem almost a shame to eat. The same exacting standards are seen in the wine list, with a strong showing of local dark, peppery Cahors. You eat either in the high-ceilinged 'classrooms' or on the geranium-bedecked terrace under towering chestnut trees. Service is attentive, yet discreet.

PRICE €€€
CLOSED Mon,Tue (Mon, Tue lunch Jul, Aug); mid-Oct to mid-Nov, first 2 weeks Mar
CREDIT CARDS AE, DC, MC, V

RESTAURANTS

THE SOUTH-WEST

R
E
S
T
A
U
R
A
N
T
S

AUDRESSEIN

L'AUBERGE

09800 Audressein (Ariège)
TEL 05 61 96 11 80 **FAX** 05 61 96 82 96

IN UNSPOILED COUNTRY close to the Spanish border, where good roads twist along wooded valleys, a culinary experience awaits you at the Auberge d'Audressein. Behind an unassuming exterior you will find food of exceptional variety and quality, served with charm and professionalism. Since late 2000 the restaurant (with rooms) has been owned by Yves and Stéphanie Atelin, who come with first-class credentials: Yves, the chef, trained with Jacques Pic and Michel Chabron as well as at prestigious addresses in the Alps and on the Côte d'Azur. Menus are wide ranging, with a price to suit every pocket. Ices come from a *maître glacier* in St Girons, and the wine list perfectly complements the food. The two dining rooms are air-conditioned, one with an open fire in winter, the other with a veranda jutting out over the river (table 'veranda 6' is the best).

PRICE €€
CLOSED mid-Nov to mid-Feb
CREDIT CARDS AE, MC, V

BELESTA

CHEZ PIERRE

66720 Bélesta (Ariège)
TEL 04 68 84 52 70

BELESTA, A TINY VILLAGE in the Fenouillèdes hills, close to the Caramany vineyards and the Roman aqueduct at Ansignan, boasts a stylishly modernized *château-musée* for its prehistoric finds, as well as this charming little restaurant, enclosed at the end of a narrow village street. It was once a garden, and has an interior cunningly glassed over and a small verandah with an old fig tree and fine views of Mount Canigou. Chef/*patron* Pierre Cubères spent many years as a *traiteur* and still makes all his own products from *foie gras* to sausage and *magret de canard*. The welcome is warm, and the food is simple, fresh and generous; perhaps a salad of *gésiers*, peppers, egg and anchovy to start, followed by a *truite aux amandes*, grilled *gambas*, or a *magret de canard* with pungent orange sauce served separately – the *magret* is enormous and you have to carve it yourself. There are aperitifs of local muscat or *grenache*, and an interesting local wine list. Don't leave without trying Pierre's own *verveine* liqueur.

PRICE €
CLOSED every eve (except by prior reservation), Wed lunch (except Jul, Aug)
CREDIT CARDS not accepted

THE SOUTH-WEST

BIRIATOU

BAKEA

64700 Biriatou (Pyrénées-Atlantiques)
TEL 05 59 20 76 36 **FAX** 05 59 20 58 21

TEN MINUTES'S DRIVE from the beach at Hendaye, Corine and Eric Duval have created a haven of civilized calm at the edge of the village of Biriatou, and a welcome escape from the bustle and crowds of the coast. An inviting terrace overlooks the wide Bidassoa valley, whose river here defines the border between France and Spain. Bakéa is a reliable hotel (a new development of 21 bedrooms, Les Jardins de Bakéa opened in 2001), but it is the restaurant which particularly appeals, with menus which represent good value and a wine list which has an interesting selection of French, Basque and Spanish bottles. Eric Duval's cooking merits a Michelin star, and specialities include *lasange d'anchois frais marinés au basilic* (in season) and *salade de ris d'agneau aux parfums de pays*.

PRICE €€€
CLOSED Sun eve, Oct to Easter; Feb
CREDIT CARDS AE, DC, MC, V

LAUZERTE

HOTEL DU QUERCY

Faubourg d'Auriac, 82110 Lauzerte (Tarn-et-Garonne)
TEL 05 63 94 66 36 **FAX** 05 63 95 73 21

THE RESTAURANT OF THIS unpretentious country hotel on the edge of Lauzerte is definitely going places. Chef Frédéric Bacou has built up a loyal following, not least because he continues to offer excellent value for money and a range of menus to suit every budget. As to his cooking, M. Bacou brings a light, imaginative touch to local dishes featuring duck and *foie gras*, local lamb, sander and game in season. Imaginative they may be, but he is careful not to produce anything which is over-sophisticated: he understands the importance of retaining the authentic tastes of simple country fare, and he strikes a happy balance. Equally true to the region is the well-chosen list of southern wines. With only a small dining area and roadside terrrace, it's worth booking in advance.

PRICE €
CLOSED Mon Jul & Aug, Sun eve, Mon Sep-Jun; early to mid-Oct, 1 week Feb
CREDIT CARDS DC, MC, V

THE SOUTH-WEST

MANCIET

LA BONNE AUBERGE

place Pesquerot, 32370 Manciet (Gers)
TEL 05 62 08 50 04 **FAX** 05 62 08 58 84

AN OUTSTANDING ADDRESS in a region of France noted for its fine food, this country inn (it also has 14 bedrooms) is much appreciated by customers from near and far. Its hosts are Simone and Pepito Sampietro, both welcoming, she elegant, he with something of the Musketeer about him. Reflecting the character of its proprietors, La Bonne Auberge is elegant yet cosy, with warm colours, old stone walls, candle and lamp light, and rows of Armagnacs glinting in their glass display case. Pepito's cooking is satisfyingly rooted in the region, and changes with the seasons. On a visit in April we were presented with a short *carte*, plus three menus: 'Bonheur et poésie de la Gascogne', 'La magie des saveurs du terroir', and 'La part des anges au parfum d'Armagnac'. Armagnac features strongly, as do (of course) *foie gras*, truffles, duck and game in season.

PRICE ©©
CLOSED Sun eve; Mon in winter; Feb
CREDIT CARDS AE, DC, MC, V

ST-SAVIN

LE VISCOS

65400 St-Savin (Hautes-Pyrénées)
TEL 05 62 97 02 28 **FAX** 05 62 97 04 95

IN A MOUNTAINSIDE VILLAGE near Lourdes, this six-generation family-run restaurant (and simple hotel) has been in the capable, and capacious, hands of Maître-Cuisinier de France Jean-Pierre St-Martin. To his inheritance of old family recipes based on top quality local produce, including mountain herbs, he has introduced inventiveness and lightness of touch. Mouth-watering menus include *galette de touradisse au foie gras, palombie en cocotte aux cèpes, merveille fourrée de fruits au Jurançon*. The food is served in a large rectangular dining room with huge picture windows, or on an attractive terrace, both with superb mountain views. Your host, who runs cookery courses and displays his talents as guest chef in top hotels abroad, has an expansive personality, full of bonhomie.

PRICE ©©
CLOSED Dec
CREDIT CARDS AE, DC, MC, V

LANGUEDOC-ROUSSILLON

LE PORTANEL

passage Portanel, 11100 Bages, Narbonne (Aude)
TEL 04 68 42 81 66 **FAX** 04 68 41 75 93

EIGHT DIFFERENT DISHES featuring eels are part of the repertoire of Didier
Marty, who runs this exceptional fish restaurant in a village house with
his wife Rose-Marie. Take your choice: perhaps *l'anguille en persillade* or
l'anguille en bourride. Whichever, the eels could not be fresher, coming
as they do straight from the Etang de Bages, the lake which stretches from
Narbonne to the sea and which the little fishing village of Bages overlooks.
If you don't like eels, there are plenty of other fish to choose from, equally
fresh, and oysters from Bouzigues. Try your fish *en croûte de sel*, or perhaps *le lessou cuit sur la peau au suc de volaille*, or *figuette
narbonnaise*. There are non-fish dishes too, including free-range chicken
and other local produce. In warm weather you eat on a terrace overlooking
the lake.

PRICE €€
CLOSED Sun eve, Mon; mid to late Nov
CREDIT CARDS AE, DC, MC, V

LA LITTORINE, HOTEL LES ELMES

plage des Elmes, 66650 Banyuls-sur-Mer (Pyrénées-Orientales)
TEL 04 68 88 03 12 **FAX** 04 68 88 53 03

LES ELMES IS A HOTEL AND RESTAURANT – La Littorine – on the winding coast
road just outside Banyuls-sur-Mer, with its own little beach. The large
airy dining room has huge picture windows, a soothing atmosphere and
attentive service. For outdoor eating, there is a shady terrace overlooking
the sea. Jean-Marie Patroux's range of menus presents a wide choice of
stylish Catalan dishes which typically combine fish and meat in surprisingly successful ways: warm oysters with artichokes, or baby squid with
morilles sauce and parmesan to start; or a main course of cod with *palourdes* (tiny clams), *boudin noir* and *fruits de mers* , or pigeon with *gambas*
(large prawns). Fish can be especially recommended as the fish market of
Port Vendres is just down the road.

PRICE €€
CLOSED Jan, Nov
CREDIT CARDS AE, DC, MC, V

LANGUEDOC-ROUSSILLON

CARCASSONNE

LE LANGUEDOC

32 allée Iena, 11000 Carcassonne (Aude)
TEL 04 68 25 22 17 **FAX** 04 68 47 13 22

WHEN YOU HAVE HAD ENOUGH of the tourists, the trinkets and the unreal
perfection of Viollet le Duc's 19thC restoration of Carcassonne's
medieval walled *Cité*, head for the less crowded *ville basse* (referred to as
Carcassonne) and this relaxing retreat. Surrounded by a pretty garden,
the flowery patio, complete with fountain, makes a cool, refreshing setting
for a lingering lunch or dinner. If the weather does not permit, don't be
put off – the warmly decorated dining room is pleasant too. Either way,
smiling waiters will serve you with Didier Faugeron's reasonably priced
classic cuisine, set out in three fixed price menus, including a brilliant
cassoulet Languedoc au confit, entremets de fraises en feuilleté, and (in
season) quail with *foie gras*. The wine list offers some of the better local
Minervois. We recommend *fondant au chocolat* for dessert.

PRICE €€
CLOSED mon lunch; Sun eve, Mon Sep to Jun; Jun; mid-Dec to mid-Jan
CREDIT CARDS AE, DC, MC, V

MOLITG-LES-BAINS

GRAND HOTEL THERMAL

66500 Molitg-les-Bains (Pyrénées-Orientales)
TEL 04 68 05 00 50 **FAX** 04 68 05 02 91

HARDLY CHARMING AND SMALL, but nonetheless amusing, this is a spa hotel
in a craggy mountain gorge, with exotic gardens surrounding a huge
lake, marble spa rooms, a swimming pool and '30s *salon* complete with
cane chairs and grand piano. The restaurant shares a chef with the adjoining Château de Riell, long famous for its stylish cuisine, but the trick is to
dine here, not at the château, where you will eat well and pay less. The
marble terrace is perfect for summer eating, though the dining room, full
of clients taking the cure, can be a bit too hushed, and service is invariably
slow. Still, excellent value menus more than compensate. They feature
local produce and fresh herbs: perhaps *gambas* grilled with pesto, served
with green pepper *coulis*, followed by salmon with coriander, or a succulent *confit de canard*.

PRICE €
CLOSED Dec-Mar
CREDIT CARDS AE, DC, MC, V

LANGUEDOC-ROUSSILLON

RELAIS DE PIGASSE

RD5, Domaine de Pigasse, 11590 Ouveillan (Aude)
TEL 04 67 89 40 98

A 17THC POSTING HOUSE on the banks of the Canal du Midi has been reno-vated in simple, chic, cutting-edge style. Cool lighting, Italian leather furniture and modern art and sculpture combine happily with the old stones and rustic views. It is the brainchild of English vigneron Bertie Eden, and makes a wonderful way to sample his excellent Minervois wines. Dine – in the cool vaulted interior or beside the tree-shaded canal – on accomplished dishes which interpret authentic regional recipes with panache, each served with an appropriate wine. Try unctuous *foie gras* with Limoux Bégude, or rabbit stuffed with snails with St Chinian Château de Combebelle, and a gorgeous muscat sorbet and red fruits with the deli-cate muscat of St Jean de Minervois. All the wines and vegetables are *biologique*.

PRICE €€
CLOSED Mon
CREDIT CARDS MC, V

LA CASA SANSA

3 rue Fabrique Nadal, 66000 Perpignan (Pyrénées Orientales)
TEL 04 68 34 21 84

CASA SANSA IS A PERPIGNAN INSTITUTION, and the best place in town to sam-ple authentic Catalan food. Tucked away in one of the narrow streets around the Castillet, the restaurant makes a good stop either for *tapas* and drinks, or a full lunch or dinner. It's best to arrive early at lunchtime since it is very popular with locals and quickly fills up. The atmosphere is warm and lively, and the decoration idiosyncratic and artistic, with every inch of the walls covered in paintings and cartoons, and lovely old Spanish tiles lining the bar. Typical dishes include a rich Catalan-style ratatouille, *pin-tade* with figs or rabbit with *aioli*. They also serve a luxurious house *foie gras* which is a meal in itself, and a truly delicious *crème catalane*, subtly perfumed with orange.

PRICE €
CLOSED Sun, Mon
CREDIT CARDS AE, DC, MC, V

LANGUEDOC-ROUSSILLON

PORT-VENDRES

FERME AUBERGE DES CLOS DE PAULILLES

baie de Paulilles, 66660 Port-Vendres (Pyrénées-Orientales)
TEL 04 68 98 07 58

Escape the busy restaurants of Collioure for this enchanting sanctuary on a small bay surrounded by vineyards just beyond Port-Vendres. Run by the vineyard, with a fixed menu to showcase the Paulilles wines, the restaurant is comfortably chic, with Spanish tiled floors and banquettes, Catalan striped fabrics and art on the walls. A large tiled patio looks out on to vineyards and the sea, and the beach is only a stroll away. Each course is accompanied by a different wine; cooling *gazpacho* with a Collioure rosé, home reared chicken and polenta with a selection of rich reds, *manchego* cheese and orange *confit* with a Rivesaltes muscat, and for dessert *tarte au chocolate noîr* matched by a rich sweet Banyuls. End your meal with one of the superb vieille Banyuls you can see maturing in glass flagons; the cheese is on sale, and you will want to buy some to take home.

PRICE €
CLOSED lunch, except Sun; Sep-Jun

ST-ANDRE-DE VALBORGNE

BOURGADE

place de l'Eglise, 30940 St-André-de-Valborgne (Gard)
TEL 04 66 60 30 72 **FAX** 04 66 60 35 56

Trained by celebrity chefs Patrick Pagès and Alain Ducasse, dashing Alain Bourgade honed his skills while cooking for the French Ambassador in Washington DC. In 1998 he came home to renovate and run his family's 17thC coaching inn. It stands beside the fountain on this mountain village's main square, with tables outside on all but the chilliest evenings. Inside, there is a soothing pastel colour scheme. Among the imaginative specialities on the fixed-price and *à la carte* menus are wheat risotto, wild mushrooms and meat juice, beef *carpaccio* with coriander, capers and shallots, grilled lamb steak with Guérande sea salt and veal shank cooked in its own juice. If you can't face the drive home, there are ten attractively decorated bedrooms.

PRICE €€
CLOSED mid-Nov to mid-Apr, dinner Mon to Thur Sep to Jun
CREDIT CARDS MC, V

AUVERGNE & MASSIF CENTRAL

GOUTS ET COULEURS

38 rue de Bonald, 12000 Rodez (Aveyron)
TEL & FAX 05 65 42 75 10

HEAD FOR THIS LITTLE SIDE STREET close to the pink sandstone cathedral for an hour or two of 'taste and colour'. In the pastel-shaded, intimate restaurant (there is also a pretty terrace for outdoor eating) you will encounter truly individual and inventive cooking. Jean-Luc Fau gives his imagination full rein, especially on his menu *'dégustation'*, but he rarely loses the plot: his dishes successfully mingle the *cuisine de terroir* with the modern and the exotic. How about *tajine de volaille en gelée aux citrons confits et confiture de courge à la cannelle*, or *carpaccio de gambas à l'huile de fleur de sureau*, or *sushis de fraises à la citronelle et lait de coco*? Certainly, this is the most inventive cooking in Rodez, indeed perhaps in all the Massif Central.

Price €€
Closed Sun, Mon; Jan; Sep
Credit cards MC, V

L'ALAMBIC

8 rue Nicolas-Larbaud,03200 Vichy (Allier)
TEL 04 70 59 12 71 **FAX** 04 70 97 98 88

THIS MINISCULE RESTAURANT near the Parc des Sources in the city centre has great charm, but can only seat 14, so you must book in advance; if at first you can't get a table, it's worth persevering. Accolades have been heaped on L'Alambic, including a Gault Millau heart and 16/20 points. In this intimate setting, Jean-Jacques Barbot and Marie-Ange Tupet make a dynamic combination, preparing fabulous, fresh food with control and sensitivity. Choose from dishes such as *panaché d'escargots*, *lardons et artichauts en petits feuilletés à la sauge* and *mijotée de lapin et crème de lentilles du Puy à la moutarde de Charroux*, and don't forgo one of the mouthwatering desserts, for example, *nougat glacé au miel d'arbousier*. Staff are friendly yet discreet.

Price €€
Closed mid-Aug to mid-Sep, mid-Feb to mid-Mar, Mon, Tue
Credit cards MC, V

PROVENCE-COTE D'AZUR

APT

BISTRO DE FRANCE

67 place de la Bouquerie, 84400 Apt (Vaucluse)
TEL 04 90 74 22 01

HARDLY A DISCOVERY (it featured in Peter Mayle's *A Year in Provence*), though it certainly feels like one the first time you eat in (or on the pavement outside) this basic town centre café with its dark, old-fashioned street frontage, and a slightly battered saucepan of something delicious is plonked on your table for you to help yourself. The cooking is plain and Provençal and mostly very good. Some dishes can be a disappointment, such as an overcooked, unimaginatively sauced pasta, but in summer we much enjoyed the *aïoli* served with a big bowl of vegetables and a sharp knife to cut them, and the *brouillade de truffes* (the house speciality) is recommended in winter, as well as game and mushrooms. Service is fast and to the point at lunch; you need to reserve for dinner.

PRICE €€
CLOSED Sun, Mon, Thur eve; mid-Mar, mid to end Oct
CREDIT CARDS MC, V

ARLES

LE GALOUPET

18 rue du Docteur Fanton,
13200 Arles (Bouches-du-Rhône)
TEL 04 90 93 18 11

IN THE CITY CENTRE, this simple bistro looks as trendy as its clientele. Above deep-red walls is a splendid open-beamed ceiling, supporting a large old brass fan – the only form of air conditioning. Black-and-white photographs line the walls and flowers in a pottery jug decorate each table. The open kitchen and genial tabby cat add to the laid-back atmosphere. Don't come here expecting *haute cuisine*; the menu is straightforward and the food robust. Dishes such as *pavé de boeuf aux mouilles*, *grosses gambas sauce américaine* and *foie d'agneau au vinaîgre balsamique* are regulars. Generous helpings and a bill that shouldn't make much of a hole in your pocket are further attractions.

PRICE €€
CLOSED Nov to mid-Mar; Sun lunch
CREDIT CARDS MC, V

PROVENCE-COTE D'AZUR

FOURNIL

5 place Carnot, 84480 Bonnieux (Vaucluse)
TEL 04 90 75 83 62 **FAX** 04 90 75 96 19

IN A TINY ROOM hewn out of Bonnieux's rocky hillside, Le Fournil is the locals' favourite restaurant. Guy Malbec's Provençal food is neither fussy nor fancy, just consistently good. It's a very individual place, both cosy and bohemian, with rough irregular walls, vibrant modern paintings and a yellow-and-green chequerboard tiled floor. In summer, tables are set outside around a handsome 17thC fountain. The cheap menu is a terrific bargain and the main menu is fairly priced, considering what it offers. They typically include lentil terrine with *foie gras* or aubergine and tomato mille-feuille as starters, followed by roast duckling, rabbit, veal or pork, cooked simply with seasonal vegetables. There is an excellent selection of local wines.

PRICE €
CLOSED Dec to early Feb, Mon, Tue lunch and dinner Sep to Dec, early Feb to Apr
CREDIT CARDS MC, V

LE JARDIN D'EMILE

Plage de Bestouan, 13260 Cassis (Bouches-du-Rhône)
TEL 04 42 01 80 55 **FAX** 04 42 01 80 70

FOR A ROMANTIC DINNER A DEUX, head for this restaurant-with-rooms en route from Cassis to the *calanque* of Port-Miou. Set back from the waterfront, tucked against the cliffs and sheltered by parasol pines, the ochre-coloured house is surrounded by a Mediterranean garden filled with pines and olive trees. From the verdant, atmospheric and permanently sheltered terrace there are views of the cape, and at night the cliffs are softly illuminated. Dishes are served on locally hand-made plates, the service is friendly and helpful, and there are sometimes musical evenings. If the food is not as seductive as the setting, it certainly passes muster. The simpler dishes are best, such as *agneau rôti aux herbes* or *dorade grillé à l'anise*, and home-made desserts. There are seven air-conditioned bedrooms, simple and homely.

PRICE €€
CLOSED Tue; early to mid-Jan, mid to late Nov
CREDIT CARDS AE, MC, V

PROVENCE-COTE D'AZUR

CASSIS

NINO

Port de Cassis, 13260 Cassis (Bouches-du-Rhône)
TEL & FAX 04 42 01 43 72

THE LAST OF THE RESTAURANTS and cafés strung out around the pretty port of Cassis with its bobbing boats and jolly seaside air, Chez Nino is also the most sophisticated and the most amusing, with the distinct air of an Italian *trattoria*. You sit on a terrace above a wall dripping with bougainvillea and beneath a blue awning in a simple, white-walled room decorated with paintings and photographs. The Italian influence extends to the friendly and amusing but prompt waiters as well as to the food. On the fairly short, mainly fish menu you will find antipasto Nino and spaghetti dishes as well as Provençal staples such as *bourride*, *bouillabaisse* (very good) and *soupe de poissons*. Lively atmosphere, good fish, fair prices; just the right place for the setting. Perfect between a morning lazing on the beach and an afternoon boat trip to the *calanques*.

PRICE €€.
CLOSED Sun in winter, Mon; mid-Dec to mid-Feb
CREDIT CARDS AE, DC, MC, V

CASTELLANE

NOUVEL HOTEL DU COMMERCE

place Marcel-Sauvairsre, 04120 Castellane
(Alpes-de-Haute-Provence)
TEL 04 92 83 61 99 **FAX** 04 92 83 72 82

THE NAME SOUNDS UNPROMISING, and the hotel is indeed as nondescript as it suggests (though bedrooms are comfortable and bathrooms recently renovated, and the owners described as 'charming'). However, persevere, because a gastronomic surprise awaits. We pass on our friends' recommendation verbatim: "What was fantastic was the food. It was early autumn and a party of hunters and their wives were at the table next to us. They told us that they have been coming to the hotel for thirty years and that the food is always marvellous. Our meal certainly was – no tricks, just good, unpretentious food well presented." You eat in a vast dining room, or outside under trees, with menus that represent unbeatable value (Michelin awards a Bib Gourmand). *Gardiane de boeuf, pigeon et foie gras rôti, pastilla de pomme et rhubarbe.*

PRICE €€
CLOSED Tue, Wed lunch; mid-Oct to Mar
CREDIT CARDS AE, DC, MC, V

PROVENCE-COTE D'AZUR

HOTELLERIE DE L'ABBAYE DE LA CELLE

place Général de Gaulle, 83170 La Celle (Var)
TEL 04 98 05 14 14 **FAX** 04 98 05 14 15

TWO BIG NAMES, top chef and hotelier Alain Ducasse and local chef/entre-preneur Bruno Clément, came together to create this new restaurant, opened with great fanfare in 1999. Together they restored an ancient pilgrim's hostel, abandoned for three centuries, to its present breathtaking architectural splendour. It stands in a tiny village nestling under the Roc Candelon, flanked on one side by the Maison des Vins for Côteaux Varois, on the other by the restored abbey, its cloisters filled with spreading mulberry trees. When the restaurant's garden has fully matured, perfection will have been achieved. The cuisine of Benoit Witz, overseen by Ducasse and Clément, matches the surroundings, with menus that change daily, and are full of flavour and delicacy. Wonderful breads and *madeleines* with coffee; thoughtful service.

PRICE €€
CLOSED never
CREDIT CARDS AE, DC, MC, V

LA PETITE FONTAINE

83610 Collobrières (Var)
TEL 04 94 48 00 12

THE VERY BEST TIME OF YEAR to visit La Petite Fontaine is on a warm autumn day when you can sit outside on the little square, under the turning trees and the washing strung out across the balconies above. Then you can savour the freshly gathered chestnuts for which the village, wedged in the Maures Massif, is renowned, as well as the booty from la *chasse – gibier* plays an important part on the menu of this family-run restaurant. All is rustic warmth and hospitality, where pretension plays no part. The wine is from the local co-operative, and the food (there are just two menus written on blackboards) is local too. Every dish is explained with passion and relish by the Fontana family, whether it be a simple starter such as *terrine* or *tarte à l'oignon*, or a more complex main dish, followed by a plate of ripe cheeses and a delicious dessert. Perfection.

PRICE €
CLOSED Sun eve, Mon; mid-Feb, mid-Sep to Oct
CREDIT CARDS MC, V

PROVENCE-COTE D'AZUR

COMPS-SUR-ARTUBY

GRAND HOTEL BAIN

rue Praguillem, 83840 Comps-sur-Artuby (Var)
TEL 04 94 76 90 06 **FAX** 04 94 76 92 24

THE GUINNESS BOOK OF RECORDS knows about the Grand Hôtel Bain – not because of its food but because it has been in the hands of the same family for a record-breaking 265 years, passed from father to son in a long, proud tradition. First in the line was Claude Bain, a mule driver who provided stabling, sheepfolds and a few rooms for shepherds and their flocks on annual trips between summer and winter pasturage. Since then it has gained steadily in reputation and today it is Claude's great-great-great-great grandson who, with his wife Elisabeth, holds the reins – a warm, happy pair, conscious of the high standards they have inherited. In the kitchen these days? Their 30-year-old son, Arnaud. Hearty and welcoming country cooking, specializing in winter in local game and truffles, using recipes passed down through the generations.

PRICE €€
CLOSED mid-Nov to Christmas
CREDIT CARDS AE, DC, MC, V

CORRENS

AUBERGE DU PARC

place du Général de Gaulle, 83570 Correns (Var)
TEL 04 59 53 52 **FAX** 04 94 59 53 54

ONE OF A CLUTCH of notable restaurants in this region owned by larger-than-life Bruno Clément, the Auberge du Parc stands in the centre of Correns, which has proudly styled itself the first 'village biologique' in France. The street entrance opens on to a pretty but perhaps too fussily decorated Regency- style dining room and a smart terrace at the rear. The clientele is knowing, and not necessarily local, and the lunchtime menu breaks the mould for people spoiled for choice: there is none. You begin with four or five dishes to share, followed by a meat course, again shared from a large platter, then a dessert. Our meal was both convivial and tasty; others have reported dissatisfaction with the choice on offer and 'tough meat'. There is a little creeper-covered arbour, perfect for lovers. If you can, approach Correns along the delightful Sourn valley.

PRICE €€
CLOSED Tue, Wed; Nov-Apr
CREDIT CARDS AE, MC, V

PROVENCE-COTE D'AZUR

GRASSE

LA BASTIDE DE ST-ANTOINE

48 avenue Henri-Dunant, 06130 Grasse (Alpes-Maritimes)
TEL: 04 93 70 94 94 **FAX**: 04 93 70 94 95

PUCE BOUGAINVILLEA cascades down the walls of this luxurious Relais et Châteaux hotel and restaurant surrounded by terraced gardens, where dollops of 'harmonie et attention' are extended right from the moment a flunky parks your car for you. Terracotta pots on stone balustrades mark your way through the perfectly restored 18thC bastide to the dining room, light and sunny, with a rose-fringed terrace. In the past the house has sheltered the rich and famous, from Joseph Kennedy in the 1930s to the Rolling Stones who lived here for a time in the 1970s, but since 1995 the owner and chef has been Jacques Chibois, a fact you won't forget since every plate and ashtray bears his initials. His culinary imagination is precocious, and despite the expense, this is an experience you are unlikely to forget or, hopefully, regret.

PRICE €€€
CLOSED never
CREDIT CARDS AE, DC, MC, V

LORGUES

LE CHRISSANDRIER

18 cours de la République, 83510 Lorgues (Var)
TEL & FAX: 04 94 67 67 15

FOR A PERFECT MORNING, pay a visit to Lorgues' Tuesday market, one of the best in the area, followed by lunch at this delightful restaurant in the town centre. Small and intimate, charmingly decorated (with a cabinet of antique wine decanters in the main dining room), it is filled with tables all through the building, from ones under bright umbrellas on the busy roadside pavement through to the pretty terrace at the back. Owners Christophe and Sandra Chabredier (he is the chef, she smiles welcomingly at front of house) describe their cuisine as 'faite de passion et de sincérité' and you really do feel that this keen young couple are giving their all. They offer a simple and inexpensive lunchtime menu, and a surprisingly extensive *carte*. Interesting vegetables to accompany, such as *petits légumes servis avec un jus d'orange aux olives niçoises*. Local wines.

PRICE €
CLOSED Wed
CREDIT CARDS MC, V

PROVENCE-COTE D'AZUR

MANOSQUE

LA BARBOTINE

5 place de l'Hôtel de Ville, 04100 Manosque
(Alpes-de-Haute-Provence)
TEL 04 92 72 57 15

YOU ARE ASSURED of an entirely feminine welcome in this charming ochre-walled restaurant, run by women, and proudly served by women too. Heavy old oak beams and worn tiled floors characterize this generous oasis, a much-appreciated discovery in an area where there are many restaurants, but not many, frankly, to recommend. Gisèle and Mireille Rey are the creators of La Barbotine, and they offer a fabulous seasonal, if simple, menu featuring Provençal vegetable dishes, fresh pasta, *pâtisseries à la maison* and – in summer – superb salads which are a meal in themselves. And look out for the delicious and sumptuous grills on the *viande* menu. There are just two menus, one featuring meat, the other vegetarian. Pretty terrace for outdoor eating, and *salon de thé* on summer afternoons.

PRICE €
CLOSED Sun
CREDIT CARDS MC, V

MARSEILLE

LES METS DE PROVENCE

18 quai Rive Neuve, 13007 Marseille (Bouches-du-Rhône)
TEL & FAX 04 91 33 35 38

ONE OF THE MOST ATMOSPHERIC and homely places to eat in Marseille, Les Mets de Provence is long-established, having first opened in 1937, and is still justly popular. Located on the second floor of the old quayside family home of the proprietor, Maurice Brun, it's right in the heart of the Vieux Port, best viewed, with its ferries and fishing boats, from the restaurant's big picture window. Rough wharfside steps take you away from the world of the sea and deposit you, once inside, firmly in the Provençal countryside. The rustic dining room has a big rôtisserie in the open hearth, and charming tables laid with prettily mismatched plates and glasses. There's no menu: M. Brun recites the offerings of the day (plenty of choice), spanning an extensive repetoire of Provençal dishes.

PRICE €€
CLOSED Sun, Mon lunch; early to mid-Aug
CREDIT CARDS MC, V

PROVENCE-COTE D'AZUR

MAUSSANE-LES-ALPILLES

MARGAUX

1 rue Paul-Reveil, 13520 Maussane-les-Alpilles (Bouches-du-Rhône)
TEL & FAX 04 90 54 35 04

WE ENJOYED THE CRISP FRESHNESS of this perfectly kept little restaurant, just off the attractive main square filled with plane trees, and with a fine fountain in the centre. You enter into a charming courtyard, where you can dine under perfectly shaped olive trees in summer. The dining room, for cooler days, looks as if it has just been decorated, very smart with its lemon yellow walls and white-clothed tables. In fact it's five years old, the creation of *patron* Jean Metraz-Brunand-Meiffre and his wife Martine. Jean, like his name, is larger than life, both in height and character, and often chats to his guests with wry humour. The menu is short, to the point, and well executed: *crespëou*, a terrine of Provençal vegetables, *artichauds à la barrigoule*, *poulet fermier* with tarragon, *pieds et paquets*.

PRICE €€
CLOSED Tue, Wed lunch; mid-Nov to mid-Dec, Feb
CREDIT CARDS DC, MC, V

MONDRAGON

LA BEAUGRAVIERE

RN7, 84430 Mondragon (Vaucluse)
TEL 04 90 40 82 54 **FAX** 04 90 40 91 01

WE LIST La Beaugravière as an interesting place to stay in this guide (see page 166) – it offers three modest, clean rooms (double-glazed to keep out the noise of the main road). However, the point of the place is the food, and we are more than happy to draw attention to it again here. Truffles are the thing: Guy Jullien is a specialist, and during the autumn truffle season, aficionados flock to his restaurant for dishes such as *foie gras de canard rôti au jus de truffes* and *pavé de boeuf sauce au vin de syrah truffé*. Whatever time of the year, the menu reflects classic regional cuisine, paying close attention to seasonal variations and good local produce. The wine list is strong on Côte du Rhône. In summer you eat on a shady terrace, in winter in the dining room decorated with illustrations of vine species. Service is prompt and attentive.

PRICE €€€
CLOSED Sun eve, Mon; mid to late Sep
CREDIT CARDS MC, V

PROVENCE-COTE D'AZUR

LA FERME STE-CECILE

04360 Moustiers-Ste-Marie (Alpes-de-Haute-Provence)
TEL 04 92 74 64 18 **FAX** 04 92 74 63 51

MOUSTIERS IS BLESSED with lovely restaurants, but Patrick Crespin's small farm is a particular delight. Its broad shady terrace looks down over slopes of asparagus, raspberries, lettuce and tomatoes to a riverbed below, while the two small dining rooms, with cream flagstones, white chairs and tables festooned with flowers are charming. Fresh local produce is the basis for Crespin's cuisine; as well as cultivating his own, he patronizes the local markets and farmers (vis. his *pigeonneau fermier de Valensole*, or *tomette de chèvre de L&L Martin*) and twice a week makes the 120 km journey to Marseille's Vieux Port fish market. An interesting innovation are his savoury ices – fresh anchovies with Ligurian olive ice cream, or roast garlic ice served with fish. Enthusiastic, knowledgeable staff.

PRICE €€
CLOSED Sun eve, Mon Sep to Jun; mid Nov to mid-Dec, Feb
CREDIT CARDS MC, V

CHATEAU DE NANS

RN560, 83860 Nans-les-Pins (Var)
TEL 04 94 78 92 06 **FAX** 04 94 78 60 46

THIS LUXURIOUS LITTLE TURRETED CHATEAU was a near ruin when it was bought by its new owners, the Bambecks, in 1998. Although there are eight bedrooms with Jacuzzi baths (and concessions for using the golf course opposite), the emphasis is on the restaurant where you dine either on the terrace under spreading trees, or in the stylish white and apricot conservatory, or in the rather darker dining room within. Statues and other artefacts are dotted about, and the artistic touches extend to the patterned plates: each dish is served on a plate specially chosen to show it off to best effect. The chef is Bruno Gazagnaire, who trained with Alain Ducasse, and his cooking is similarly light and refined, with a Provençal slant: witness *fraicheur d'écrivisses en mini ratatouille* or *dos de loup rôti au jus s'olives et basilic*. Don't miss the *gratin de fraises de bois*.

PRICE €€€
CLOSED Mon; also Tues in winter; mid-Nov to mid-Dec, mid-Jan to mid-Feb
CREDIT CARDS AE, MC, V

PROVENCE-COTE D'AZUR

LE BRUIT DE LA MER

Port de la Rague, 06210 La Napoule (Alpes-Maritimes)
TEL 04 93 49 57 47

ITS EXTERIOR SEEMS UNASSUMING ENOUGH, but this restaurant enjoys a stunning and unforgettable view over the Mediterranean. The best time to appreciate it is at dinner: it's positioned on the furthest promontory of the port, and as the sun begins to sink, the lights of Cannes across the bay begin to twinkle, against a backdrop of the looming Iles de Lérins, and the brooding Alps in the distance. As for the noise of the sea (*bruit de la mer*), that comes to you in the guise of the gentle clank of halyards against masts in this modern but pleasant harbour. The view wins the day, but the food won't disappoint. The fish, as you would expect, is the freshest possible, and served according to the day's catch with a wide selection of sauces and accompaniments. If you can't decide, ask what the chef recommends.

PRICE €
CLOSED Sun, Mon, Tue, Wed, Thur eve in winter
CREDIT CARDS AE, DC, MC, V

MAS DES GERANIUMS

San Peyre, 06650 Opio (Alpes-Maritimes)
TEL & FAX 04 93 77 70 11

THERE IS SOMETHING TRULY BEGUILING about lunch on the wide sloping terrace of this old favourite (we first visited over 20 years ago, and, in spirit at least, little has changed). As well as simple food, it once offered simple bedrooms in the house, a traditional Provençal *bastide*, but now, under chef Michel Creusot, concentrates on the food alone. It is well named, you think, as you relax at one of the tables under shady trees and awnings, surrounded by bright geraniums. Ask for one on the highest level to get the best view of the old village and the golf course below. Although there is, inevitably, a mainly Provençal flavour to the food (such as *filets de rougets à la Provençale*) M. Creusot comes from Burgundy, and therefore *escargots*, *poulet de Bresse aux morilles* and the like also make a showing on the menu.

PRICE €
CLOSED Tue, Wed Sep-Jun; Wed, Thur lunch Jul Aug; mid-Nov to mid-Jan
CREDIT CARDS MC, V

PROVENCE-COTE D'AZUR

PÉGOMAS

RELAIS DU PAS DE L'AI

route de Tanneron, 06580 Pégomas (Alpes-Maritimes)
TEL 04 93 60 98 47 **FAX** 04 93 42 81 84

LOOKING FOR PEACE AND QUIET? Here is a tiny oasis of tranquillity amid the brazen bustle of the Côte d'Azur. Though it lies between Grasse and Cannes, it feels as though it's in the middle of nowhere, lost in a little valley which is as lovely in February, when it is covered in yellow mimosa, as it is in summer. There are fine views from the terrace. As for the food, it is described as 'gastronomique' although we would prefer to call it good standard Provençal. The delightful family who have owned the place since it started 12 years ago are endearingly enthusiastic: "La terrine de foie gras! C'est une merveille!". Also notable are the *confit de canard* and *risotto de gambas*. An unpretentious place with a genuinely rural feel where you can get away for a few hours before rejoining the madding crowd.

PRICE €€
CLOSED Mon, Tue lunch in summer, Sun, Mon, Tue eve in winter
CREDIT CARDS AE, MC, V

ST-JEAN-CAP-FERRAT

LE SLOOP

Port de Plaisance, 06230 St-Jean-Cap-Ferrat
(Alpes-Maritimes)
TEL & FAX 04 93 01 48 63

WE FIRST HEARD about Le Sloop when Andrew Lloyd-Webber confessed to the Sunday Times that it was his favourite restaurant in the South of France. What distinguishes it? Though it's one of a string of restaurants overlooking the new port, it's a clear cut above the others, both in design and cooking. It has the feel of a sophisticated cruise ship, whether you are sitting on the deck under sunshades, or inside the bright dining room. The menu offers excellent choice and value, and Alain Thericocq's cuisine has a knack of being unpretentious yet original. Recently we enjoyed a *salade d'homard mozzarella et avocat au basilic*, and to follow *dorade entière au four à la Niçoise avec fleurs des courgettes*. Desserts include interesting combinations of *chaud-froid* using the same fruits in differing ways. Service is always attentive, however busy the restaurant.

PRICE €€
CLOSED Wed, Thur lunch; mid-Nov to mid-Dec
CREDIT CARDS AE, DC, MC, V

PROVENCE-COTE D'AZUR

HOTELLERIE DU COUVENT ROYAL

place Jean-Salusse, 83470 St Maximin-la-Ste-Baume (Var)
TEL 04 94 86 55 66 **FAX** 04 94 59 82 82

ST MAXIMIN USUALLY gets shot past on the motorway to the coast, but you may have glimpsed the silhouette of its grandiose basilica as you sped by. The attractive market town huddles round it (don't miss the darkened skull of Mary Magdalene in the 4thC crypt), and its adjacent 13thC convent. It's most pleasant to stroll through its lovely shady cloisters, and then to dine in the attractive restaurant in what was once the Chapter House. Stylishly restored, it has huge windows inserted into vaulted walls, giving both light and a great view of the cloisters. It's large-scale, with large tables and comfortable chairs to match. In summer you can sit outside in the cloister garden. The cooking is desribed as 'tendance Provençal' but has a delicate touch, with a hint of the orient in its use of coriander, saffron and spices. The wines are mostly local.

PRICE €€
CLOSED Sun eve, Mon
CREDIT CARDS AE, DC, MC, V

AUBERGE DE TOURRETTES

11 route de Grasse, 06140 Tourrettes-sur-Loup (Alpes-Maritimes)
TEL 04 93 59 30 05 **FAX** 04 93 59 28 66

TALENTED YOUNG CHEF Christophe Dufau and his Danish wife Katrine opened this restaurant-with-rooms in the shell of a typical village inn just a couple of years ago. Though it's close to the hotspots of the Côte d'Azur, Tourrettes is an unassuming village high in the hills, and from the airy open-plan restaurant with its glassed-in terrace, there are great views over unspoiled wooded hillsides down to the coast. The decoration is simple, stylish and unstuffy; clean, contemporary lines, warm tiled floors, shades of white, natural linen tablecloths, much wood and an olive tree in a terracotta pot. The reasonably priced food has real flair, and uses plenty of local ingredients including herbs from the garden. Dishes might include lobster terrine *en gelée* flavoured with orange, or perhaps chicken stewed with pickled lemons. Also featured as a place to stay on page 173.

PRICE €€
CLOSED Mon, Tue Oct to May; mid-Jan to mid-Feb
CREDIT CARDS AE, DC, MC, V

PROVENCE-COTE D'AZUR

AUBERGE FLEURIE

0106 route de Cannes, 06560 Valbonne (Alpes-Maritimes)
TEL 04 93 12 02 80 **FAX** 04 93 12 22 27

AN OLD FAVOURITE, run for many years by Jean-Pierre Battaglia, who trained at L'Oasis in La Napoule before acquiring his own place. He has now been joined in the kitchen by Lionel Debon, who has his own list of credentials, including La Pyramide at Vienne. What impresses here are the reasonable prices, especially for the cheapest of the *prix fixe* menus, and Michelin awards a Bib Gourmand for 'good food at moderate prices'. Signature dishes include *rosace de rougets en gelée de crustacés*, *Saint-Pierre cuit sur la peau à la fleur de sel*, and *pigeonneau rôti aux morilles*. You eat either (according to weather and availability) in the dining room of the old *auberge*, or – preferably – on the shady terrace. This is a popular place (book ahead), with an agreeable buzz on busy evenings.

PRICE €€
CLOSED Mon; Sun eve, Mon Sep-June
CREDIT CARDS AE, MC, V

L'OURSIN BLEU

11 Quai de l'Amiral Courbet, 06230 Villefranche-sur-Mer
(Alpes-Maritimes)
TEL 04 93 01 90 12 **FAX** 04 93 01 80 45

THE VILLEFRANCHE RESTAURANT everyone knows is La Mère Germaine, but our insider reports that it is getting stuffier and more expensive year by year. "I'd still go there for an evening celebration," she writes, "but, for a relaxed, delicious lunch beside the water, I've switched to L' Oursin Bleu, only opened a couple of years ago". The owners are young enough to be keen – their aim, they say, is to create "une ambience conviviale" – and their chef is the passionate Jérôme Deloncle, who favours seafood (as you'd expect at a harbourside restaurant) with an extra touch of spiciness and imagination; witness his *grosses gambas laquées au kumbava*, or the *crumble de thon rouge*. As for desserts, my advice is to forget the rest, good as they are, plump for the *moelleux au chocolat coeur liquide* and go straight to heaven.

PRICE €€
CLOSED Tue
CREDIT CARDS AE, DC, MC, V

THE RHONE VALLEY

DOMAINE DE CLAIREFONTAINE

38121 Chonas l'Amballan (Isère)
TEL 04 74 8 81 52 **FAX** 04 74 58 80 93

A HANDSOME 18THC HOUSE in splendid parkland, once the residence of the bishops of Lyon, situated just outside Vienne. Owned by Philippe and Laurence Giradon, it's a hotel and restaurant which is run on family lines and without pretension, with a genteel, faded air redolent of a more refined era. Philippe Giradon specializes in a mixture of traditional and modern cuisine – among his classics are roast lobster (*homard Breton, sauce américaine allégée*) and lamb seasoned with rosemary, as well as *trilogie de foie gras en dodines* and *millefeuille de pommes et figues* (in season). The pretty air-conditioned restaurant is painted yellow and has a beamed ceiling, flagged floor and French windows that open out on to a garden terrace. If you stay the night, go for one of the large double rooms – modestly priced for their size.

PRICE €€€
CLOSED Sun eve, Mon, Tue lunch; mid-Dec to mid-Jan
CREDIT CARDS AE, DC, MC, V

HOTEL DE LA POSTE

place de la Mairie, route Napoléon, 38970 Corps (Isère)
TEL 04 76 30 00 03 **FAX** 04 76 30 02 73

T HERE IS A WARM, intimate and friendly atmosphere at this notable hotel and restaurant in Corps, a busy tourist centre within reach of skiing and walking. The exterior sets the happy tone, with its pink walls, blue awnings and bright geraniums in window boxes. Nothing inside disappoints. The two dining rooms are cosy and welcoming, with antique country furniture, colourful fabrics and paintings on the walls. Service is smiling and friendly, and the cooking of M. Dulas draws people from miles around (and a Bib Gourmand – good food at moderate prices – from Michelin). You might choose *pantagruélique farandole de hors d'oeuvre avec saladiers de palourdes*, followed by *gigot d'agneau*, roast quail or smoked duck salad, with a delicious pâtisserie for dessert. Inexpensive wine list.

PRICE €€
CLOSED Jan to mid-Feb
CREDIT CARDS AE, MC, V

HOTEL & RESTAURANT NAMES

In this index, hotels and restaurants are arranged in order of the most distinctive part of their name; very common prefixes such as 'Auberge', 'Hôtel', 'Hostellerie' and 'La/Le/Les' are omitted, but more significant elements such as 'Château', 'Domaine' or 'Moulin' are retained.

Hotel & Restaurant Names

HOTEL & RESTAURANT NAMES

HOTEL & RESTAURANT NAMES

HOTEL & RESTAURANT NAMES

Hotel & Restaurant Names

HOTEL & RESTAURANT LOCATIONS

In this index, hotels and restaurants are arranged by the name of the city, town or village they are in or near. Hotels located in a very small village may be indexed under the name of a larger

HOTEL & RESTAURANT LOCATIONS

HOTEL & RESTAURANT LOCATIONS

HOTEL & RESTAURANT LOCATIONS

Hotel & Restaurant Locations

Hotel & Restaurant Locations

SPECIAL OFFERS

Buy your *Charming Small Hotel Guide* by post directly
from the publisher and you'll get a worthwhile discount. *

Titles available:	Retail price	Discount price
Austria	£9.99	£8.50
Britain	£10.99	£9.50
Britain's Most Distinctive Bed & Breakfasts	£9.99	£8.50
France	£11.99	£10.50
France: Bed & Breakfast	£9.99	£8.50
Germany	£9.99	£8.50
Greece	£10.99	£9.50
Ireland	£9.99	£8.50
Italy	£11.99	£10.50
Mallorca, Menorca & Ibiza	£9.99	£8.50
Paris	£10.99	£9.50
Spain	£9.99	£8.50
Switzerland	£9.99	£8.50
Tuscany & Umbria	£9.99	£8.50
USA: Florida	£9.99	£8.50
USA: New England	£9.99	£8.50
Venice and North-East Italy	£9.99	£8.50

Please send your order to:
> Book Sales,
> Duncan Petersen Publishing Ltd,
> 31 Ceylon Road, London W14 OPY

enclosing: 1) the title you require and number of copies
> 2) your name and address
> 3) your cheque made out to:
> Duncan Petersen Publishing Ltd

*Offer applies to UK only.

SPECIAL OFFERS

If you like *Charming Small Hotel Guides* you'll also enjoy Duncan Petersen's *Versatile Guides/Travel Planner & Guides*: outstanding all-purpose travel guides written by authors, not by committee.

Titles available:	Retail price	Discount price
Australia Travel Planner & Guide	£12.99	£10.50
California The Versatile Guide	£12.99	£10.50
Central Italy The Versatile Guide	£12.99	£10.50
England & Wales Walks Planner & Guide	£12.99	£10.50
Florida Travel Planner & Guide	£12.99	£10.50
France Travel Planner & Guide	£12.99	£10.50
Greece The Versatile Guide	£12.99	£10.50
Italy Travel Planner & Guide	£12.99	£10.50
Spain The Versatile Guide	£12.99	£10.50
Thailand The Versatile Guide	£12.99	£10.50
Turkey The Versatile Guide	£12.99	£10.50

Travelling by car? Duncan Petersen's *Backroads* driving guides include original routes and tours – avoid the motorways and main roads and explore the real country. Full colour easy to read mapping; recommended restaurants and local specialities; practical advice on where to stop, visit and picnic.

Titles available:	Retail price	Discount price
Britain on Backroads	£9.99	£8.50
France on Backroads	£9.99	£8.50
Italy on Backroads	£9.99	£8.50
Spain on Backroads	£9.99	£8.50

Please send your order to:

Book Sales,

Duncan Petersen Publishing Ltd,

31 Ceylon Road, London W14 OPY

enclosing: 1) title you require and number of copies

2) your name and address

3) your cheque made out to:

Duncan Petersen Publishing Ltd

*Offer applies applies to this edition and to UK only.